THE
MERCHANT TAYLORS
OF YORK

a history of the
Craft and Company from the fourteenth to
the twentieth century

EDITED BY

R.B. DOBSON & D.M. SMITH

ON BEHALF OF THE
COMPANY OF MERCHANT TAYLORS
OF THE CITY OF YORK

BORTHWICK TEXTS AND STUDIES 33
2006

ISBN-13: 978-1-904497-16-5
ISBN-10: 1-904497-16-0

Published 2006
Borthwick Publications
University of York
Heslington
York
YO10 5DD

CONTENTS

ABBREVIATED REFERENCES

BI	Borthwick Institute, York
BL	The British Library, London
Cal. Pat. Rolls	*Calendar of Patent Rolls*
EHR	*English Historical Review*
Freemen's Register	Register of the Freemen of the City of York, ed. F. Collins (2 vols., Surtees Society 96, 102, 1897–1900).
Giles	Katherine Giles, *An Archaeology of Social Identity: Guildhalls in York c.1350–1630* (British Archaeological Reports, British Series 315, 2000)
Johnson	Bernard Johnson, *The Acts and Ordinances of the Company of Merchant Taylors in the City of York* (York, 1949)
Mennim	A. Michael Mennim, *The Merchant Taylors Hall, York* (York, 2000)
MTA	Merchant Taylors' Archives
RCHM	Royal Commission on Historical Monuments, *The City of York. vol. V. The Central Area* (1981)
REED	Records of Early English Drama
Rotuli Parliamentarum	*Rotuli Parliamentorum: ut et petitiones et placita in parliamento* (6 vols., Record Commission, 1783–1832)
Swanson, *Artisans*	H. Swanson, *Medieval Artisans: an urban class in late medieval England* (Oxford, 1989)
Test. Ebor.	*Testamenta Eboracensia* eds. J. Raine snr & J. Raine jnr (6 vols., Surtees Society 4, 30, 45, 53, 79, 106, 1836–1902)
TNA	The National Archives, Kew

VCH York	*Victoria County History: A History of Yorkshire: The City of York*, ed. P.M. Tillott (Oxford, 1961)
YASRS	Yorkshire Archaeological Society Record Series
YCA	York City Archives
YMB	*York Memorandum Book* eds. M. Sellers (vols. 1–2); J. W Percy (vol. 3) (3 vols., Surtees Society 120, 125, 186, 1912-73)
YML	York Minster Library
York Civic Records	*York Civic Records*, eds. A. Raine (vols. 1–8); D. Sutton (vol. 9) (9 vols., YASRS 98, 103, 106, 108, 110, 112, 115, 119, 138, 1939 –78)

LIST OF ILLUSTRATIONS

14 Section of the Little Hall, looking to the north and showing the variations in the existing trusses. The ties run past the arch-braces. Reproduced by permission John Baily.

15 The east side of the Hall and and Almshouses as exposed by excavation of the previously lost church and cemetery of St Helen-on-the Walls, Aldwark, in 1973-74. Reproduced with permission of York Archaeological Trust.

INTRODUCTION

R.B. Dobson & D.M. Smith

The Hall of the Company of Merchant Taylors of York, built six centuries ago just within the north-eastern section of the medieval city wall, has never been one of the most visited monuments in a much visited city. Encased in seventeenth-century brick and once located in one of the most destitute sections of an impoverished city, it was until recently not even very easy to find. Only with the demolition of the Rose and Crown in 1949 and the Ebor Tavern twenty years later, the two Victorian public houses which commanded the narrow alleyway into its precincts, was the Hall at last properly visible from the street. Now that it is surrounded by a dense conglomeration of modern small-scale housing (which has only replaced dilapidated slum property in the area during the last twenty years), at first sight the Hall still has comparatively little to attract the passing visitor. However, in York, even more than in most other English cities, appearances can be deceptive; and passing tourists who take the trouble to walk 500 feet east down Aldwark from Monk Bar will find themselves facing one of the four surviving great medieval guildhalls of the city, quite as significant memorials to the city's past as its parish churches, its castle, its walls, its late Victorian railway station and almost as its Gothic cathedral. Very dissimilar in appearance although those York guildhalls are, the external and internal fabric of all four (the civic Common Hall, long known more simply as York Guildhall); the Hall of the Merchant Adventurers in Fossgate; the Hall of the religious fraternity of St Anthony at the end of Aldwark; and the Hall of the Merchant Taylors) remains remarkably intact, preserving a quartet of medieval town halls unsurpassed elsewhere in Britain.

The Masters, Court of Assistants, Members and Clerks of the present day Merchant Taylors who have commissioned this new collaborative survey of the development of their guild for over six hundred years are well aware that they owe the existence of their Company to the survival of their Hall. Had it not been for that survival — rather against the odds — it seems more or less inconceivable that the Company of Merchant Taylors would itself have outlasted the abolition of its economic monopolies and privileges by the Municipal Reform Acts of the 1830s. Very few of the ninety members who constitute the Company of Merchant Taylors at the beginning of the second Millennium are practising tailors; but they would all agree that their most important role, their single greatest responsibility, is to preserve the Hall as scrupulously as possible for the enjoyment of posterity. Nevertheless this volume is not primarily an architectural study of the Merchant Taylors' Hall itself. The latter has in fact received very detailed and specialist study in very recent years, most obviously in Mr Michael Mennim's highly illuminating *The Merchant Taylors' Hall, York* and Dr Katherine Giles's extremely original *An Archaeology of Social Identity: Guildhalls in York, 1350–1630*, both published in the year 2000. Under such intensive analysis, what might seem a comparatively simple building has proved to be nothing of the sort; and in his own sophisticated last chapter of this collection of essays, Dr John Baily, late Clerk of the Company, not only summarises the state of recent research on the building but employs his detective powers to reveal how many important new secrets the Taylors' Hall has to offer to the attentive visitor.

However important its architectural features, what gives the Taylors' Hall a central place in the history of York and Yorkshire is that it is the only one of the four surviving York guildhalls which developed into the religious, convivial, charitable, social and economic headquarters of a manufacturing craft or mystery. The economy of pre-industrial York, like that of nearly all European towns, rested absolutely on the small-scale production of goods for personal consumption and on their sale by retail from the houses and workshops in which they were made. Economic historians have often been slow to emphasize that the most plentiful of the many manufacturing crafts that honeycombed the pre-industrial town were those associated with clothing. Of these much the most numerous were the tailors. As will emerge very clearly from the statistical evidence used by the authors of this volume, from the late fourteenth to the late eighteenth centuries the art of tailoring, the production of fine domestic apparel, was always the largest profession among the citizens and freemen of York.

Accordingly the primary purpose of the following essays is to convey a sense of the economic and social activities of the York tailors and their womenfolk as these changed dramatically from century to century. The contributors to this volume naturally hope that the present members of the Merchant Taylors' Company (exactly ninety in number as this collection of essays goes to press) will enjoy this account of the labours of their predecessors, labours very different from their own. We hope moreover that this book may have a wider interest still. Its first five contributors are all academic historians, associated either now or in the recent past with the History Department of the University of York. As they have all an active research interest in the history of the city, they have naturally seen it as their main task to place the life and work of its tailors fully in the context of the economic and social history of the city as a whole. Urban historians of England, and of Europe too, have almost always tended to devote much more attention to mayors and merchants than to tailors and seamstresses, despite the fact that it was on the labouring skills of its manual workers that a town's economy depended absolutely. This collection of essays attempts to redress the balance and rescue thousands of York's artisans and craftsmen from undeserved oblivion.

Any history of a medieval guild that is still flourishing six centuries later is bound to have a commemorative function too. To some extent this volume is meant to mark the 620th anniversary of the York tailors as an organised and self-regulating community, but with the proviso that no one will ever know for certain quite how, when and why the numerous tailors of the city decided to create their own fraternity. Nor do we know for certain when those tailors, in association with other craftsmen, sponsored the building of the great Hall of St John the Baptist, since the Reformation the Merchant Taylors' Hall. Indeed the foundation of both fraternity and Hall prove more or less impossible to understand without some knowledge of the positive explosion of craft and other guilds in late medieval York as a whole. As Dr Heather Swanson shows in her cogent survey of some very complex problems, many of the issues surrounding the early history of craft guilds remain remarkably obscure, above all for lack of direct documentary evidence. What is certain is that in early 1387 no less than 128 York master tailors assembled, probably in the city's Guildhall, to register their earliest surviving ordinances. Whether or not these ordinances replaced now lost regulations, in many ways they emerge, probably not coincidentally, at a period when at long last English society was becoming increasingly literate and reliant on an ability to read and write. Whether literate or not, many of the 128 tailors who had been present at the confirmation of their ordinances in 1387 were involved in the construction of their massive Hall by 1415 or a little earlier. How appropriate, after all, that the single largest craft guild in late medieval York should have left to posterity the largest and least damaged craft guildhall in the medieval north of England.

Unfortunately, whereas the early fabric of the Hall survives, the guild's records only begin to do so from the reign of Elizabeth I. Before 1551 any attempt to write a history of the York tailors is bound to be an exercise in making bricks with far too little straw. Admittedly, the ordinances and several other references to the guild are preserved in the City of York's Archives while the incomparable record holdings of the National Archives at Kew occasionally throw light on the activities of the tailors. Still insufficiently exploited too are the many tailors' wills and testaments preserved in the long series of probate registers now in the custody of the Borthwick Institute for Archives. The Borthwick Institute also holds on deposit the archives created by the York tailors themselves. Apart from a series of registers containing guild ordinances and the like, the most informative sequences of documents tend to be Court Minute Books (from 1641), Apprenticeship Registers, Minute Books, Membership Records and Account Books. All these sources are described in detail in Professor David

Smith's *A Guide to the Archives of the Company of the Merchant Taylors of the City of York* (Borthwick List and Index, 12, 1994), supplemented by his *The Company of Merchant Taylors in the City of York: Register of Admissions, 1560–1835*, published in the same series in 1996.

Readers of the four chapters in this collection which carry the story of the Merchant Taylors from 1551 to the present day will soon appreciate that they are all based on the Company's almost completely unpublished archives. In his chapter on the period between 1551 and 1662 Dr William Sheils seizes the opportunity to produce an exceptionally vivid account of the geographical origins of York tailors before examining the responses of the Company to the vicissitudes of civic and national politics. In the subsequent chapter, dedicated to the usually neglected period between 1662 and 1776, Dr Simon Smith is able to develop several of these themes with much statistical expertise, thereby not only shedding very new light on membership trends and the importance of women tailors to the Company's welfare but also placing the economic challenges facing the York tailors against a national background of 'the new social history of guilds'. Professor Edward Royle deserves our particular gratitude for contributing not just one but two chapters to this volume, so carrying the history of the York tailors through the Victorian age to the present day. For many historians and tailors alike, this was a period in which the Company threatened to become an 'old useless relic of the past, with little spirit and less hope'. Professor Royle does equal justice, no easy matter, both to the degradation of the mid-nineteenth century Company (when only a handful of members ever bothered to enter the interior of their dilapidated Hall) and to the recovery of its fortunes from the 1930s onwards – under the leadership of their then Clerk, Mr H.E. Harrowell, a prominent York solicitor and Justice of the Peace. Since the extensive restoration of the Hall in that and the following decade, its membership has risen from to less than 30 in the 1940s to 90 in 2005. Among the latter there are now three lady members, thus reviving a tradition of female membership of the Company which – as Dr Smith shows below – was crucial to its welfare during the eighteenth century. Thanks to the generosity of one member of the Company, the latter's charitable activity (directed towards relieving financial hardship among practitioners of arts and crafts in the city) has also been revived in recent years; and it is hard to believe that the Hall itself has ever appeared more attractive since it was first constructed some six centuries ago.

We are grateful to all the contributors to this volume for the alacrity with which they accepted an invitation to write for this collaborative venture. Our most sincere thanks to them for the time and trouble they have taken to place their expertise at the Company's disposal. Ms Sara Slinn of the Borthwick Institute for Archives has been a source of invaluable support and guidance during the preparation of these essays for publication. For assistance in our search – not easy – for visual representations of the Taylor's Hall were are indebted to Barbara Wilson, Frances Mee and the staff of York City Art Gallery. We are grateful too to the successive Masters of the Company (Messrs Owen Wetherell, Peter Smith, Nigel Peel, Richard Baldwin and Graham Wilford) as well as to the members of the Court of Assistants who encouraged us to complete this volume, in particular Richard Stanley, past Master and a former Clerk. Thanks should also go to the Company's Clerk, Ms Jo Risely-Prichard, for all her help, as well as to Dr John Baily, previous Clerk. Apart from writing the last chapter in this book, John Baily is the main inspiration behind its composition. It was Dr Baily who observed in the late 1990s that Mr Bernard Johnson's detailed but somewhat inaccurately titled *The Acts and Ordinances of the Company of Merchant Taylors of the City of York*, written shortly after the author was Master in 1946–48, was both out of date and out of print. Whether this is a worthy successor it is not for us to say: we are only too conscious that 'guild history' proves a difficult genre of historical writing – and one which often raises more questions than it resolves. However we have no doubt that these essays do reveal the way in which the history of the Merchant Taylors of York can throw significant new light on the economic and social forces which influenced the development of a town now celebrated as England's most important 'historic city'. And for those who believe that history has few more pleasurable spectacles to offer than astonishing and unexpected reversals of fortune, the great Taylors' Hall in Aldwark still poses question which words alone cannot adequately answer.

Barrie Dobson
David Smith

CRAFTS, FRATERNITIES AND GUILDS IN LATE MEDIEVAL YORK

H. Swanson

Today the most familiar public face of the crafts and fraternities of late medieval York is the magnificent cycle of mystery plays, evolved in the later middle ages to celebrate the feast of Corpus Christi. Performing the cycle was a huge undertaking, commencing at dawn and running on well after dark, when the mercers' pageant of The Last Judgement was performed in a blaze of torch-light. The whole elaborate performance, whilst having profound spiritual significance, was also designed to make manifest to contemporaries the scale and variety of York's enterprise. It gave evidence of how many flourishing crafts there were in the city, and how prosperous the trading operations of the most potent of those crafts, the mercers. The complex of meanings inherent in the plays is an indication too of the variety of the functions performed by the various associations of craft, fraternity and guild in the city in the later middle ages.

Upwards of fifty different craft associations eventually came to be involved in the processions and pageants of Corpus Christi. Indeed so complex had the ceremony become that by the fifteenth century it was spread over two days. Whereas on Corpus Christi day itself the pageants were presented by the crafts, the procession on the following day was led by a different kind of association, the Corpus Christi Guild. Membership of this guild cut across that of the craft associations, attracting people from all over the city, and beyond. There were three of these big civic guilds in late medieval York, the other two being the combined Guild of St. Christopher and St. George, and the Guild of St. Anthony; of the three, Corpus Christi was the largest and the most prestigious. In addition to the civic guilds there was a large number of smaller fraternities and guilds within the city. The majority of these small fraternities were based on the parish rather than looking city wide for members, but some were attached to one of the numerous houses of religious orders scattered across York. In all therefore, there was a plethora of associations which the men and women of late medieval York might join, depending on their resources, occupations and personal connections.

All these associations, craft, guild and fraternity, had some shared aspirations, and can be defined as 'groups of men and women joining together for communal purposes, and bound to each other by common ties of loyalty'.[1] They provided mutual support for both the living and the dead, in the form of convivial gatherings in this life and provision for the soul, to hasten its uncomfortable passage through purgatory, in the next. But given such a broad definition, these associations could look remarkably different. The scale of the mutual support given by each association varied greatly across place and time, depending on the membership and the kind of resources and power that those members wielded. As a result they acquired a variety of different functions depending on the particular aspirations of their members, and depending on the society in which that guild, fraternity or craft flourished. A further potential source of confusion arises from the fact that in different countries the terms had different connotations. At one extreme, the wealthiest and most powerful guilds in autonomous towns in continental Europe, for example the mercantile guilds of Florence, controlled the government, set foreign policy, controlled taxation, administered justice. Mutual support for the living in these cases meant establishing a political regime that supported those who controlled commerce and industry. In England the powerful centralising monarchy meant that no city or town was autonomous and that even the most potent London companies could not exercise this kind of authority. A guild or a fraternity in an English provincial town exercised a certain amount of power locally if its membership comprised the civic elite, but a small parish fraternity had neither significant local clout or, indeed, aspirations to do anything more than offer immediate local support.

However, despite the elastic nature of the terms craft, guild and fraternity, we can say pretty confidently that in late medieval England a clear distinction existed in people's minds between fraternities and guilds on the one hand and crafts on the other, for the two types of association did have somewhat different objectives and priorities. Generally speaking guild and fraternity were interchangeable terms; they were associations whose membership was voluntary in contrast to craft associations which came to be compulsory by the later middle ages. Hence it is convenient to deal with each in turn, taking first the guilds and fraternities, before turning to the crafts.

Guilds and fraternities were usually associations of lay men and women; clergy were not excluded from them, but those such as York's Corpus Christi Guild, founded by chaplains and run by clergy, were the exception. Because the nature of the guild or fraternity depended on who its members actually were, it is not surprising that they had a fairly fluid existence. The Guild of St. Anthony was dynamic and 'even predatory': it poached members from the Holy Trinity Guild based in the Dominican Priory in 1418; absorbed the Paternoster Guild in 1444-6; merged with the Guild of St. Mary and St. Martin at around the same time, as senior partner in the merger.[2] The Corpus Christi Guild, although originally founded by chaplains, came to attract the socially aspirant; membership brought the heady prospect of metaphorically rubbing shoulders with the city and county elite. The Guild of the Holy Trinity began as a fraternity within the hospital of St Mary and Jesus in Fossgate, but eventually came to take over the entire enterprise.

This fluidity is one of the reasons that counting numbers of guilds and fraternities is a little difficult. Another was the informality of many of them, as the English crown found out when trying to make a survey of all guilds in 1388-9. This was a time of political crisis when guilds fell under suspicion for being potentially subversive secret societies, though greed at the thought of acquiring guild assets was another powerful motive behind the survey. But the returns from the enquiry are not as helpful as they might at first seem and the survey is a better indicator of the government's suspicions than of the number of guilds that existed. The very informality and transience that made the government so suspicious, made the guilds difficult to track down then and makes it equally hard to locate them now. The 1389 returns give only two guilds for York, the Paternoster Guild and the Guild of St. John the Baptist; it seems very unlikely that there were no others at that date. Where they survive, references in church-wardens' accounts or parochial guild accounts, can fill out the picture, but for York evidence to supplement the skimpy 1389 returns has to come mainly from 15th century wills. But wills too have their limitations, for will makers were only a small minority of the population in the later middle ages, so bequests to guilds and fraternities are unlikely to give us the full number of fraternities.

The nature of the surviving evidence for guilds and fraternities also gives a somewhat slanted perception of their function. The returns that were made to the 1389 enquiry suggest that guilds were keen to downplay anything that could remotely smack of subversion, in order to keep themselves out of trouble; consequently they were likely to emphasize the religious aspects of the guild rather than any social or occupational functions it had. As for wills, the testators were almost invariably on their death-beds, when their minds were focused on the rapidly approaching trials of purgatory. They were therefore more likely to highlight the role of the guild in providing prayers for their souls, than to dwell on the jolly times to be had eating and drinking together. But both aspects of guild life deserve equal attention, indeed cannot be completely separated. The sense of community was expressed in religious ritual; furthermore the boundary between the living and the dead was perceived as a very porous one, active kinship extending to those beyond the grave.

But before looking in more detail at what a guild or fraternity did for its members, something needs to be said about the way it was organised – though with the smallest fraternities there was likely to have been little or no formal organisation at all. Both men and women could be members, though in some places there were single gender guilds (though no evidence in fact survives for them in late medieval York); they were usually associated with stages in the life cycle, for example young men's or widows's guilds. Men and women were not however equal members of guilds and guild officials were virtually always men. The number of officials varied with the size of the guild: a small parish guild like St. Anne's in St. Margaret's church, Walmgate, had only two wardens, whereas the large Corpus Christi Guild had a master and six keepers. These officials were elected from the membership, but election often meant being chosen by and from amongst the 'best', the most prestigious members of the guild. This was an almost inevitable reflection of social relations in what was an intensely hierarchical society, and it was, also inevitably, open at times to abuse: there was a major legal enquiry when in 1533 members of the St. Christopher Guild became aggrieved at the way that elections in the guild had been cornered by a clique who then ran the guild for their own profit.[3]

If guild meetings were held, members were expected to turn up, payment of a fine either in cash or in wax to sustain the guild lights being the punishment for failure to do so. Very few guilds had their own hall, and these mainly date from the fifteenth century; others must have met in hired rooms or in the churches where they maintained the light to their patron saint. Some kind of financial contribution was often expected of members. A guild might charge an entry fee and members paid quarterage, that is a subscription made in instalments. So for example, the members of St. Anne's guild paid quarterage varying from 1d. to 6d. depending on means. Entrants to the Corpus Christi Guild paid 'what their consciences dictated'; perhaps unsurprisingly the average fell from 2s. 7d. in 1415 to under 2d. in 1540.[4] Though by no means always taxing sums, the fact that some payment had to be made inevitably meant that it was the most vulnerable, the destitute, who were excluded from this form of support, unable to afford even the most minimal contributions.

Central to a guild's activity was religious ritual, directed to either a patron saint or focused on the attributes of God, for example the Holy Trinity. The obligation on guild members was to reduce the time spent by their fellows in purgatory. Everyone was destined to spend some time there as no one could perform adequate penance in this world for sins committed. To this end all guilds sustained a candle or light before the altar or image of their patron who was to intercede for them. Guild members would get their brothers and sisters off to a good start in the next world through a decent, well attended funeral, and subsequent memorial masses. The ordinances of the Carpenter's fraternity of 1482 specify:

'yf ony of the said fraternite dy, the said bredirhode shall gyfe for a trentall of messis to be dooyn for hys sawll in the said Freir Austens, vs'.[5]

If the guild were affluent it might support a permanent chaplain, though only a small minority of guilds, such as the three big civic guilds of York, could afford to do this. On the strength of their investment in property, the Guild of St. Christopher and St. George, for example, supported two chantry priests, to say masses daily throughout the year for the members of the Guild. Processions and performances mounted by the large civic guilds attracted the attention and hence prayers of a much wider audience, and gave in turn a spiritual benefit to that audience through their involvement. These events could be entertaining as well as spiritually and morally instructive: in the Paternoster Guild's play of the Lord's Prayer 'virtues commended' was likely to be soberly presented but 'vices and sins reproved' gave plenty of scope for lively extemporization.[6]

The large increase in the recorded number of guilds and fraternities in the late middle ages is very probably associated with the growing desire of the laity to take steps to secure their own salvation. Arguably the late medieval church was 'demand led' with the laity prepared to pay for good works which brought grace, participating in the mass being one of the most spiritually potent of these good works. The gift of grace was of course available to all through the sacraments administered by the parochial clergy, but the fraternity or guild gave the opportunity of what might be called a 'bespoke' service in this respect. The lay members could dictate the terms on which they employed priests to say masses for them, could decide for themselves the most efficacious forms of ritual and charity — as far as funds extended.

However we should not see parish guilds and parish clergy in competition with each other; they seem largely to have existed in co-operation rather than opposition. How many guilds a single parish sustained varied a great deal. The abundance of York's parish churches, and their small size, meant that there were unlikely to be more than one or two fraternities attached to each parish. This contrasted with a town such as Doncaster where the one parish church had 18 fraternities attached to it.[7] Guild members were likely to be the most spiritually active members of the parish — for we certainly should not imagine all medieval men and women were diligent church-goers. Clearly there were bound to be some problems, human nature being what it is, and it is probable that there were some tough little cliques among the parish fraternities, indulging in spiritual one-up-man-ship or jockeying for social position. But an avowed intention of many guilds was to order behaviour and diffuse tension, so that the guild of St. John the Baptist was characteristic in having procedures for reconciling quarrelsome members.

The reference to reconciling quarrels draws attention to the important role guilds performed in acting as a form of social cement. That men and women could be members of several guilds reinforced this role, creating interlocking networks that helped stabilize society, for guilds offered support and assurance against an uncertain existence as well as a certain death. They were all the more valuable in towns, the honey pot for migrants. Through guilds and fraternities many of these immigrants could be integrated into urban society where there was no family network to support them. Hence the guild was one of the fundamental social units of the late medieval town. At a minimum members would get together to share a meal, a very simple one for the members of St. Anne's guild who bought bread, cheese and beer to celebrate All Saints. In contrast, by the sixteenth century, the St. Christopher Guild was accustomed to feast on venison given to them by the Scrope family.[8] Cooks and other victuallers might be encouraged to join a guild, in return for their contribution in kind to the feast.

The solidarity fostered amongst members of the guild was shown in practical help towards members who had fallen on hard times. The ordinances for the York carpenters' fraternity made provision that:

> 'yf ony of the said fraternite fall to povert, so that tha may not wyrk, or happyn to be blynd, or to leis thar gudes by unhapp of the world, then the forsaid breyrhode to gyffe tham iiiid every weke, as long as tha liff, by way of almusse'.[9]

Charity was specifically for guild members and did not extend to the wider public; if donations were given to the poor at funerals it was because their prayers were considered to be particularly effective, and the gesture was largely symbolic. Practical assistance to guild members also came in the extension of credit, or the granting of loans, something that must have proved particularly valuable to those without family or influential connections. Of course the influential also used the networking possibilities of guild membership. William Barton, skinner, who died in 1435, was a member of the Guilds of Corpus Christi, St. Christopher, Paternoster, St. Mary of the skinners and St. John the Baptist of the tailors.[10] This might be a mark of exceptional devoutness, but at the same time Barton was probably cultivating as many useful connections as possible amongst potential partners and customers.

Membership of the three large civic guilds, and very probably many of the parish guilds was drawn from a wide variety of occupations, and the help given was not contingent on membership of a particular craft. However there were good reasons for the members of the same craft to form their own fraternity. Geographical proximity was one. Most pin makers for example lived in the parish of St. Crux and we know that the pinners sustained a light in that parish church from the awful years of the Black Death onwards. Even when scattered across the city, shared experience would bring members of a craft together in mutual support. To this end members of a craft might found a new guild, or they might take over an existing one, as the mercers seem to have done with the Holy Trinity Guild. But guilds and fraternities were not exclusive to one craft, though that craft might dominate its proceedings and determine its main objectives. Neighbourliness, marriage, mutual business interests would make a rigid policy of exclusion counterproductive.

Nor was there necessarily only one guild formed by members of a craft. The cordwainers (shoemakers) paid for a candle in the Minster, but some of them also supported a fraternity of St. Mary at the Carmelite Friary. By the early sixteenth century yet another guild of cordwainers dedicated to St. Augustine had appeared at the Austin Friars.[11] This might be accounted for by the sheer number of cordwainers scattered across the city. It might also represent the development of splinter groups; for example where there were large numbers of servants in a craft they might form their own fraternity to protect their interests. Although we should not exaggerate the gulf that existed between small masters and their servants, there undoubtedly were some very severe antagonisms at times. So in the 1430s the cordwainers' servants used their fraternity to agitate for better terms and conditions; the masters in turn hastened to the city council complaining of the servants' 'illicit meetings and prohibited confederations at the Friars'.[12]

However closely a fraternity might be connected with one craft it was not wholly identical with it. Membership of the fraternity was voluntary, as the carpenters made quite clear:

> 'every man of the said occupacion within the said cite shalnot be
> compellid ne boundyn to be of the said fraternite ne brodirhod, ne noyn
> to be thar of bot soch as will of thar free will'.[13]

In contrast, obedience to the regulations of the craft as set out by the city council was mandatory. The carpenters' ordinances make a distinction between the regulations of the fraternity and those governing the production and sale of goods undertaken by the 'occupacion' of carpenters. 'Occupacion' was in fact only one of several different terms used to describe members of the same craft; they might also refer to themselves as belonging to an 'arte', 'artificium', 'crafte' or mystery, and it is under any one of these names that they appear in the copious ordinances recorded by the city council.

But though craft and fraternity were perceived as two separate entities, in practice they were often closely related. In many of the craft ordinances recorded by the city council the dedication to a candle or light remains embedded. The pinners, like the cordwainers, required new apprentices to contribute to the fraternity candle on starting work. The tailors, as did many other crafts, required fines to be paid in the form of wax. But whereas the self-regulation of the craft fraternities was designed for the mutual support of members, the ordinances for crafts enrolled by the city council tended to be made of sterner stuff. It may be that these ordinances were initiated by the crafts themselves, seeking better guarantees of their authority to regulate their own internal affairs. What seems more likely is that the council saw them as a good way to control the work force and to legislate for consumer protection. The varied self-help arrangements of artisan fraternities and associations provided a base which was adapted by the civic authorities and turned into a comprehensive administrative system for the enforcement of trading standards and labour relations. Supervision of the ordinances was to be made by searchers appointed by the craft and with authority over all practitioners of that craft. In order to explain how this systematisation came about it is necessary to go back to the first appearance of guilds in York, in the twelfth century, when there was already a connection with commerce.

One of the first urban institutions recorded in York, as elsewhere, was the guild merchant, granted to the city in the mid-twelfth century. This was a trading association that gave privileges, such as reduction of toll, to its members and was designed to protect the interests of those living in the town against outsiders. It also, inevitably gave its members a commercial advantage over non-members living in the town. We do not know how widely it threw its net, though it did include some artisans, but there would always be a substantial section of the townspeople who could not afford to join. From the start the people who most benefited from the guild merchant were the wholesale dealers, and there was deliberate discrimination against some artisans, particularly those in the cloth making industry. It is probably because the large scale dealers used their privileges to try and gain control over all transactions in the most valuable commodities, that groups of artisans formed their own guilds in the twelfth century. This is certainly true of the weavers whose guild in York dates from 1163. It may also be true for the guilds of cordwainers (1160), glovers and leather workers (1181) and saddlers (1181). All paid sums of money to the crown for official recognition. But the battle against predatory merchants was one that they could not win and most of these guilds rapidly disappear from the records. We only know the fate of the weavers' guild which was already dreadfully in debt by 1214.

Because of its regulatory role the guild merchant had a certain amount of judicial power over commercial matters. In this respect it predated and for a time paralleled in some degree the emerging organs of urban government. As these latter grew more complex, and acquired greater judicial authority, there was a decreasing rationale for a separate guild merchant to regulate trade, particularly as the same people were likely to be found in control of both guild and government. Hence the guild merchant faded out in York in the thirteenth century. With this change came another, as the freedom of the city came to take the place of membership of the guild merchant as a means of 'counting in' the economically privileged. But though the guild merchant went, guilds remained a way of creating and reinforcing common bonds – sometimes in pursuit of very dubious objectives. The people of York complained in 1301 about an ostensibly religious guild, founded by Andrew de Bolingbroke, a complaint which was entirely justified. The guild was actually the cover for a clique who were manipulating civic government to their own advantage, by rigging the tax system and diverting money to their own pockets. Amongst the fifty-four members of the guild were a few wealthy artisans, including two tailors; it is rather disillusioning to find also that it included Richard Tunnock whose illegal activities presumably helped him fund the 'bellfounder's window' in York Minster.[14]

When craft associations emerge in the records again in the fourteenth century, it was the city council and not the crown which was the body authorising and regulating them. The earliest of these ordinances are those of the girdlers, dating from 1307, but surviving because transcribed when a new set of girdlers' ordinances was enrolled in 1417. Whereas guilds of artisans had been a potential source of antagonism in the twelfth and thirteenth centuries, by the late fourteenth and fifteenth centuries craft associations had become politically acceptable. The gradually changing attitude to artisans is evident from the 1330s onwards in York, beginning with a transformation of the significance of the freedom of the city. Access to the franchise had become very restricted by the thirteenth century and some categories of artisan, like the weavers, were excluded from the freedom altogether – a legacy of the hostility between manufacturer and wholesaler that had existed in the textile industry since the twelfth century. However from the 1330s access to the freedom began to widen, and after the Black Death the stream of new entrants became a positive flood. This was by no means an act of altruism on the part of the city council. The city needed to attract a skilled workforce, particularly after the devastation of the Black Death, and extending the freedom was one way of doing this.

But from the council's point of view, this granting of privileges towards artisans had to be paralleled by a system of stringent control over their operations. We see therefore from the later fourteenth century onwards a policy of regulating the York crafts and systematically recording those regulations in the civic records. The perceived need to regulate became more acute with the huge changes following on the Black Death, when a shortage of labour encouraged mobility and drove up wages. National legislation of 1363–4 aimed, in conjunction with the Statute of Labourers of 1351, to keep control of the urban labour force. It specified that 'artificers, handicraft people, hold them every one to one mystery, which he will chose betwixt this and the said feast of Candlemas, and two of every craft shall be chosen to survey, that none use other craft than the same which he hath chosen'.[15] Hence the great list of craft ordinances surviving from medieval York is not just evidence of the range of manufacturing in the city; it is witness to the enthusiasm of the city council for acting on this legislation and regulating, as far as possible, everything that moved.

Craft organisations were not therefore spontaneous and democratic. They may well have been a pre-existing fraternity mediating relations between craft members, but this was licked into a different shape by the council. In line with the requirements of Edward III's legislation, two searchers answerable to the council were appointed for each craft. The searchers were responsible for inspection of goods, enforcing terms of employment and ensuring attendance at the compulsory craft meetings. The greater part of the fines for breach of any of these regulations went to the council.

The enrolled regulations were almost completely uninterested in whether the craft feasted or prayed together; these things should not affect the smooth running of the market. As long as there was no trouble, the only aspect of the craft's social activities that the council was interested in was their ability to put on a play at Corpus Christi. There is the occasional, illuminating, exception. The marshalls (whose work was originally the shoeing of horses) and the smiths were constantly at each others throats in the fifteenth century, to the exasperation of the civic authorities. Despite the fact that the two crafts were by this time doing virtually the same work, they persisted in maintaining different identities, expressed in devotion to different saints. After lengthy arbitration the mayor and council ruled in 1443 that:

> 'every maister of the said craftes shal com to Seint William chapell upon Ouse brigg every yere, to thair devyne service of Seint Loy, upon the morn after Missomerday ... and com to thair mete al togeder upayn of vid... And also that every man of the said craftes shal com to messe at the said chapell every yere upon the morn after Seint Andrewe day'.[16]

The communion wafers may have stuck in their gullets and they probably ate with gritted teeth at the feast, but they had to do it.

Another telling detail comes in the ordinances of the carpenters' fraternity. Members of the fraternity were expected to come together twice a year to pay their subscriptions and participate in the fraternity masses at the Austin Friars. But any that:

> 'is absent and not thar, shal pay a pound of wax to the behove of the said fraternite, and vid. to the behove of the chambir of thys full nobill cite, withowt he have a resonabill excuse'.[17]

All breaches of fraternity rules similarly entailed a fine payable in part to the council. The justification for this can be found in a statute of 1436 which required all guilds to register their ordinances with the civic authorities.[18] But it is only the carpenters' fraternity that we know about in any detail; the almost complete silence on the subject of all other craft fraternities is frustrating. We cannot assume that there was a fraternity or guild associated with each of the recorded crafts; on the other hand because of the specific bias of the existing records, we cannot assume that there was not. Moreover it is clear that, whatever the artisans felt, in the minds of the council fraternity and mystery were linked and both subject to their control.

One occupational group has been left out of the above account – that of the merchants. The most successful merchants controlled the city government in the later middle ages. There was no formal constitution restricting power to these people; it was their wealth and control of trade which allowed a small group of men to retain power amongst themselves. Membership of the ruling councils was by co-option which ensured that the existing elite could restrict access to their circle to those who were deemed acceptable. This meant absorbing ambitious and successful artisans from individual crafts into their number, something that could be done painlessly. Merchants had, therefore, no need of a separate craft organisation; the regulation needed to forward their business was made by the city council that they controlled. However they did maintain two searchers as a means of quality control and very possibly to keep smaller scale merchants and potential rivals in line.

So what was the genesis of the Mercers' Company, which obtained a royal charter in 1430? This is by no means clear, though it was founded through the efforts of the leading brethren of the Holy Trinity hospital in Fossgate, and almost certainly in close association with that hospital. The very obscurity of the origins of both hospital and company, and the constant changes of name by which the former was known, are salutary reminders of the fluidity of fraternity and guild organisation. A fraternity of Jesus Christ and the Blessed Virgin Mary, founded in 1357 had become the hospital of Holy Trinity and St. Mary by the late fourteenth century and was more commonly referred to as Holy Trinity hospital by the early fifteenth century. The brethren of this hospital, listed in 1420, were largely mercers. Mercers by the fifteenth century were probably not dealing in commodities that were significantly different from those handled by merchants; hence the retention of the name may signal a group which saw themselves as having a distinct social identity. For the brethren of Holy Trinity were not in the 'top flight' of York merchants.[19] The establishment of the company may well have been in part to put the Holy Trinity hospital on a more secure footing; but equally it could serve the interests of a group who were on the fringes of power, increasing their prospects of both economic and political success by providing a base for shared enterprise. The company they formed was clearly distinct from the craft associations of artisans. Certainly it shared similar objectives of overseeing the smooth running of business, but its ordinances did not have to be enrolled before the mayor and defaulters were brought before the company's own courts. Equally significantly, any fines levied were kept by the company and did not have to be shared half and half with the city council.

If the aim of the foundation was in part to acquire status, it was amply rewarded. Founder brethren went on to civic greatness as chamberlains and mayors, and the company began to attract members from among the governing elite, so that by the 1470s it was indeed the top people's club, the social arm of the civic government. But this social function was underpinned by hard-headed economic considerations. That the mercers acquired their charter as the 'worthy companye of the noble craft of mercers' is instructive.[20] It follows practice which had been adopted in London from the mid-fourteenth century onward, where, it has been suggested, the use of the word company indicated a change in perception, with members emphasising commerce more than commensality.[21]

The full array of manufacturing and mercantile associations was on display at Corpus Christi. As noticed earlier, the celebration of the feast of Corpus Christi gave rise to so huge a spectacle that it had to take place over two days, the pageants on the first day, the Corpus Christi procession on the second. Participation in the pageants was the only aspect of the ritual life of the crafts that the city council got really exercised over. The council had very probably initiated the play cycle and was certainly determined to control it; it was an important way of articulating their vision of the city, a display both of economic strength and spiritual unity, the people of York as the visible body of Christ. The performance thus carried a whole series of messages – spiritual and moral teaching, civic pride, the hierarchical order of society, civic harmony – all of which could be synthesized in theory but which in practice might come into conflict. The gap between the council's aspirations and the ability of the crafts to deliver was one source of tension; another was that between the presentation of an ordered hierarchy and the conflicting interests of different crafts.

In order to sustain the pageants virtually everybody was required to contribute, even when they had no craft organisation. The masons came to be responsible for the pageant of the Purification of the Blessed Virgin Mary, but not without financial help from the unskilled and semi-skilled:

> 'labourers of this city yearly henceforth, viz the Faggotbearers, Gardeners, Earthwallers, Pavers, Dikers and Groundwallers with earth shall pay and deliver each year ... 13s. 4d. to aid the expenses of that pageant'.[22]

The labourers were in return not to be obliged to contribute to anyone else's pageant. It looks as if the poor labourers had been pressurised from a number of quarters to help fund a show that would not bring down mayoral wrath, for the civic records are full of complaints by the crafts about the costs of putting on a pageant. These complaints never met with sympathy from the council. Furthermore the mayor and council kept strict control of all stages of the production:

> 'yerely in the tyme of lentyn there shall be called afore the Maire for the tyme beyng iiii of the moste Connyng, discrete and able playeres within this Citie to serche, here and examen all the plaiers and plaies [and] pagentes thrughoute all the artificeres belonging to corpus christi Plaie'.[23]

Any performers found not up to scratch were not allowed to perform. Mayor and council also set the route, the order of performance, the times of performance, and imposed fines on any craft that disrupted proceedings.

It was the craft as a whole, not the fraternity, that was made responsible for the pageant. But the effort involved in the production, the processing and performing together in public, must have help give the craft a sense of identity beyond that which could be imposed by the enforcement of regulations. In this respect the Corpus Christi play may have worked towards the merging of identity of mystery and fraternity.

The idealised organic whole of the city presented in the plays was one that was based on an acute sense of social hierarchy. Harmony was sustained when everyone knew and kept to their place, though this perception of the social order as recorded by the literate does not necessarily faithfully tell us how it was perceived from the bottom upwards. Neither were all agreed as to their relative place in the hierarchy. Hence whilst the plays and procession were aimed at demonstrating the operation of the city as a harmonious whole, there could be furious fighting going on between participants. So for example, trouble between cordwainers and weavers over precedence disrupted the festival between 1490 and 1493.[24]

The status accorded to different occupations was not entirely related to the product or the profitability of the craft. Equally the relative standing of crafts varied somewhat from town to town; fullers in Winchester in the late fourteenth and early fifteenth century were high status artisans, in York they were amongst the poorest. An important factor in fixing status was whether a group of artisans had a stake in the wholesale trade, or whether they were restricted to piecework and small-scale retailing. The Winchester fullers had managed to escape the limitations of the small scale and had joined the mercantile elite, whereas the York fullers did not. The hostility to the weavers encountered earlier effectively excluded them from the profitable wholesale trade; the occasional individual might prosper enough to become a merchant, the status of the entire craft was not lifted as a result. This contrasts with the success of the tailors' craft whose interests increasingly merged with those of the drapers. There was prejudice against other manufacturing occupations as well. Medieval towns had scores of leather workers; perhaps as a direct consequence cordwainers were held in deep suspicion. The fact that they were constantly at odds with the tanners cannot have helped their reputation. Tanners too were suspect, very probably because the value of their product made them a potential commercial threat to merchants, whilst the smell of it made them socially unacceptable. For much the same reasons, and for their association with blood, butchers were usually regarded as social pariahs.

Changes in the economy in the later middle ages brought a number of changes to the standing of different crafts. Throughout the country the Black Death of 1348-9 brought a savage reduction of the population; recurring plagues kept the population low for the next 150 years. The resulting labour shortage has already been seen as one reason for changing the policy towards admissions to the freedom of York. Labour shortages also drove up wages. In terms of individual living standards, higher wages meant more lavish patterns of consumption and some artisans profited as a result, and their greater prosperity facilitated social climbing. But whereas artisans such as pewterers and tailors could become substantial and well respected citizens, other crafts continued to face deep prejudice. Even though people ate much more meat, the butchers could never be really acceptable, and suspicion of them got deeper as they got richer.

But the economic consequences of a low population that resisted recovery were complex, and resulted in a downturn in some significant respects. The growing wealth of certain groups of York artisans must been seen in the context of a drastic reduction in the scale of the urban textile industry and a decline in mercantile fortunes. The weaving of woollen cloth, which had boomed in York in the late fourteenth and early fifteenth century, contracted thereafter. It has long been suggested that the restrictive practices of the craft organisations drove manufacturing industry into the country. But one of the outstanding characteristics of the York weavers' guild was its failure to take a successful stand against the merchants who controlled the marketing of cloth; so if the intensity of urban regulation was discouraging, this cannot be imputed solely to the craft. With the contraction in manufacture came a contraction in the export trade. The growing output of the textile centres in the West Riding did not pass through the hands of York merchants but was exported by Londoners. And it was not only the cloth trade that diminished, the later middle ages saw all overseas trade concentrated in London, to the detriment of provincial merchants.

The city of York in the late fifteenth century was as a result experiencing acute economic difficulties, and civic finances were in a desperate state. One result of this was to alter the balance of power in the city. It was no longer just a case of wealthy individual artisans seeking to join the merchant class which had controlled civic government for so long. Whole occupations, those whose market had enabled them to avoid the consequences of the economic downturn, were now seeking better representation in civic affairs. The constitution of 1517 gives a good insight into the relative status of the city's crafts. A distinction was made between major and minor crafts; major crafts were represented on the council by two members, minor crafts by one. All other crafts, which in theory had previously had a voice in the common council, were excluded from formal representation. Amongst the major crafts were mercers, drapers, grocers, tailors, dyers, goldsmiths. Included amongst the minor crafts were some of the newly prosperous, innholders and pewterers, as well as glovers, armourers and ironmongers who had a long established place in the city's economy. The small group of glaziers was deemed a major craft, as there were a number of wealthy and influential men amongst them; the numerous butchers were (probably reluctantly) included among the minor crafts. Tanners and cordwainers were excluded completely.

By the early sixteenth century much had conspired to make craft organisation ubiquitous. Systematic regulation, the communal effort of the pageant, the battle for representation in difficult times all gave rise to a formal structure through which craft aspirations were expressed. Craft-based fraternities were very probably increasingly subsumed under this organisation. But even greater changes were in the offing with the Protestant Reformation, which can quite legitimately be seen as a revolution. Religion had touched every aspect of urban life; the dismantling of Catholicism transformed urban society. One aspect of this change was the abolition of the religious fraternities that had bound people together. Henceforth the only way that occupational groups could express their common purpose and sense of solidarity was through the craft organisations regulated and authorised by the city council.

Notes

1 V. Bainbridge, *Gilds in the Medieval Countryside: Social and Religious Change in Cambridgeshire c.1350–1558* (Woodbridge, 1996), p.19.

2 D.J.F. Crouch, *Piety, Fraternity and Power: Religious Gilds in Late Medieval Yorkshire 1389–1547* (York, 2000), p.141.

3 E. White, *The St. Christopher and St. George Guild of York* (Borthwick Paper 72, York, 1987), p.11.

4 Crouch, *Piety, Fraternity and Power*, p.187.

5 YMB, vol. 2, ed. M. Sellers (Surtees Society 125, 1914), p.279.

6 REED, York, ed. A.F. Johnston and M. Rogerson, 2 vols (Manchester, 1979), pp.310,732,693.

7 Crouch, *Piety, Fraternity and Power*, p.124.

8 P. Hoskin, 'Some late 14th century gild and fabric wardens accounts from the church of St. Margaret, Walmgate, York' in *The Church in Medieval York* ed. D.M. Smith (Borthwick Text and Calendar 24, York, 1999), pp.85–6; White, *St. Christopher and St. George Guild*, p.15.

9 YMB, vol. 2, p.279.

10 BI, Probate Register 3, ff.408v–409.

11 Crouch, *Piety, Fraternity and Power*, p.134.

12 YMB, vol.1, p.191.

13 YMB, vol.2, p.278.

14 G.O. Sayles, 'The dissolution of a gild at York in 1306', EHR, 55 (1940)

15 *Statutes of the Realm*, vol.1, 37 Edward III c.6.

16 YMB, vol.2, p.181.

17 YMB, vol.2, pp.278–9.

18 *Statutes of the Realm*, vol.2, pp.298–9.

19 L.R. Wheatley, The York Mercers Guild 1420–1502 (York University MA thesis, 1993) p.127.

20 *The York Mercers and Merchant Adventurers, 1356–1917*, ed. M. Sellers (Surtees Society 129, 1917) p.34.

21 P. Nightingale, *A Medieval Mercantile Community* (London, 1995) p.240.

22 REED, York, p.778.

23 REED, York, p.109.

24 *York Civic Records*, vol.2, ed. A. Raine (YASRS, 103, 1940) pp.56–8,70,73–4,90, 93–4,96–100.

Plate 1 'The Merchant Taylors Hall from the Bar Walls, Aldwark', showing the medieval original west gable of the Hall: coloured drawing by E. Ridsdale Tate, 2 October 1914.

Plate 2 'Merchant Taylors Hall from the City Walls', showing the east gable of the Hall: ink and pen drawing by E. Ridsdale Tate, 19 May 1904.

Plate 3 The Great Hall, looking west, drawn by Arthur Gill, apparently when the Hall was being re-panelled in or about 1940.

Plate 4 The west end of the Great Hall before and after its extensive renovation in the 1940s and 1950s.

Plate 5   The position of the Merchant Taylors Hall, as shown on the first Ordnance Survey Map of York, surveyed 1850.

Plate 6 Millennium Group of all the Company in 2000 A.D. The portrait, of each of the 70 members was painted individually by the artist, Peter Mennim.

Peter Smith, the new Master, leads the Taylors' procession to their annual Guild Service at All Saints, Pavement, on Charter Day in June 2001.

The Great Hall set for dinner.

Plate 7

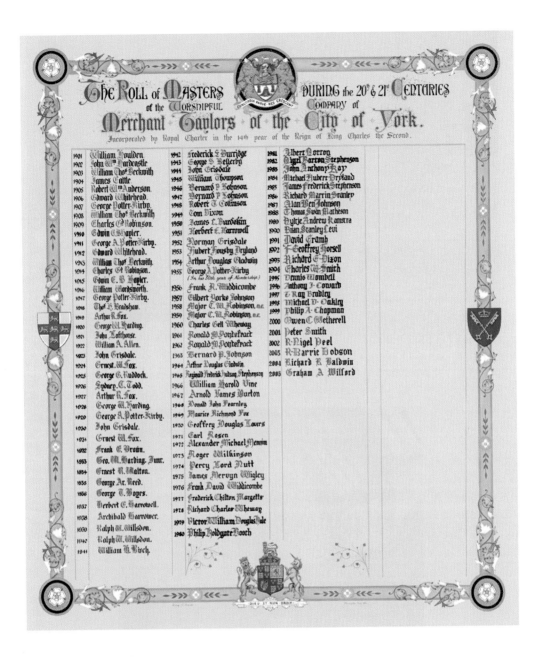

Plate 8 Roll of Masters of the Company since 1901.

THE TAILORS OF MEDIEVAL YORK: FROM CRAFT TO COMPANY

R.B. Dobson

The origins of the Merchant Taylors of York, like those of virtually all the guilds, fraternities, crafts and companies which once honeycombed the towns of medieval and early modern England, are not only impenetrably obscure but raise questions which will always be impossible to answer. Quite how and why did a comparatively modest medieval fraternity come to acquire one of the largest urban halls of fifteenth-century England and then continue to survive – and sometimes even flourish – for over six hundred years since it came to birth ? Historical ignorance has of course its compensations; and it is many years ago since Marc Bloch, the famous French medievalist, reminded historians that minute study of an acorn doesn't necessarily do much to make them understand the intricacies of the resulting oak tree.[1] That said, and although the craft or mystery of the tailors of York emerged out of the mists of unrecorded history, at least one moment in time seems more important for its mysterious development than any other.

In the spring of 1387, during the mayoralty of one of York's formidable overseas merchants of the period, William Selby, the city councillors agreed to enter in their official register a lengthy document in Norman French they styled the '*Ordinances des Tailleurs*'.[2] By the late fourteenth century the registration of such craft ordinances in the so-called Memorandum Books of the city of York was common enough and seems indeed – as in other major English towns – to have become almost compulsory. More unusually, the York tailors' ordinances of 1387 are prefixed by a list of no less than 128 names, those of the master tailors (*mestres taillours*) who allegedly consented to the detailed regulations which followed. Not surprisingly, all these York tailors were males and almost eighty per cent held surnames derived from place-names within forty or fifty miles of the city itself. On the assumption, not too questionable, that as late as the reign of Richard II such toponymic surnames still provide an approximate guide to the geographical origins of the tailors in question, the latter were overwhelmingly recruited from York and the surrounding villages and small towns of Yorkshire. To that extent the most enduring social dynamic in the history of the York tailors had already been established.[3] Although they occupied homes and workshops (normally identical) in the city of York, until the early nineteenth century these were usually men – and sometimes women – who were usually recruited from the city's local villages to serve what was largely a county and not just an urban market for the finest woollen clothing Yorkshire could supply.

The 1387 tailors' ordinances are however even more invaluable in providing the first surviving incontrovertible evidence that the tailors of York were by that date a coherent and organised professional community of readily identifiable members, united in the pursuit of certain common objectives and subject to self-regulation and to the imposition of penalties for any infringement of the rules and regulations they produced. What Bernard Johnson, the author of the first detailed history of the Merchant Taylors' Company, wrote over half a century ago still stands: 'this is the first document definitely dealing with tailors as a Gild: previous to this we have mention of tailors, but only as isolated individuals'[4] It is in fact unlikely that the York tailors of 1387 would have been regarded — by themselves or by others — as a craft 'guild', that highly ambiguous word. However, they certainly saw themselves as members of a relatively well articulated communal 'Taillour crafte', craft being the usual English translation of the Latin word 'ars' or the French word 'artifice', the latter employed in the original text of these first surviving ordinances themselves.[5] Not that these ordinances of 1387 were necessarily the first such rules the tailors of York ever compiled. Medieval urban craft ordinances are notoriously difficult to interpret, partly because they are rarely arranged in what would now seem a logical manner and especially because they tend only to survive as later and much expanded recensions of earlier and now totally lost regulations. As the detailed clauses of the York tailors' ordinances of 1387 and later themselves demonstrate to perfection, these are historical sources which often tell us disappointingly little about their members' daily routines and conditions of work. Rather they tend to focus on issues which had led to previous controversy and conflict, and especially on those offences against craft practice which warranted a monetary fine. Indeed under close examination, the York tailors' ordinances of 1387 are primarily devoted to setting the levels of such fines (usually ranging from 6d. to £2) for acts of craft malpractice and insubordination.

Nevertheless the revelations offered by the 1387 Ordinances are crucial to the understanding of how the late fourteenth-century York tailors' craft had emerged and was able to maintain its cohesion. As in many late medieval English craft associations, supreme authority within the fraternity of York tailors was exercised by an all-powerful group of searchers. At York these were 'four good men, loyal to their art' who were elected annually by a compulsory assembly of all the master tailors in the city on the feast day of St. James the Apostle (25 July). Any tailor who disobeyed or proved 'rebell to the serchors' was immediately liable to a fine of 40d.; and it was these four officers (no master is mentioned in the 1387 ordinances) who summoned general meetings of the craft, who organised its annual pageant on the feast of Corpus Christi every summer, and who supervised the standard of the clothing produced in the many tailors' workshops scattered through the city.[6] To an extent now hard to appreciate and often unduly neglected by historians of craft guilds, it was this power of search which probably did more than anything to bind the craft together. In the late medieval city of York as in the much more complex urban world of late medieval London, 'the meaning, extent and effectiveness of search is arguably the key to understanding the nature of the companies' hold over the city's economy'.[7] As in London too, it is striking that in practice the early ordinances of the York tailors seem considerably less concerned about the quality of the clothes produced by their members than by an intense desire to regulate and control the number of tailors at work in the city. Thus in 1387 it was decreed, to take only one example of the 'restrictive practices' ubiquitous at the time, that 'no stranger (i.e. non-member of the craft) 'sew in no place bot opynle in a mester shope'.[8] The York master tailors were themselves prohibited from enrolling more than a very few apprentices, no doubt one of the reasons why theirs was not an occupation which tended to produce large individual fortunes, even when the city's late medieval economy was probably at its most buoyant during the years around 1400. All in all, the impression left by these ordinances is of a very large craft indeed, obsessed by the dangers of overproduction and a consequent adverse effect on the livelihood of tailors already established in the city.

More surprisingly perhaps, the tailors' ordinances of 1387, like those of almost all York crafts of this period, make it abundantly clear that the fraternity was directly accountable to the mayor and council of the city sitting in their chamber on Ouse Bridge. Not only were the four searchers themselves made answerable to the mayor for any failure to 'do ther duti' but they were also required to inform the civic authorities of the shortcomings and delinquencies of master tailors throughout the city. It is even more noticeable, as in other surviving York craft ordinances, that the proceeds of nearly all fines imposed on defaulting tailors were to be shared (usually in two equal portions) between the four searchers on the one part and the city chamber on the other. Such a division was common practice in many English towns. There is no doubt, as soon as evidence begins to survive, that English town councils were at pains to exercise close supervision on both the internal constitutional as well as the economic activities of the craft guilds. When the tailors of Exeter had the temerity to acquire a charter of incorporation from Henry VI without the consent of the mayor and council of that city, the latter fought a long and ultimately successful campaign to have the charter annulled. In the city of York, however, the most striking demonstration of the power exercised by the York mayor and council over the city's crafts is their requirement that the latter's searchers should 'sustain and maintain' the costs and expenses of the tailors' annual Corpus Christi pageant from the proceeds of the contributions they were obliged to collect from every master tailor.[9]

Thanks to the survival of the official civic register of the York Corpus Christi play (written in the 1460s or 1470s), that play has become firmly established as the city's greatest contribution to English literature. It is equally important to stress that until and indeed beyond the onset of the Reformation that play was the most important agency for the communal religious ideology of both city and individual crafts. As in the case of the other York crafts, the tailors' obligation to 'put on their own play' every June undoubtedly did a very great deal to strengthen the craft's sense of identity and common purpose during the economic and religious vicissitudes of the two centuries between the 1370s and the final performance of the Corpus Christi cycle in 1569. Moreover, by 1415 the tailors had been given the responsibility of staging one of the concluding and most ambitious of the fifty-one plays in the cycle, namely 'The Ascension of the Lord to Heaven', with a large cast of Jesus, the Blessed Virgin Mary, St John the Evangelist, eleven apostles and two angels.[10] The origins of the city of York's huge and celebrated Corpus Christi play cycle are almost as mysterious as that of its many guilds; but as the first surviving documentary reference to those plays and pageants is as late as 1376, it is tempting to suppose that the civic council may have inaugurated the cycle as a whole shortly before that date in the knowledge that what seems to have been much the most expensive theatrical production in late medieval England could already be sustained by compulsory participation and financial levies from fifty or so of the town's most substantial crafts. One might well go further still and agree with Dr Heather Swanson that not only did the York city council initiate annual productions of the Corpus Christi play cycle as a whole but they probably did so (perhaps even as a primary motive) in order both to publicly identify the craft affiliations of its citizens and to exercise effective economic and political control over their potentially unruly and even subversive fraternities. To the tailors of York themselves, however, the annual progress of their play of the Ascension through the streets of York at the feast of Corpus Christi had a more simple and positive role to play: between the 1370s and 1560s here was the ideal opportunity in the civic year to display their high status in the city as well as their commitment to Biblical Christianity.[11]

However, for the historian of the Merchant Taylors of York, as for the student of almost all English urban craft fraternities, the extent to which their guild was originally created and fostered from above by the civic authorities rather than (as is traditionally believed) by enthusiastic voluntary association on the part of the craftsmen themselves is a very controversial and even contentious matter. It will probably always remain so for the simple reason that 'in general industrial organisation in York is undocumented before the fifteenth century'.[12] The absence of civic administrative records at York from before the 1370s is indeed a grave misfortune and hides from us forever the critical stages in the emergence of new forms of late medieval craft organization. Thus the first York Memorandum Book, invaluable (as we have seen) in preserving the earliest surviving texts of craft guild ordinances, only begins in 1376; the earliest surviving city chamberlains' account roll was compiled in 1396–7; and the first of the great archiepiscopal probate registers dates from 1389 to 1396.[13] Accordingly it is only after the 1370s that the history of York can be written from its own self-generated archives.

In the case of the city's tailors, as in that of the great majority of English urban occupational guilds, such a grave deficiency of original evidence is worse compounded by the disappearance of the medieval records of the craft itself. The earliest administrative record surviving in the present Merchant Taylors' archive is a small parchment register of 1560 (sometimes confusingly called the Calf Skin Roll), comprising only 15 folios and containing the oaths to be sworn by the beadle, master, incoming members and other officers of the Company.[14] Not a single York Tailors' Court Minute Book, Apprenticeship Register or Master's Account Book (the three standard components of most craft guild archives) survives before the reign of Elizabeth I. Although probably only a few late medieval York tailors were fully literate, it is inconceivable that their craft failed to conduct some of its business by means of written record. By 1486, for instance, not only the major City of London livery companies but also the York barber-surgeons were capable of producing highly elaborate registers.[15] No such medieval 'guild books' survive for the York tailors although it is clear from one of the city's 'house books' that in 1530 'the records of Saynt John Hall' (now completely disappeared) did contain tailors' apprenticeship registers. Perhaps some of these early records still survived as the so-called 'other olde Bookes as formerlye' delivered from one master to the next in the late seventeenth century; but if so, they have long since vanished into oblivion. So too have the personal 'books of debts' (*libri debitorum*) in which many York tailors (like John Carter in 1485) kept their own detailed record of money owed to them.[16] Any attempt to write the history of the York tailors' guild before the Reformation is therefore doomed to be an exercise in making bricks with very little straw indeed.

That said, there can be no serious doubt that from as early as the city's foundation in 71 A.D. groups of tailors must have played an important and numerically significant role in the economic activities of Roman Eboracum, then Anglian Eoferwic and — especially — Viking Jorvik. The celebrated excavation of the Coppergate site by the York Archaeological Trust in the 1970s made it abundantly clear that the latter supported a well-established textile industry before the Conquest. Somewhat unfortunately, the archaeological evidence for craft industry in York during the century after William I's Conquest of the North in 1066–70 has proved to be less easy to interpret, largely because the occupations pursued by the Norman inhabitants of the excavated housing in the town can often prove highly uncertain.[17] However, although the compilers of Domesday Book in the 1080s were notoriously indifferent to the existence of specialised labour in English boroughs, a unique entry in Little Domesday reveals that in the comparatively small town of Bury St Edmunds tailors were among the seventy-five craftsmen (in the company of bakers, brewers, washerwomen, shoemakers, robemakers, cooks and porters) serving the great abbey there.[18] It is hard to believe that major regional centres like York did not count many more tailors still among their residents by 1086. The twelfth century was also the period when the personal surname of 'Tailor' or 'Taillour' first became extremely widespread throughout English society, a surname – derived from the Old French *tailleur* – whose popularity outlasted the middle ages to become the fourth commonest second name in England and Wales by the 1850s.[19]

Needless to say, the exceptional popularity of the craft surname 'Tailor' or 'Taylor' is itself a reflection of the numerical ascendancy of the tailors' profession in the medieval and pre-industrial English town. On the whole most of the many studies of English and indeed European urban centres have failed to give enough emphasis to the extremely large numbers of townsmen and townswomen who gained their livelihood from the tailoring and other clothing professions. The main reason for such neglect is no doubt that tailors tend to leave few material remains to posterity of either the clothes they once made or indeed the – comparatively few and simple – tools of their trade. Moreover the practice of tailoring was often so dispersed and fragmented within a town's walls that it can sometimes prove almost invisible to ourselves today. In the words of William Cunningham over a century ago, 'Of all kinds of skilled labour, tailoring is the most likely to maintain its character as a household occupation; and the migratory character of the household would militate against the organisation in England of large workshops.'[20] However, and despite the fact that the skills of the medieval tailors have tended to receive infinitely less attention than that of the weavers, fullers and other crafts involved in the manufacture of woollen cloth, they were quite as crucial to the economic welfare of nearly all substantial English towns. Only after this volume was planned has it become apparent that previous neglect of English 'clothing culture' may be about to be redeemed. Meanwhile, it is important to remember, in Heather Swanson's words, that one of the major attractions – perhaps indeed the most important reason – for 'coming to market in York must have been the sheer availability of well-made clothes'.[21]

That particular comment must have been as applicable to the twelfth as the fifteenth century. Indeed the York tailors of the early 1450s probably believed, and were certainly prepared to inform the royal government, that a chaplain had prayed continuously for the souls of their predecessors for the previous three hundred years (*per trescentos annos iam elapsos*).[22] However, as we have seen, there is no direct evidence that the tailors of York were properly consolidated within some form of guild organisation before the fourteenth century. For whatever reason, probably the still unregulated nature of their mystery, the early medieval tailors were therefore apparently not one of those few York crafts (most prominently the weavers) who were from the twelfth century onwards described as 'guilds' in governmental records, usually because they were given some form of monopoly rights in exchange for becoming liable to the king's 'geld', in other words subject to financial exploitation by the Crown.[23] It is therefore hardly surprising that documentary allusions of any sort to York tailors before the fourteenth century are very rare and very uninformative, like the cryptic references to 'tailors of York' in a royal exchequer memoranda roll of 1274-5. [24]

Much more revealing are the ordinances imposed on the York crafts by Edward I's government in 1301 in an attempt to protect the royal officials and soldiers then resident within the city (in preparation for military campaigns against the Scots) from embezzlement by the local tradesmen. Although tailors figure less prominently in these ordinances than one might have expected, the maximum prices at which they could sell many of the clothes they produced were set at levels favourable to the purchaser. Accordingly a 'triple gown' was not to be sold for more that 12d. and three furred garments were to be priced at 18d., in direct confirmation – if such were needed – that at least some York tailors were then catering for the luxury clothing market.[25] However, it may be more significant still that already by 1301 the royal government could be confident that the York mayor and council had it within their power to impose price-fixing on the tailors as on the other crafts. As far as the very limited evidence allows us to know, there had probably never been a time when the tailors of York or indeed any other craft guild could withstand the economic authority of the city government for long.

Indeed it was due to an initiative by the mayor and aldermen of York and not of its crafts in their own right that in 1272 we can at last begin to know the names of the tailors and the other tradesmen of the town. Thanks to the survival of the first great York Freemen's Register, undoubtedly the most precious item in the City Archives, from that year onwards to 1671 there exists an authoritative and more or less complete list of all the individuals who became citizens of the town, together with a one-word description of their respective professions or occupations. For a few years, between 1272 and 1306, the Freemen's Register admittedly provides a less than complete record of those who 'entered the liberty of the city of York'.[26] Even so, during those thirty-four years, fifteen tailors (almost half the number of recorded workers in the textile crafts in York) were designated as tailors. In the very first year of the Register (1272) Richard de Hepesingham, *cissor*, emerges as the earliest identifiable freeman tailor in the history of the city; and a year later he was followed into the freedom of the city by another 'taylour', John de Burton by name, who bore a surname later to be celebrated in the annals of the Yorkshire and English clothing industry.[27] However it was during the forty years before the catastrophic outbreak of the Black Death in the early summer of 1349 that the Freemen's Register begins to reveal the full extent of the tailors' growing numerical ascendancy in the economy of the city. Between 1307 and 1349, when an average of some fifty to sixty new freemen were admitted to the liberty of York every year, three or four of these new citizens were usually described as tailors. During that period as a whole 110 York tailors became citizens, more than any other craftsmen in the town except the cordwainers (making shoes) and the mercers.[28]

It was however during the following half century, not long after the first devastating attack of the Black Death, that the York tailors can be seen moving into a position of absolute primacy among the crafts of York. Between 1350 and 1399, recurrent attacks of bubonic plague created such high levels of mortality in the city that new craftsmen tended to be entered into the freedom of York in unprecedently great numbers and at great speed to avoid the collapse of the city's manufacturing industry. Never can it have been easier to become a tailor of York than in the decades immediately after the Black Death first savagely depleted the ranks of the citizens. Between then and the end of the fourteenth century no less than 374 tailors, many more than from any other craft, became freemen of York.[29] As the city's tailors self-evidently needed to sell through the 'open windows' (a contemporary phrase) of their shops and houses to survive, it was essential for them to be registered as freemen of the town — for only then were they allowed to sell retail within the city. Accordingly there can be no reasonable doubt that the York Freemen's Register preserves the names of the vast majority of the city's master tailors from the fourteenth century onwards. Such a conclusion is indeed indirectly confirmed by the evidence of the records of national taxation, above all by the famous returns of the notorious 1381 Poll Tax. Although the latter survive for only twenty-eight of the forty-one medieval parishes of the city, they identify seventy-three York tailors, many more than any other group of tradesmen in the city except for a group of seventy-five under-privileged weavers resident in the town.[30] It follows that from the 1380s onwards the tailors were always likely to be the single largest manufacturing craft in the town , still attaining an average intake of eight to ten new members a year in the early Tudor period.[31]

The city of York was not at all untypical in this respect. To take only one example, according to the 1381 poll tax returns for Oxford, fifty-two tailors were householders there, far and away the largest group of tradesmen resident in the borough.[32] Almost all these Oxford tailors employed at least one servant, a reminder that in York too the tailors' apprentices and servants (who probably included several women seamstresses) constituted a very large proportion of the city's population. So numerous were those that in 1387 the master tailors of York felt it necessary to prohibit their own servants from unauthorised meetings and dealing in clothes.[33] All in all, it can hardly be an exaggeration to suggest that the making of comparatively fine clothing was the primary human activity of the late medieval and early modern English and indeed European town. As late as the mid-nineteenth century, shortly before the introduction of the mass production of ready-made clothing transformed the industry, there were some 74,000 male tailors in England, perhaps almost double that number if one includes women. The latter, with their smaller fingers, regularly sewed the waistcoats and usually the button holes of male and female apparel. In York itself, during the five hundred years from the 1350s to the 1850s there were few decades in which the tailors failed to be the most common manufacturing craft in the town.[34]

However perhaps the York Freemen's Register and the city's taxation records are even more valuable for placing the tailors within the broader context of the other textile and clothing trades in the town. No attempt can be made here to describe the varying fortunes of the many and various craftsmen (most notably the weavers, fullers and dyers as well as the tapiters or chaloners, specialising in worsteds) who were engaged in the complex processes which led to the production of woollen cloth itself. It is certainly true that not long after 1400 the tailors of York were gradually forced to look further and further afield for that cloth itself as the city's own weaving industry continued to contract in the face of growing rural competition, not least from the textile centres of the nearby West Riding. However, it was even more significant that from the late fourteenth century onwards medieval England's most valuable manufacturing industry, the production of woollen broadcloths, was protected from overseas competition by heavy royal customs duties on the export of raw wool. There was accordingly little likelihood of the York tailors ever being seriously deprived for long of their essential raw material, the bales of dyed woollen cloth required for their working benches.[35] They were potentially much more vulnerable to the danger that their relations with their suppliers might be disrupted by the city's drapers, specialised cloth merchants who bought wholesale and sold mainly to the domestic market. As Dr Heather Swanson has shown, in many ways the history of the clothing industry in late medieval York might be written in terms of a struggle for economic power and influence between the city's tailors and drapers.[36] However, although the latter were often York burgesses of considerable wealth and prestige (as many as six drapers but only one tailor were elected mayor of the city between 1350 and 1500), they never possessed a guild hall nor even a properly organised guild structure. As their numbers began to decline sharply during the fifteenth century, so several drapers joined the mercers' guild while many others became increasingly associated with the tailors. Although the relationship between the two crafts remained complex and often contentious until the early Tudor period, there were many occasions on which 'the good men of the hole crafts and occupacons of drapours and taillours within the Citie' co-operated closely, especially when faced with growing competition from 'foreyn drapours of the countrey'. In 1492 the latter were required to 'have tables sett oppenly in Thursday market and theire sell there cloths by retale' so that they could be properly inspected by the tailors' and drapers' four searchers.[37] In the City of London and several other provincial towns the drapers, even in the twenty-first century, are still a force to be reckoned with. In York, by contrast, they eventually lost their separate corporate identity within the tailors. On 26 June 1551 the two crafts, long closely linked with one another, were at last legally united under one annually elected master and four searchers as 'the companye or feloshipe of tailors and drapers within the Citie of Yorke'.[38]

As will be seen at the close of this chapter, the eventual absorption of the York drapers into the Taylors' Company need occasion no great surprise. In all late medieval towns the fortunes of a particular craft and its position within the hierarchy of civic guilds were often highly volatile, dependent upon a host of different economic, political and personal influences. By the end of the fifteenth century, the city of York itself seems to have contained more craft guilds than its declining population and manufacturing capacity could readily support. However, a century earlier, when the York tailors' craft was emerging from obscurity, the city's primacy as the north of England's leading marketing centre had naturally encouraged a high degree of specialisation in the labour force and – as a direct result – the formation of several other if much lesser clothing crafts. In particular, the production of such specialised clothing items as stockings, headwear and ecclesiastical vestments was – at least in theory – the province of the hosiers, cappers and vestment makers respectively. However, in practice many of the stockings (predominantly woollen) produced in York were the work of the city's tailors rather than its hosiers. Although by at least 1415 the latter were capable of sponsoring their own pageant in the Corpus Christi play cycle, there were in fact never many of them at work in the city. Thus between 1350 and 1399 only seven hosiers are recorded in the civic Freemen's Register, a figure which rose only gradually thereafter to a climax (such as it was) of ten between 1500 and 1524.[39] During that same quarter-century the number of York citizens categorised as makers of headgear was not so very much larger, comprising sixteen cappers and five hatters. Here again, the manufacture of yarn or woollen hats, caps and bonnets had traditionally often fallen to the lot of York's tailors. By 1500 or so, however, the increasing popularity – under Dutch influence – of woollen headwear created a growing demand for specialists in the manufacture of hats and caps.[40]

However, neither the cappers, the hatters nor indeed the members of any other craft remotely challenged the dominance of the York tailors over the most important clothing centre in the north of England. Thus, although a small parchment register of 1591 containing the ordinances of the York Embroiderers, Vestment Makers, Cutters and Drawers in 1591 is one of the more precious items now within the Merchant Taylors' Company archives, only a few members of these four crafts are ever recorded as such in surviving civic records.[41] Thus, despite the church of York's status as the ecclesiastical headquarters of northern England, between 1490 and 1549 only six vestment makers became freemen of the city. It would certainly seem, in Dr Swanson's phrase, that there was no 'feverish sewing of ecclesiastical garments' either immediately before or after the Reformation.[42]

Only in the case of the widows, wives and daughters of the city does the Freemen's Register seriously under-represent and indeed distort the realities of the city's occupational structure. However, although there is no doubt that the prosperity of the tailors of York rested very heavily indeed upon the labour of the female members of their households, the latter had little or no opportunity (except perhaps when widows) to wield much influence over the organisation of their craft or indeed their own working conditions.[43] What they could do was hope to become sisters – and as such integral members – of another type of fraternity altogether, the religious guild of St. John the Baptist. By the 1380s, if not before, that guild was beginning to provide the tailors of late medieval York with novel and very challenging opportunities for fellowship. Despite its size and prominence, this 'fraternitas seu gilda in honore Sancti Johannis Baptiste in Civitate Eboracense' was to fall victim of the Protestant ideology of the English Reformation and to disappear for ever in 1545-6. Nevertheless, by a curious irony, the modern Company of Merchant Taylors actually owes more to the achievements – and especially its surviving Hall – of that comparatively short-lived religious fraternity than it does to the labours of the medieval tailors of the city themselves. It is accordingly to the highly problematic history of the once great York fraternity of St. John the Baptist that this chapter must now turn.

* * * * * * *

Like the precise origins of the tailors' craft, so those of the York guild of St. John the Baptist are lost beyond recall. Indeed had it not been for a unique royal investigation of 1388-9 into the proliferation of guilds throughout the country as a whole the emergence of the 'guild or fraternity' (the words were used interchangeably) of St. John the Baptist in York would remain totally mysterious. On 1 November 1388, under pressure from the parliamentary Commons, alarmed at the profusion of new and unauthorised guilds during the thirty years since the Black Death, Richard II's government took the unprecedented step of ordering the officers of all guilds in the kingdom to provide written returns certifying their origins, composition, privileges, constitutional practices, property and possessions.[44] The survival rate of these returns among the archives of the royal chancery is notoriously poor; so it is a piece of unexpected good fortune that of the thirteen original certificates to survive from Yorkshire, two were compiled at York, one on behalf of the city's Paternoster guild and the other for the fraternity of St. John the Baptist. The latter, written on a single parchment membrane and still in excellent condition, was authenticated at York on 22 January 1389 by the seal (now lost) of Master Richard de Thoren or Thorne, then vicar-general of Archbishop Thomas Arundel.[45] The choice of Thoren as sponsor of the guild was in fact particularly appropriate. As one of the handful of residentiary canons of York Minster, he must have had detailed knowledge of a fraternity whose most specific obligation was reported as 'to burn a candle on all Sundays and feast days before the altar of St. John the Baptist in the cathedral church of the blessed Peter of York for the praise and honour of Almighty God and St. John the Baptist himself'.[46] It must have been at this altar in the Minster too that the brothers of the guild were reported to support a chaplain to celebrate masses every year for themselves and their predecessors. Much more burdensome was the commitment (said to be 'the first burden on the said guild') to pay 7d a week to any brother of the guild who had been reduced to poverty. Although the fraternity of St. John the Baptist held no lands, rents or possessions of any kind in 1388, the return of that year makes it clear that the guild was sufficiently well organised (under an unspecified number of *custodes* or wardens and a group of twelve councillors) to raise financial contributions from its members and to enforce fines or even expulsion on negligent or rebellious brethren. Above all, however, the return of 1389 leaves no doubt at all that when it is first exposed to view, for the fraternity of St. John the Baptist as for all religious guilds of the period, 'the basic purpose was devotional'.[47]

In many ways, however, the account of the guild of St. John the Baptist provided by the return of 1389 is more interesting for what it omits rather than for what it includes. All allowances made for the fact that in the history of guilds arguments *ex silentio* are always hazardous, it is certainly important to stress that in 1389 there was no mention of women members, of a hall, of a chapel, or of how long the fraternity had existed.[48] It is more significant still that the return of that year includes no reference to the tailors or to any other York craft. As no list of the members of the fraternity of St. John the Baptist survives for any period of its history (and as there is indeed as yet no direct proof that it actually existed long before 1386), it is more or less impossible to trace the process whereby it became closely and eventually exclusively associated with the York clothing trades in general and with the York tailors in particular. However it seems not unlikely that in their dedication to St. John the Baptist the York tailors were following a national as well as local trend. During the second half of the fourteenth century the tailors of many of the major English provincial towns were similarly involved in establishing or enhancing fraternities dedicated to the Baptist.[49] Nor perhaps can it be coincidental that much earlier in the century (between 1315 and 1333) it was an exceptionally prominent York tailor Alan Segold, heavily involved in money lending and credit transactions with the York Minster clergy, who registered a bond of 40s. with the 'keepers of the light of St. John the Baptist' in the cathedral.[50] In 1386, two generations later, the will of a York tailor called John de Sevenhouse included a bequest of 10s. to 'the guild of the tailors of the Blessed John', not only the first surviving reference to a guild with that name but also direct evidence that the fraternity of St. John the Baptist was already being associated with the tailors of the city.[51] Four years later, on 21 December 1390, it was another York 'taillour', Peter de Barleburgh, who combined a bequest of 2s. to the fabric of York Minster with a legacy of 3s. 4d. 'capellano gilde sancti Johannis Ebor' fraternitatis mee', the first known reference to a chaplain of the guild.[52] There seem to be only two possible explanations for such an association: either the guild of St. John the Baptist was founded *de novo* by the tailors of York or an already important religious guild in the city was adopted by the tailors who gradually took it over and administered it in their own interests.[52] Of these two hypotheses the second seems the most likely, not least because membership of St. John the Baptist's guild was never confined exclusively to the city's tailors. Between the 1380s and the dissolution of the guild in the 1540s at least seven drapers as well as several litsters or dyers and other craftsmen are known to have made testamentary bequests to the '*fraternitas Sancti Johannis Baptiste*' in a way which makes it virtually certain that they had been members of that fraternity. [53]

In any event the tailors of York can hardly have failed to profit enormously from their association with a patron saint as famous as Christ's celebrated precursor. In late medieval England, as throughout Christendom, John the Baptist was an exceptionally popular saint, with no less than 496 churches dedicated in his honour, a total only exceeded by the Virgin Mary, All Saints, and Saints Peter and Michael.[54] The familiar if complex image of an ascetic and somewhat forbidding figure, dressed in animal skins and holding a long cross in his left hand while pointing with his right hand to the Lamb or *Agnus Dei* (lying on a copy of the Gospels) must have been well known to all the inhabitants of late medieval Yorkshire. Indeed in York itself that image of the Baptist continues to gaze at its beholders even now from the stained glass windows of the

Minster and several of the city's surviving medieval parish churches. Even more remarkable, and in some ways the most startling of the Baptist's relics in medieval England, was the charger on which his severed head had been placed after his execution on Herod's orders at the instance of the seductive Salome. However doubtful its authenticity, this charger was preserved in the York parish church of All Saints Pavement until 1386, in which year it was surrendered to Richard II and so joined the English monarchy's collection of relics.[55] It is therefore hardly surprising that St. John the Baptist was the patron of a remarkably large number of late medieval religious guilds, not only in East Anglia and the south but in the Midlands, from Walsall to Lichfield, and in Yorkshire, from Hull to Richmond in the North Riding.[56] Quite when and why John the Baptist became the more or less universal patron saint of every tailors' guild in late medieval England remains a mysterious issue. However there can be little doubt that it was the observances of the powerful tailors' fraternity of the city of London which, as in so many matters of prestige and status over the centuries, set the decisive precedents for their counterparts in provincial towns. According to London's most famous antiquary John Stow (himself a late Elizabethan merchant taylor), a mystery of 'Taylors of the Fraternity of St. John the Baptist', under the authority of a master and four wardens, had already emerged in London by 1300.[57] During the following two centuries, new entrants to tailors' guilds throughout England were therefore increasingly likely to be required to combine their loyalty to their fraternities with devotion to a common patron saint. In the absolutely explicit words of the Exeter tailors' ordinances of the 1470s, 'ye shall swere that ye shall be gode and trew to the fraternyte of Syn John the Baptyste of Taylors within the Cyte'.[58]

So popular was the veneration of St. John the Baptist among the tailors and other craftsmen in late fourteenth-century York that it could hardly be satisfied for long by the lighting of candles and occasional devotional acts at the solitary altar of St John the Baptist in York Minster. Above all, it seems clear that by the 1390s the guild, increasingly dominated by the tailors of the city, was now determined to have its own chaplain, or at least a chaplain under its authority. Such is much the most likely explanation for a notarial instrument of 25 June 1396 still surviving in the archives of the York Merchant Adventurers. By the terms of that document Thomas Horneby, William Kepwyk and William Wortelay, all citizens of York, all members of the guild of St. John the Baptist and all drapers or tailors too, founded a perpetual chantry of one chaplain within the recently established hospital of Jesus Christ and St. Mary in Fossgate.[59] Not too surprisingly, this complex stratagem, whereby the fraternity of St. John the Baptist did secure a chaplain devoted to its needs but only in return for the obligation to administer a hospital as well a chantry within what is now the Merchant Adventurer's Hall, soon disappeared without trace. By the late 1390s the ambitions of the fraternity of St. John the Baptist – and of the tailors of York – had become much grander still.

By any standards the erection – in the years just before or more probably just after just after 1400 – of the massive '*aula fraternitatis sancti Johannis Baptiste*', the present great Merchant Taylors' Hall, proved to be the single most decisive event in the history of the guild. Although the history of almost all medieval English civic buildings is very poorly documented, it is especially frustrating that nothing will ever be known for certain about precisely when, why and by whose hands this largest if architecturally most conventional of all York's four surviving medieval guildhalls was actually constructed. However a detailed report on the earliest surviving roof timbers in the Hall made by the Dendrochronological Laboratory of the University of Nottingham in 1991 has suggested a felling date of 1413–14.[60] Not much later, on 2 December 1415, there is incontrovertible documentary proof of the existence of the hall of the fraternity of St. John the Baptist – when the mayor and commonalty of York leased to four tailors and a litster a substantial section (six ells) of the ditch or moat immediately within the city walls 'where it abutted on the land and hall of the same fraternity'. To be more precise, the lease in question seems to have been of a quite narrow strip of land, bounded by the existing Hall of St. John on the northeast and running between a tenement belonging to Guisborough Priory on the south and a fence erected by a Thomas Crofton on the north.[61] As for the important question of why the fraternity of St. John the Baptist in association with the tailors of York should have built their remarkable hall in so comparatively obscure an area of the city (north-east of Aldwark, south-west of the city walls and immediately to the north-west of the long vanished church of St. Helen-on-the-Walls), there can again certainly be no easy answer. Not that the absence of clear-cut documentary or archaeological evidence has inhibited some extremely interesting and ingenious conjectures on such issues during recent years. Especially notable is the first full-length study of the Merchant Taylors' Hall by a professional architect, Mr Michael Mennim, who has at last placed that building firmly in the context of the many other 'hall houses' of later medieval England. [62]

More radical and provocative still has been Dr Kate Giles's re-interpretation of the origins of the Merchant Taylors' Hall within her invaluable comparative study of all York's surviving medieval guildhalls. Might it be, for instance, and as Dr Giles has suggested, that the fraternity of St. John the Baptist and the tailors of York 'shared the use of buildings on the site in the late fourteenth century' before the present hall was actually built? [63] Perhaps so; but it has to be said that all the arguments which rest on the supposition that what Professor David Palliser has called the 'enigmatic Peter or Pear Tree Hall' (recorded as 'Pertrehall' and 'Petrehall' respectively in the official city surveys of the custodies of York's walls in 1380 and 1403) was associated in some way with the fraternity of St. John the Baptist seem less than conclusive.[64] Perhaps – or perhaps not – future archaeological investigation may throw light on these inscrutable issues. Meanwhile it may be as well to remember that neither of the only two properly professional excavations ever conducted at or near the Merchant Taylors' Hall produced clear evidence of the early use of the site. When Mr Dudley Waterman excavated a trench through the floor of the hall in 1949 (with 'an enthusiastic band of volunteers, including ladies on the History staffs of local colleges and members of Bootham School'), he merely unearthed the medieval city bank and a mortar floor with cobbles below, and one Roman tile. In 1991, forty–two years later, the York Archaeological Trust's excavation of a single trench immediately to the north-west of the present hall exposed a complex series of now demol-ished buildings which appear to have been constructed as late as the sixteenth and seventeenth centuries. Some of the structures revealed by this trench may conceal the remains of earlier buildings which were once used as service accom-modation for the Hall of c. 1415; but as fifteenth-century levels were not reached it must be hazardous to assume so. All in all, the hypothesis that these buildings might comprise an earlier hall of the guild of St. John the Baptist, to which the present hall was added later, remains highly uncertain, on the whole a not alto-gether likely shot in the dark.[65]

* * * * * * *

By any standards, the most critical moment in the long history of the tai-lors of York self-evidently occurred when they were confident of securing suffi-cient funds to build a massive new hall, within which their administrative and convivial functions, together with the religious and charitable obligations of the fraternity of St. John the Baptist, could be brought literally together under one – very large – roof.[66] It is indeed absolutely obvious that when completed shortly before 1415, the *aula sancti Johannis Baptiste* (as it was almost always known until the Reformation) totally transformed the status and scale of the activities associ-ated with both his fraternity and the craft of tailors. With its five large bays, separated from a single two-storey service bay on the north-west by a still remark-ably intact screens passage, this fraternity hall must have been originally de-signed for much fraternal eating and drinking. As in modern times, so in the later middle ages, by no means all the feasts held in the Hall were necessarily confined to members of the guild. It seems probable that within a very few years of its construction the long tradition of leasing the hall to others for a variety of large public and social occasions was already well established. Thus in 1442–3 it was the chamberlains of the city who paid the wages of two carpenters (for two and a half days at 6d. each a day) to erect a 'barr' or bench within the hall. Twelve years later, during the summer of 1454, the city chamberlains spent almost a shilling on the construction of another wooden 'barr'. On this occasion the partition was needed so that Richard, duke of York, '*protector Anglie*', and his fellow Yorkist justices could sit in judgment on suspected traitors and criminals in the hall.[67] Nor can there be any doubt that the spaciousness of St. John's Hall must have made it an attractive locale for a wide range of public festivities and entertainments within the city. Large feasts, accompanied by the civic waits or musicians, were certainly a feature of the 'taler hall' by the end of Queen Elizabeth's reign. Although the Merchant Taylors' Hall only became the first cradle of professional theatre in the city of York as late as 1705, large numbers of strolling players, mimes and musicians visited the cathedral city in the century and more before the Reformation. Several of these 'variety acts', often staged in the civic Guildhall or Common Hall, are likely to have appeared at the Taylors' Hall too, long before the first authenticated performances by minstrels there in 1595.[68]

Much more significant for the tailors of York was the use of St. John the Baptist's Hall as what might almost be termed the administrative centre of the clothing industry within the city. Unfortunately, and as already mentioned, the business records of neither the individual tailors nor of their fraternity have left any significant trace to posterity. However, a fleeting reference of 1498 to a the copying of a bill or document 'afore the sersours in the Taillour Hall' reminds us that the four searchers of the guild continued to exercise their central role of controlling the detailed operations of the city's clothing trades until and beyond the Reformation. The same document makes it inadvertently clear that as late as the 1490s there were some, but by no means all, 'sersours that couth rede'.[69] That said, by 1530 official registers of apprentices accepted by York tailors were systematically preserved (but are alas long since vanished) 'emongs the records of St. John Halle'. By that date, on the eve of the Reformation, circumstantial evidence might suggest that at least a quarter or so of all master tailors could read a little but write considerably less.[70]

It was probably only in the reign of Elizabeth I that the guild's official business came to be primarily conducted in a large timber-framed chamber, of highly uncertain date, projecting south-west of the main body of the hall. Now known as Little Hall, this supplementary structure was in regular use as the 'Counsel House' or — more fittingly still — as the 'Counting House' of the Company throughout the seventeenth century. A recent hypothesis that the Little Hall may have been 'in essence a fifteenth-century building', with a chapel at floor level and a chamber above' is highly conjectural.[71] Nevertheless very central indeed to the purposes of the pre-Reformation fraternity of St. John the Baptist was an altar where masses could be regularly recited for the souls of deceased brethren and their kinsfolk. That altar may itself have been a more or less permanent fixture soon after the construction of the hall; but how far it was enclosed within a structurally separate chapel, inside or outside the present Hall, seems uncertain. In 1489 the tailor William Akers or Acres bequeathed two yards of 'paynted clothe' to be made into 'an alter clothe in St. John Chappell' and between 1503 and 1530 there is intriguing testamentary evidence of building work on a 'new chapel' in St. John's Hall. For the fraternity of St John and the York tailors themselves no doubt a chaplain was even more important than a chapel; and there seems every likelihood that they could provide enough funds to maintain their own chaplain fairly continuously from the 1380s to the Reformation. One tailor, Peter de Barleburgh, bequeathed 3s. 4d. as early as December 1390 'to the chaplain (capellano) of the guild of my fraternity of St. John of York'; and other references suggest that the tailors employed their own chaplain for many if not all of the years until the destruction of all the English chantry foundations in the 1540s.[72] Thus in October 1446 Archbishop John Kempe licensed 'the brothers and sisters of the guild or fraternity of St. John the Baptist next to the parish church of St. Helen in the Werkdike' to appoint a suitable chaplain to celebrate divine office in their 'manse or habitation there' for the following three years. Nearly twenty years later, in September 1465, Archbishop George Neville made a similar grant with two significant variants in wording, namely that the chaplain should only hold office at the archbishop's pleasure and that the latter's licence was now addressed to the Warden (Gardianus) as well as the brethren and sisters of the guild.[73]

The formal institution of an annually elected office of Warden or Master was obviously a critical moment in the constitutional and administrative evolution of all important medieval guilds. For the tailors of York that moment came when on 10 February 1453 Henry VI's government granted fifteen of their representatives perpetual incorporation (communitas perpetua et unum corpus in re et nomine) by a licence under the royal privy seal. Henceforward the brothers and sisters of this 'community' were to elect one Master and four Wardens on the feast of the Nativity of St. John the Baptist (24 June) every year. Now awarded the privilege of its own common seal, inscribed with the figure of its patron saint, the guild henceforward enjoyed the right to plead in all law courts within the kingdom and also to hold lands and tenements up to a value of £5 a year in order to sustain its chaplain.[74] Although one of the primary obligations of the latter was to pray for the souls of Henry VI and his wife, Queen Margaret of Anjou, it is hardy likely that the award of these highly important privileges to the York tailors was the result of any personal initiative on the part of those two Lancastrian monarchs. First pioneered by the leading London livery companies in the late fourteenth century, such grants of incorporation to major borough guilds and companies had gradually become quite common. Admittedly in 1453 the tailors of York must have been highly gratified to receive the corporate status which their rivals, the even more prestigious 'worthy companye of the noble craft of mercers in the citie of York', had acquired twenty-three years earlier.[75] More significantly still, the royal grant of incorporation of February 1453 implicitly fused the fraternity of St. John the Baptist and the tailors' mistery into one legal entity. Drapers, haberdashers and others would continue to join the Baptist's fraternity for many years to come; but there could no longer be any doubt that the tailors of York would inherit the traditions and procedures of that fraternity, as indeed they still do to the present day. Although alas the original document has failed to survive, the royal licence of February 1453 is unquestionably the most important legal enactment in the long history of the York tailors. In course of time the latter would carry their new privileges to their logical conclusion and — in imitation of the example set by their London counterparts in 1503 — evolve into a duly constituted company of 'Merchant Taylors'.[76]

By a strange irony the rise of the tailors' fraternity to a higher legal and social status in York than ever before was accompanied by a period of harsh and prolonged economic recession in the city. Quite when the manufacturing capacities of the city of York began to be seriously inhibited by what Professor John Hatcher has recently called the late medieval 'great slump' remains a very controversial matter. However there is no doubt that from the 1450s the mayor and civic council of York were becoming increasingly obsessed by what they later called (to Richard III in September 1483) 'the dekay and grete poverte of the said Cite'. Nor did those aldermen, in addressing Henry VII four years later, have any doubt that their basic misfortune was declining numbers: 'there is not half the nombre of good men within your said citie as ther hath beene in tymes past.'[77] The tailors could hardly remain immune from such a sustained period of economic decline caused by the continued attrition of the Yorkshire population. It has indeed been argued that 'the fact that the tailors shared in the falling fortunes of the manufacturing crafts is an indication of a general sag in the prosperity of the city'.[78] Nevertheless, and as has been seen, the York tailors suffered less than most sections of the city's manufacturing trades. Although the number of tailors admitted to the city's freedom fell from 280 in 1400–49 to 234 in 1450–1509, during the half-century between 1525 and 1575 this figure rose to 266 and then again (much more substantially) to 390 between 1575 and 1624.[79] As these figures suggest, in demographic terms the tailors of York survived the economic crises of the fifteenth and sixteenth-century English economy surprisingly well, partly no doubt as a result of a dramatic decline in the number of York drapers, with whom they were to be amalgamated in 1551.[80]

Meanwhile, during the last medieval century, between their charter of incorporation in 1453 and the dissolution of the English chantries nearly a hundred years later, the tailors of York preserved a modestly successful, if rarely dynamically entrepreneurial, position within the trades of the city. On the evidence of early Tudor subsidy accounts, as of the Poll Tax returns of 1377–81 many years earlier, few York tailors were wealthy enough to be liable to high rates of taxation. What these sources do reveal is that in the early sixteenth as in the late fourteenth centuries the houses of the tailors (unlike those of the metal-workers and tanners) were dispersed widely throughout the centre of the city. The great majority of York's tailors lived scattered along the city streets north-east of the Ouse, with the highest concentrations usually in the more commer-cialised parishes of St. Sampson and St. Martin, Coney Street.[81] This impression of dispersal throughout the city is fully confirmed by the evidence of the wills of York tailors copied into the archiepiscopal probate registers now at the Borthwick Institute in York. Of the eighty-four surviving wills of fifteenth-century York tailors preserved in these registers, four were made by women, all of these wives or widows of male members of the company.[82] Only a small handful of women tailors, like Alice Hoipe, a native of Scarborough in 1479 who had married a tailor of that town, were apparently assured or prosperous enough to leave a last will and testament to posterity.[83] As Dr Jeremy Goldberg has argued, the eco-nomic welfare of working women in late medieval towns may often have been at its least wretched during periods of labour shortage, most obviously in the after-math of the Black Death. Certainly when Margaret, an obscure seamstress who had migrated to York from Knaresborough, made her will in January 1398, she was sufficiently prosperous to leave 6s. 8d. to the city's Carmelite friars as well as several small bequests to her kinsfolk. Much more critical, however, for the for-tunes of the late medieval York tailoring industry as a whole was the enthusi-asm, probably increased enthusiasm, for fine clothes so conspicuously revealed throughout York and Yorkshire in nearly all female, and especially widows' wills to survive. In August, 1479, to take a typical example, a sacristan's widow called Janet Candell naturally bequeathed her 'best gown with my hode' to her parish church of St Sampson's; but she left the other items in her large collection of various cloaks, kirtles and other clothes – as well as a remarkably lavish supply of bed linen – to her many female friends.[84]

It is hardly surprising that the surviving wills of male tailors from the 1380s to the Reformation are much more informative as well as much more numerous than those of their wives, widows and daughters. Although such York tailors made comparatively brief and conventional wills, quite typical of all the York manufacturing trades, they provide a uniquely valuable insight into their family and social connections as well as their religious and other priorities. Even more revealing but unfortunately much less likely to survive are the probate invento-ries prepared by the executors in accordance with the desires of the deceased testator. Only a hundred or so of these probate inventories survive from the huge diocese of York before the year 1500; but of these one is without question the single most revealing source for the operations of the York tailors' craft in the fifteenth century. This lengthy inventory of the goods, debts and above all the household contents, was compiled on the instructions of the executors of John Carter, tailor, on 14 September 1485, only a fortnight after he had made his last will and testament.[85] Carter himself had been admitted to the freedom of the city as a 'taillor' in 1454-5; and by the time of his death thirty years later he must have been one of the most patronised tailors in York. The inventory of John Carter's goods is now best known for its revelation that his premises were packed with cloth no longer manufactured in the city of York but rather in the West Riding. His copious stocks of Halifax tawny, Halifax green, Halifax russet, and black Halifax kersey testify in minute detail to the early triumphs of the West Riding textile industry at the expense of the weavers and dyers of York itself. Nor does any other document give a more vivid impression of a tailors' crowded environment, with hall, buttery, chamber, parlour, kitchen and work-shop all full either of clothes in the process of being made or of clothing ready to be sold. More surprising perhaps is the way in which John Carter's inventory reveals extremely extensive living and working quarters, nearly all full of hang-ing space for clothes as contrasted with very few tools of the tailor's trade. Ac-cording to the inventory, the only tools in John Carter's workshop were a shap-ing board, trestles, two pressing irons and two pairs of shears — the latter how-ever so fundamental to the tailor's craft that their unauthorised importation from abroad was often prohibited. [86]

Not all York tailors were as confined to their workshops as seems to have been so with John Carter. As in the case of all late medieval English towns for which evidence survives, notably in the city of London, the business acumen and social connections of a small élite of citizens sometimes enabled them to emerge from the comparative obscurity of their craft to high urban status, wealth and civic office. To that process one or two tailors of York certainly conformed, sometimes with the outcome of abandoning the tailor's fraternity and its guild. Perhaps the most striking fifteenth-century example is 'William Girdelyngton, taillour' who was admitted to the freedom of the city in 1405-6. In 1440-41 Girlington became the only tailor to hold the Mayor's office in fifteenth-centuryYork; but when he made his will three years later he styled himself 'civis et draper'. As we have seen, the social and economic distinction between drapers and tailors was by no means unbridgeable. As a wealthy draper, Girlington's career was in some ways indistinguishable from that of an overseas mercer or merchant too. He stored and sold copious quantities of cloth from his shop in Feasegate, and at his death declared his intention to provide each poor person in the town with a complete set of bed linen.[87] In the early Tudor period a very few tailors, as well as rather more drapers, achieved even greater fame and for-tune. Outstanding among these were two near contemporaries, William Coupland and Richard White, whose biographies provide the most fitting epi-logue to the history of the tailors of medieval York. Both Coupland and White, the first a native of York and the second from Edlingham in Northumberland, were admitted to the freedom of the city as tailors, in 1521-2 and 1529-30 respectively. Very early in his career Coupland developed a general mercantile business, trading so successfully in corn and lead that when he eventually died (in 1568) he was worth over £1,000. As Mayor of York in 1553-4 and again 1568-9, Coupland had the misfortune to preside over the city during the early and acrimonious phases of a Protestant regime which he clearly abhorred. By contrast, Richard White, Mayor in 1552-3, seems to have accepted the religious revolutions of the 1530s and 1540s with equanimity. A great owner of household property in the city, his own residence was a timbered house adjoining the Minster Close which he was still leasing from the dean and chapter at the time of his death in 1558. As the first effective Master of the united guild of drapers and tailors in 1551, White was especially well placed to guide the new company into the new religious age. By actually leasing for his own use half the Tailors Hall after it had been vacated by the defunct guild of St. John the Baptist, he could not only do that but presumably also profit materially from the destruction caused by the Reformation.[88]

The prominent careers of William Coupland and Richard White would of course have been inconceivable among the tailors of York before the early sixteenth century. The overwhelming impression left by the bequests of members of the tailors' fraternity in the fifteenth and early sixteenth centuries is of their dedication to their families, to their parish churches and to other time-hallowed and thoroughly conservative religious and charitable causes. Very few York tailors or their wives would ever have contemplated being buried anywhere except in their parish churches, to the restoration of whose fabric they usually contributed a few shillings. Other small bequests to the repair of York Minster or to one or other of the four York mendicant convents (most frequently the Carmelites) were also extremely frequent. Nor did loyalty to the tailors' fraternity preclude tailors from making gifts to other religious guilds, like that of Corpus Christi, in a gild-invested city. However the guild of St. John the Baptist naturally held pride of place among the city's tailors. Between 1386 and 1546, but naturally not later, record of at least forty testamentary bequests, most of them by tailors or drapers, to the fraternity of St. John the Baptist survives among York's long sequence of probate registers. Most of these legacies were of comparatively small sums of a few shillings or less, quite often to pay for torches to be carried in funeral and other processions.[89] A much more intriguing bequest was that of William Gyslay who in June 1446 left 3d. to the 'pauperibus in le masyndewe Sancti Johannis Baptiste' next to the church of St. Helen-on-the-Walls.[90] This Maison Dieu or almshouse, however humble and more or less completely undocumented until the seventeenth century, did at least survive the catastrophe which befell the religious guilds of England in the late 1540s and was to have a long and charitable future ahead.

The same cannot, for good or ill, be said of its parent body, the fraternity of St. John the Baptist itself. The latter was probably informally dissolved in 1545, the year in which official documents begin to refer to the 'Taylors' Hall' in place of 'the Hall of St John'. In any case, as the guild of St. John , like the other York fraternities of St. Martin, St. Anthony and the Paternoster, had certainly disappeared by 1548–9, the details of their wealth and endowments were never included in the royal chantry returns.[91] Nothing alas can ever be known for certain about the way in which the tailors of York reacted to the religious holocaust of the 1530s and 1540s. Perhaps, after all, they were wise to keep a low profile. During those two decades it seemed to many contemporaries that so major an onslaught on the confraternal life of the religious fraternities would lead to the destruction of trade guilds too.[92] At least the York tailors had the consolation of realising that their hall had never been built for religious purposes as such and that the demand for the clothing they provided was in no danger of complete collapse. No doubt, like most tradesmen in most ages, nearly all those tailors ('very poore men' according to the city council in the reign of Queen Elizabeth) were to remain obscure individuals for many centuries to come. However, they responded to a radically new age in a new way, not least by joining forces with the drapers of the city only a very few years later. When on 27 October 1550 the 'occupacons of taylours and drapers then present in the Counsell Chambre on Ouse brigg' subjected their new united status for approval by the Mayor and Council, a new stage in their long and complex struggle for prosperity and survival had begun.[93]

NOTES

1 M. Bloch, *Apologie pour L'Histoire ou Métier d'Historien* (Cahiers des Annales, 2, Paris 1949), p.7.

2 YCA, Reg A/Y. ff.37v–39; YMB, I, 94–101.

3 For a comprehensive guide to the geographical as well as family origins of the merchant tailors after 1560 (derived from the Company's Abled Masters' Books), see D. M. Smith, *The Company of Merchant Taylors in the City of York: Register of Admissions 1560–1835* (Borthwick List and Index, 16: 1996). Their toponymic surnames leave no serious doubt that all the craft guilds of late medieval York, like those in every English town 'drew much of their population from comparatively close by': see S. Reynolds, *An Introduction to the History of English Medieval Towns* (Oxford, 1977), p.70; C. Galley, *The Demography of Early Modern Towns: York in the Sixteenth and Seventeenth Centuries* (Liverpool, 1998), pp.6–8, 11–13; and W. Sheils, below, pp.59, 63.

4 Johnson, p.7.

5 YMB, I, 96–9. Henry VI's letters patent of 10 February 1453 conferring corporate status on the 'fraternity, and 'perpetual guild' of the York tailors implies that before that date they were only members of an 'art' or 'mistery': (*Cal. Pat. Rolls, 1452–61*, p.105; Johnson, p.121).

6 YMB, I, 96–100.

7 The many guild ordinances surviving from late medieval York make it clear that all crafts were required to employ searchers,usually four or two elected annually: see YMB, II, pp.166–7, 194–5, 206–7, 208–10. For the anxiety of the London tailors' guild in 1450 that the ability of their searchers to exercise 'due service and correction' might be prejudiced by craftsmen who produced garments hidden away in rented attic rooms, see M. Davies, 'Artisans, Guilds and Government in London', in *Daily Life in the Late Middle Ages*, ed. R. Britnell (Stroud, Gloucestershire, 1998), p.158.

8 YMB, I, 99.

9 *Rotuli Parliamentorum* VI, 219–20; M. Kowaleski, *Local Markets and Regional Trade in Medieval Exeter* (Cambridge, 1995), pp.100–1; Swanson, *Artisans*, p.119; cf. C. Phythian-Adams, *Desolation of a City: Coventry and the Urban Crisis of the late Middle Ages* (Cambridge, 1979), pp.111–12.

10 *The York Play: a facsimile of British Library MS Additional 35290*, ed. R. Beadle and P. Meredith (University of Leeds, School of English 1983), ff.236v–240v, 354; R. B. Dobson, 'Craft Guilds and City: the Historical Origins of the York Mystery Plays Reassessed', pp.99–104, in *The Stage as Mirror: Civic Theatre in Late Medieval Europe*, ed. A.E. Knight (Woodbridge, Suffolk, 1997).

11 H. Swanson, 'The Illusion of Economic Structure: Craft Guilds in Late Medieval English Towns, *Past and Present*, 121 (1988), p.44.

12 E. Miller, 'Medieval York', in *VCH York*, pp.87–95.

13 YCA, Reg. A/Y 1, f.2; *York Chamberlains' Accounts*, pp.1–8; BI, Prob. Reg, I; D.M. Smith, *A Guide to the Archive Collections of the Borthwick Institute of Historical Research* (Borthwick Texts and Calendars, 1 (1973), p.156.

14 Smith, *Guide*, pp.6–7; Johnson, pp.49–51.

15 BL, Egerton MS 2,572, ff.1, 17. Not surprisingly, a guild or company's prospects

of making and preserving its own written records were much enhanced after it acquired a Clerk, an office not recorded in the employ of the York tailors' fraternity before the1560s: see Johnson, p.51; *The Merchant Taylors' Company of London: Court Minutes, 1486–1493*, ed. M. Davies (Stamford, 2000), pp.8–12.

16 MTA, Account Book 1 (1665-1712), f.117v; *York Civic Records*, 3, p.130.

17 P. Walton, 'Textiles, Cordage and Raw Fibre from 16-22 Coppergate', in *The Archaeology of York: The Small Finds, 17/5* (York Archaeological Trust, 1989), pp.318–41, 422-4. Cf. *Medieval Archaeology*, 47 (2003), p.371, for comments on this issue in a review of *Finds from Medieval York*, ed. P.J. Ottaway and M.S.H. Rogers in *The Archaeology of York: The Small Finds 17/15* (York Archaeological Trust, 2002).

18 *Domesday Book: A Complete Translation*, ed. A. Williams and G.H. Martin (London, 2002), pp.1248-9; H.C. Darby, *Domesday England* (Cambridge, 1977), pp.288, 309, 367.

19 B. Cottle, *The Penguin Dictionary of Surnames* (Harmondsworth, 1967), pp.278-9. The use of the word 'Taylor or 'Taylur' (both derived from the Anglo French 'tailleur') as a surname first appears in record sources towards the end of the twelfth century: see P.H. Reaney, *A Dictionary of British Surnames* (London, 1958), p.316.

20 W. Cunningham, *The Growth of English Industry and Commerce during the Early and Late Middle Ages* (5th edn., Cambridge, 1910), p.245.

21 *Medieval Clothing and Textiles*, I, ed. R. Netherton and G. R. Owen-Crocker (Woodbridge, Suffolk, 2005); *Clothing Culture, 1350–1650*, ed. C. Richardson (Aldershot, 2004); Swanson, *Artisans*, p.45.

22 *Cal. Pat. Rolls, 1452–61*, p.465; Johnson, p.121.

23 *VCH York*, pp.43-4; *Cal. Pat. Rolls, 1345-38*, pp.199-200 (an inspeximus of Henry II's charter granting the York weavers *gildam suam*). The precise origins of medieval craft guilds in York and elsewhere remain almost as mysterious as they were when Lujo Brentano first reviewed the meagre evidence as long ago as 1870 in *English Gilds*, ed. Toulmin Smith (Early English Text Society, Original Series, No.40), pp.cxiv–cxxiv.

24 TNA, E159/49, membs. 11d, 17d, 31 (references I owe to the generosity of Professor David Smith).

25 *York Civic Ordinances, 1301*, ed. M. Prestwich (Borthwick Paper 49, York, 1976), p.15.

26 YCA, Book C/Y (1272-1671); *Freemen's Register*, pp. vii–xviii; R.B. Dobson, 'Admissions to the Freedom of the City of York in the Later Middle Ages', *Economic History Review*, 2nd ser., 26 (1973), pp.1–22.

27 *Freemen's Register*, pp.1-10.

28 Ibid., pp.11–41; Dobson, 'Admissions to Freedom', p.22; *VCH York*, pp.114-15.

29 *Freemen's Register*, pp.42-103; *VCH York*, p.114.

30 *The Lay Poll Tax Returns for the City of York in 1381*, ed. N. Bartlett, in *Trans. East Riding Antiq. Soc.*, 30 (n.d.). p.13.

31 Galley, *Demography of Towns*, p.190; cf. D. Palliser, *Tudor York* (Oxford, 1979),

pp.163-4.

32 *VCH, County of Oxford, I: City of Oxford* (1979), pp.45-7.

33 YMB, I, 97-8.

34 Galley, *Demography of Towns*, pp.34-5, 190; *VCH York*, pp.218, 259.

35 For the classic account of how, from the mid-fourteenth century onwards, England was transformed from being 'an exporter primarily of raw materials into an exporter primarily of manufactured [i.e. woollen] products', see E.M. Carus-Wilson, *Medieval Merchant Venturers* (London, 1954), pp.239-64. Cf. H. Heaton, *The Yorkshire Woollen and Worsted Industries* (2nd edn., Oxford, 1965), pp.68-88.

36 Although Swanson (*Artisans*, p.49) rightly emphasises the often 'artificial nature of the division between the tailors and drapers', tailors were rarely expected to travel out of York whereas drapers regularly did so in search of cloth and other merchandise, e.g. to Stourbridge Fair near Cambridge in the sixteenth century (*York Civic Records*, 6, p.63),

37 *York Civic Records*, 2, pp.90-1.

38 The new ordinances of the united Tailors and Drapers of York, largely derived from the tailors' ordinances of 1387, were presented in October 1550 and approved by the mayor and council in 1552: see Johnson, pp.128-32; W. Sheils, below, pp.53-4.

39 *Freemen's Register*, pp.42-245; *VCH York*, p.114; Galley, *Demography of Towns*, p.190.

40 Galley, *Demography of Towns*, p.190; R. B. Dobson, 'Aliens in the City of York during the Fifteenth Century', in *England and the Continent in the Late Middle Ages: Studies in Memory of Andrew Martindale* (Harlaxton Medieval Studies, 8 (2000), p.266.

41 Smith, *Guide*, p.21. The register is most remarkable for its intricate early Tudor stamped leather binding (Johnson, pp.123-6).

42 Swanson, *Artisans*, p.51.

43 For a somewhat more optimistic view, see P.J.P. Goldberg, *Women, Work and Life-Cycle in a Medieval Economy: Women in York and Yorkshire, c.1300-1520* (Oxford, 1992). Between 1300 and the Reformation it was however extremely unusual for more than one or two women, usually seamstresses or chapwomen, to be granted the freedom of York in any civic year (*Freemen's Register*, pp.8-250).

44 D.J.F. Crouch, *Piety, Fraternity and Power: Religious Gilds in late medieval Yorkshire, 1389-1547* (Woodbridge, 2000), pp.13-44.

45 TNA, C.47/46/455; Johnson, pp.118-19; *English Gilds*, ed. Toulmin Smith, pp.137-40, 146-7. For a brief account of Canon Richard Thorne, see M. Aston, *Thomas Arundel: A Study in Church Life in the reign of Richard II* (Oxford, 1967), pp.295-6.

46 TNA, C47/46/455.

47 Ibid. and see Crouch, *Piety, Fraternity and Power*, p.31.

48 Johnson, pp.118-19.

49 By 1400 St. John the Baptist was becoming the patron saint of tailors' guilds everywhere in England. For two prominent examples, see Richard II's letters patent of 16 October 1398 authorising the brethren of the fraternity of St. John the Baptist at Bristol to found a chapel (Bristol Record Office, No. 4954); and the establishment of a tailors' guild of the Baptist at Hull by the 1380s (*VCH East Riding of York*, I, *The City of Kingston upon Hull*, 1969), pp.58, 168, 397).

50. YML, Ms(1)a, f.4v: a reference I owe to H. Swanson, 'Craftsmen and Industry in Late Medieval York' (University of York, History Department, D. Phil thesis, 1980), p.383.

51 Ibid., p.79. Dr Swanson rightly points out that this and other references prove that Johnson (p.26) was quite mistaken in suggesting there is no evidence of the York tailors' special devotion to St. John Baptist before 1423.

52 BI, Prob. Reg. 1, f.17

53 BI, Prob.Regs, 2, ff.79, 192, 426, 577; 3, f.408; 5, f.327; 8, f. 3.

54 D. Farmer, *The Oxford Dictionary of Saints* (Oxford, 1978), pp.215–16. The only parish church dedicated to the Baptist in medieval York, near the south end of Hungate, was disused by 1519 and sold in 1550: RCHM, *City of York*, V, *The Central Area* (1981), p.149.

55 See, e.g., RCHM, *York, The Central Area*, pp.8, 17, 18, 21, 22, 34, 38, 42. For a characteristic example, at St Martin's, Micklegate in 1407, of the numerous parish chantries dedicated to St John the Baptist, see *The York Sede Vacante Register 1405–1408: a Calendar*, ed. J. Kirby (Borthwick Texts and Calendar 28, York, 2002), p.45. Cf. *Cal. Pat. Rolls, 1385–89*, p.194; *VCH York*, p.371.

56 V. Bainbridge, *Gilds in the Medieval Countryside: Social and Religious Change in Cambridgeshire, c.1350–1558* (Woodbridge, 1996), p.37; Crouch, *Piety, Fraternity and Power*, pp.24,31, 34, 37, 46, 92, 239.

57 W. Herbert, *The History of the Twelve Great Livery Companies of London* (2 vols, London, 1834–7), II, pp.390–1; *The Merchant Taylors' Company of London: Court Minutes, 1486–1493*, ed. M. Davies (Stamford, 2000), pp.3–5. Although direct evidence is lacking, there is little doubt that the creation of the fraternity of St. John the Baptist at York was heavily influenced by the remarkable rise to prominence of the London fraternity of that name, also inseparably associated with the tailors' craft, in the late fourteenth century: see M. Davies and A. Saunders, *The History of the Merchant Taylors' Company* (Leeds, 2004), pp.14–27.

58 *English Gilds*, pp.316–17.

59 D.M. Smith, *A Guide to the Archives of the Company of Merchant Adventurers of York* (Borthwick Text and Calendar 16, York, 1990), pp.9–10.

60 K. Giles, *Archaeology of Social Identity: Guildhalls in York, c.1350–1630* (British Archaeological Reports, British Series 315, 2000), p.39. This work is much the most learned, if inevitably sometimes speculative, survey of the many complex general issues.

61 YMB, III, 54. Cf. *Merchant Taylor Hall, Aldwark, York: A Concise Report on the Archaeological Evaluation* (Historical Buildings Services, 1991), p.10.

62 A. M. Mennim, *The Merchant Taylors Hall, York* (York, 2000); and see J. Baily,

below, **pp.**83-98.

63 Giles, *Archaeology of Social Identity*, pp.36-45.

64 RCHM, *City of York*, II, *The Defences* (1972), pp.17-18; D.M. Palliser, Introduction to *The Church of St Helen-on-the Walls, Aldwark*, ed. J.R. Magilton (York Archaeological Trust, 10/1, 1980), pp.5, 14.

65 D. Waterman, 'Excavations in the Hall of the Merchant Taylors, Aldwark, York', *Yorkshire Architectural and York Archaeological Society* (1949-50), p.15; *20th Annual Report, 1991-1992* (York Archaeological Trust) p.21; *Merchant Taylors Hall ,Concise Report*, p.11.

66 See Giles, p.56.

67 *York City Chamberlains' Account Rolls, 1396-1500*, ed. R.B. Dobson (Surtees Society, CXCII, 1980) pp.26, 99.

68 YCA, CC.1 (1446-50); CC1a (1448-83); Johnson, pp.109-13; *VCH York*, p.533; S. Rosenfeld, *The York Theatre* (London, 2001), pp.1-3.

69 *York Civic Records*, 2, p.136.

70 Ibid., 3, p.130; Palliser, *Tudor York*, pp.173-4.

71 RCHM, *York, The Central Area*, pp.90-1; Johnson, p.103; Giles, p.43.

72 BI, Prob. Reg., 1, f. 17; 5, ff.463v-464; Giles, p.42.

73 BI, Reg. 19 (Kempe), f.193v; 22 (Neville), f.49r - references for which I am grateful to Professor David Smith.

74 TNA, C. 66/477, memb. 11, transcribed by Miss D.A. Leech in Johnson, pp.121-3; *Cal. Pat. Rolls, 1452-61*, p.105.

75 *The York Mercers and Merchant Adventurers, 1356-1917*, ed M. Sellers (Surtees Society, CXXIX, 1918), pp.33-6.

76 Davies and Saunders, *Merchant Taylors' Company*, p.22. The York tailors' company was only formally constituted as 'the Master, Wardens, Assistants and Fellowship of Merchant Taylors in our said citty of Yorke' by Charles II's letters patent of 26 April 1662 (BL, Additional MS 8935; Johnson, p.141). See below, p.68.

77 *Cal. Pat. Rolls, 1446-52*, pp.221-2; *York Civic Records*, 1, p.82; 2, p.9; cf. D. M. Palliser, 'Urban Decay Revisited', in *Towns and Townspeople in the Fifteenth Century*, ed. J.A.F. Thomson (Stroud, 1988).

78 R.B. Dobson, 'Urban Decline in late medieval England', *Transactions of the Royal Historical Society*, 5th ser. 27 (1977), pp.18-21. Cf. *VCH York*, p.89. P. J. P. Goldberg, 'Mortality and Economic Change in the Diocese of York, 1390-1514', *Northern History*, XXIV, (1988), pp.38-55.

79 *VCH York*, p.114; Galley, *Demography of Towns*, p.194.

80 Swanson, 'Craftsmen and Industry', pp.77-81; and see below p.54-5.

81 N. Bartlett, 'The Lay Poll Tax Returns for the City of York in 1381', *Trans. East Riding Antiq. Society*, XXX (unpublished), pp.1-79.

82 E.g. BI, Prob. Reg, 1, ff.26, 61.

83 BI, Prob. Reg. 5, f.110.

84 BI, Prob. Reg. 2, f.14; *Test. Ebor.*, III, 245-6.

85 *Test., Ebor.*, III, 300–4; edited in translation by P.M. Stell and L. Hampson in *Probate Inventories of the York Diocese, 1350-1500* (privately printed, c.1999), pp.287–94.

86 *Probate Inventories*, pp.287–94; cf. Swanson, *Artisans*, pp.47, 77, 103, 120, 144, 159.

87 *Freemen's Register*, p.108; *Test. Ebor.*, II, 93–5; J. Kermode, *Medieval Merchants: York, Beverley and Hull in the Later Middle Ages* (Cambridge, 1998), pp.79, 205, 298, 302.

88 *Freemen's Register*, pp.243, 249; *The House of Commons, 1509–1558*, ed. S. T. Bindoff (History of Parliament Trust, 3 vols, 1982), I, 715–16; III, 605.

89 E. White, 'Probate Bequests to Guild of St. John the Baptist', tabulated in Giles, pp.101–4.

90 BI, Prob. Reg. 2A, ff. 128v–129.

91 Indeed most urban religious guilds in Yorkshire seem to have disappeared 'before the dissolution process was complete': see Crouch, *Piety, Fraternity and Power*, pp.236–43.

92 I.W. Archer, 'The Livery Companies and Charity in the Sixteenth and Seventeenth Centuries,' in *Guilds, Society and Economy in London, 1450-1800*, ed. I.A. Gadd and P. Wallis (London, 2002), p.15.

93 *York Civic Records*, 5, pp.57–62; 6, p.37; Johnson. p.128.

THE COMPANY OF TAILORS AND DRAPERS, 1551-1662

W.J. Sheils

The legislation of Edward VI's reign removing the religious functions of the fraternities and the associated decline in their ceremonial obligations at Corpus Christi and other liturgical festivals precipitated a reconsideration of the function of the craft guilds. Furthermore these socio-religious changes were being implemented at a time of economic difficulty for the city, and for the nation as a whole. York itself experienced a series of epidemics between 1549 and 1552, probably intensified by bad harvests and malnutrition, with the result that, during the 1550s the population of the city was reduced by about a third from its already low figure of 8,000.[1] It was against this background of religious change and economic distress that the two guilds, of tailors and drapers, decided to formalise their earlier co-operation and to amalgamate under a new set of ordinances. This was not, however, a marriage of equals. The tailors were far more numerous but the drapers, whose membership was sufficiently small for them to be discharged from their obligations to contribute a pageant to the cycle of mystery plays in 1551, were generally much wealthier individuals active in business on a national scale. They traded with merchants in London and attended national fairs, and were at the centre of the regional distributive network comprising important cloth towns such as Kendal.[2]

The new ordinances were first presented on 27 October 1550 and were passed by the mayor and corporation two years later. The clauses relating to the tailors follow closely the ordinances of 1387 for regulating apprenticeship, maintaining quality and uncovering fraud, but removed references to expenditure on Corpus Christi and the prohibitions on unlawful assembly and livery. There were modest changes, however, which proved significant for the regulation of the craft; these were the removal of the obligation for apprentices to be examined by the searchers of the company and the imposition of fines on those masters elected to office and refusing to serve. In the case of a Master of the company this was fixed at 40s. and for a searcher at 10s., and the sums received were to be shared equally between the corporation and the poor artificers. Both articles are indicative of an important shift in emphasis observed elsewhere in early modern England, and were as much concerned with the discipline of members and officers as with the maintenance of standards of craftsmanship.[3] This can be further seen in those ordinances referring to the drapers, where there is little attempt to control quality and much effort to exclude competition. The drapers were essentially concerned with maintaining their monopoly of trading within the city, especially against their competitors from Kendal, who were only permitted to trade wholesale. In addition other traders from outside York had to pay a tax, called pageant silver, if they sold more than three yards of broad cloth or six of narrow, and they were not allowed to sell their wares in the streets or inns of the city but only at Thursday Market or in the Common Hall, where the searchers of the company could oversee the cloth for sale. The searchers had the right to impound deficient cloth or cloth sold illegally and the income received from the sale of such cloth was to be shared equally by the corporation and the company, which could use its share either in the repair of its hall or in the relief of poor colleagues or their families.[4] Having completed these ordinances with a requirement from the master and the searchers, two for the tailors and two for the drapers, to uphold the company's regulations, and setting fines on those craftsmen who disobeyed the master or searchers, the new company compiled oaths to be sworn by its officers and free craftsmen, which were recorded in a volume around 1560.[5]

The amalgamation made the tailors and drapers the second most important craft group in the city after the merchants and mercers, joining them with four members on the Common Council of the city.[6] They dominated the clothing trades of the city, which accounted for about a quarter of the city's freemen for most of the period under discussion; in the years between 1550 and 1575 the tailors alone were the largest group of new freeman with 152 admissions whilst in the final quarter of the sixteenth century they and the drapers combined accounted for 209 admissions, over twenty more than the next largest occupational group, the merchants and mercers.[7] This dominance continued into the early part of the seventeenth century, although by the 1650s diversification of the local economy, and York's growing role as a centre for consumption, meant that the place of the tailors and drapers in the local economy was being challenged by the victualling and distributive trades.[8] In a period which has been described generally as one of economic growth and recovery for the city after the crises of the early and mid sixteenth century, members of the company, albeit some way behind the merchants in importance, were at the centre of that revival. Not only in its economic life but also in political affairs.[9]

The charting of the company's history in this period is assisted by the survival of records which are not available for earlier periods, most importantly the register of abled masters from 1560 and the register of apprentices from 1606.[10] From these sources we can identify over 1900 individuals who began as apprentices in the company, of which just over 850 became masters and served the company between 1560 and 1660.[11] The overall pattern to be observed from these sources is of a consistent level of recruitment of seventy to eighty new masters each decade, of which about one-sixth were drapers and the vast majority tailors. This pattern was disrupted somewhat by the demographic crisis of the early seventeenth century, which led to a skills shortage and special initiatives to ensure that numbers were sustained.

Table of apprentices and masters 1560–1660

	APPRENTICES				MASTERS			
	T	D	Unidentified	Total	T	D	Unidentified	Total
1560–9						69		69
1570–9						68	4	72
1580–9						74	1	75
1590–9						59	8	67
1600–9	99	19	3	*121**	64	7	25	96
1610–9	245	32	8	285	69	12	28	109
1620–9	222	35	3	260	58	10		68
1630–9	220	31	6	257	61	14	3	78
1640–9	100	33	10	143	64	16	2	82
1650–9	182	33	10	225	64	12		76

T = tailor   D = draper

* Note: The apprentice register starts in 1606

The peculiar circumstances of the early seventeenth century data will be dealt with later, but the overall impression from these figures is of a stable craft community holding its own within the local economy. This, however, hides a modest but noticeable relative decline towards the end of the period as the local economy diversified and the population of the city increased, a situation which is also reflected in the freemen's registers where the proportion of clothing trade entrants dropped from a consistent figure of c. 24% of total admissions in the years between 1550 and 1625 to about 16% in the years after 1640.[12] From the company's records the decline is more noticeable in the register of apprentices than in the masters' register, but this may also owe something to the disruption of the Civil Wars in the 1640s, when recruiting individuals from outside the city was likely to be especially difficult, and record keeping may have been more fitful. The other point to emerge from the table is that the ratio of apprentices to masters was approximately 2.5:1, with 1066 apprentices being recorded between 1606 and 1650 and 413 masters between 1610 and 1660, and that this ratio applied equally to tailors and drapers. This may underestimate the normal ratio, as the figures for the years after 1605 and the disrupted years of the 1640s show that apprentices at those times had a better chance of becoming a master than at other times, and it may be that the normal pattern was closer to 3:1, a figure which is also reflected in the ordinances which forbade any master to have more than three apprentices at any one time.

Of course the path from apprentice to master was subject to many vicissitudes, the death of or absconding by an apprentice being the most common and sometimes recorded in the registers, where very occasionally it was also noted that an individual had left his apprenticeship to take another craft.[13] This was very unusual, however, and it can be assumed that most apprentices completed their term and remained for a time in the employment of a master. Indeed, as in the case of Nathaniel Buck in 1625,[14] it was sometimes explicitly stated in the indentures that an apprentice would continue to serve his master for a fixed period after completing his apprenticeship. Overall about half, or a little under half, of those completing apprenticeships were eventually admitted as masters of the company, usually within five years of serving their time, but this left a sizeable number of craftsmen who remained unfree of the company. Many of these men must have worked for master craftsmen in the city as paid employees, and a few may have set up within the ecclesiastical liberties of the city where they did not have to pay for freedom or adhere to company rules. A sizeable proportion may have returned to their home towns to ply their trade, and never intended to set up in the city itself. This was probably the case with apprentices from other towns in the county, such as Richmond, Pickering, Malton, Ripon and Stokesley, which regularly provided apprentices to the company, very few of whom became masters. Some of these, such as Christopher Chapman, son of a Hull alderman and apprenticed to Robert Askwith in 1617, or Henry, son of Edward Gower, of Richmond, gentleman, were from families among the elite of their own home towns and no doubt returned there to work. Members of the company therefore, in addition to standing at the centre of a regional distribution network for its products, provided training for craftsmen not only in the city but in towns in the North and East Ridings.

The decision to become a master depended, therefore, on opportunity and individual circumstance, and there was clearly a hierarchy in operation. Apprenticeship to well established masters such as the MP Robert Askwith, or alderman Robert Hemsworth, both drapers, was much sought after for their sons by local gentry and fellow aldermen, as it would provide both the training and the connections necessary to set up as a master. These connections could lead to mutually advantageous reciprocal arrangements, as in the case of Gabriel Freeman, son of a gentleman from Malton, who was apprenticed to Robert Askwith in 1614 and in his turn took on another member of the Askwith family, Samuel, as an apprentice in 1623.[15] Social status was therefore an important factor both in gaining an advantageous apprenticeship and in becoming a master but, in the absence of status, kinship and local connections were also important. If we take the years 1620–24 as a sample, of the 107 apprentices registered at that time, seven were apprenticed to their fathers and a further 27 came from the city and were presumably known to their new masters. Of those coming from further afield at least four were apprenticed to masters with the same surname and this must represent a minimum figure for kinship recruitment. Almost half the apprentices in these years, 47 out of 107, came from either the city or villages in the vale of York, and this strongly local pattern of recruitment confirms information from other leading towns such as Norwich.[16] Those coming from further afield, just over half of the total, reveal a strong bias to the north, principally Ryedale and the dales, with a smattering from east Yorkshire and a significant minority from the smaller towns of the county, mostly in the North Riding but including Keighley and Tadcaster in the West Riding. Beyond the county individual apprentices were recruited from Westmorland, Cumberland, Durham, Lincolnshire and, more surprisingly, Wiltshire, in that case apprenticed to a prosperous draper.[17] The overall impression gained from the sources is one of a stable recruitment pattern within which apprentices from York and its immediate hinterland were more likely to become masters than those from further afield. Though buffeted by external factors such as plague and Civil War, the crafts offered attractive careers to the sons of families fairly well established in local rural society and the market towns of Yorkshire, and masters were sufficiently prosperous and trade sufficiently brisk for them to take on enough apprentices to secure a profitable future for the crafts in the city, or at least for their leading practitioners.

Within the company itself the drapers were the most prosperous group and dominated the office of Master for most of the period. Only eighteen out of the eighty one craftsmen who became masters of the company between 1560 and 1661 were described as tailors, and while a few early masters were called both tailor and draper it is likely that, as in the case of John Dyneley, a city alderman and master of the company in 1562 and 1568, the drapery business was more important than tailoring. Of the tailors who became masters of the company only three were elected on more than one occasion, William Sunlaye in 1591 and 1603, James Godson in 1602 and 1614, by which date he was described as a "gentleman" in the register and had presumably distanced himself somewhat from the practice of his craft, and Thomas Campleshon in 1612 and 1622.[18] Notwithstanding their numerical superiority the tailors were clearly the junior partners in the company for almost all of the period, and this impression is reinforced by the fact that they had something of a resurgence in the management of the company's affairs in the disrupted years between 1641 and 1661, when seven tailors were elected Master. These years encompassed the Civil War, Interregnum, and Restoration, when political loyalty may have been as important to gaining office as social or economic position, and covered a period in which internal trade was itself disrupted and the clothing trades within the city were in relative decline.

The amalgamation of the two crafts not only provided the drapers with a hall, which they had not had hitherto, but provided the new company with prosperous members who could make use of and had the means to maintain the building. The drapers soon assumed leadership of the new company and from the few references we have to decisions taken by the company during these years, these seem to be controlled by drapers, as in 1578 when fines were set for those masters who absented themselves from the annual Midsummer feast; members present at that meeting were Robert Askwith, Christopher Maltby, Thomas Gibson, Richard Burton, William Gilmyn, and William Beckwith, all of whom were drapers, and the tailor John Sargeantson.[19] The drapers dominated the Mastership of the company, occupying the office in four years out of five through-out the century after 1560, but the lesser office of searcher, of which there were four appointed annually, two for the tailors and two for the drapers, was shared out more equally with each group generally regulating its own area. It was the searchers who carried out the daily work of checking on quality of goods, of overseeing apprenticeships, and ensuring that the social and ceremonial life of the company ran smoothly. They were, in effect, the executive officers of the company and for the smaller independent craftsmen, the filling of this often onerous position was the summit of their ambition; this was especially true of the tailors, whose opportunities to rise higher in the company were limited. Among these men were loyal servants of the company such as Richard Hall: admitted a master tailor in 1581 he served as searcher on eight occasions in the next thirty-three years, for the tailors in 1586, 1593 and 1603, for the drapers in 1590 and 1600, and for the hosiers, who had merged with the company in the mid 1580s, in 1597, 1604 and 1606. And there were others, most of whom, like him, never achieved higher office, although the tailor John Hudles eventually became Master of the company in 1597, twenty five years after being admitted and having served five terms of office as searcher in the different crafts.[20] It is craftsmen like these, about whom we know little more than the bare outlines of their working lives, who formed the backbone of the society at this period, as at any other.

Mention of these men brings us to consideration of the career patterns of the individuals who comprised the company at this time. Entrance to the crafts was almost always through serving as apprentice to a free master, usually for seven years, though occasionally eight or nine are specified, perhaps in consid-eration of the age of the candidate. Sometimes the apprenticeship arrangements were interrupted by the death of the employer and alternative arrangements had to be made, though few were as unlucky as Thomas Emerson, son of a York haberdasher, who was apprenticed as a tailor to Thomas Bell, Robert Lunde and Anthony Hurwoode in succession, the first two dying on him. Such acci-dents could extend the period of apprenticeship, and in Emerson's case it took him nine and a half years from his first entry on 24 June 1621 to serve his indentures and a further four and a half years to be admitted a master tailor.[21] Setting up as an independent master in York or elsewhere was the ambition of most apprentices but the process depended a lot on personal circumstances and opportunity. There was, therefore a wide variation in the amount of time which elapsed between starting an apprenticeship and becoming a master craftsman. We have data on this from 1606, but there are problems of interpretation. The demographic crisis of 1604–5 makes the period before 1620 an unreliable guide to normal practice and the data from the Civil War period suggests that registration of apprentices may have broken down somewhat at that time, which leaves the information from the 1620s and 1630s, a relatively stable period in York's economic history, as our best guide to normal practice.[22]

From the surviving registers we can identify with certainty forty four individuals, apprenticed in the 1620s who subsequently became masters, and from these can draw some conclusions. The first thing that strikes one is the essentially local recruitment pattern: twenty of the new apprentices were from the city itself and another ten were either from suburban parishes like Acomb and Clifton or from villages in the vale of York, such as Newton upon Ouse or Riccall. Of those who came from further afield, most came from the dales area to the north and west. There were very few indeed from either the West or East Ridings, where the growing towns of Leeds and Hull presumably provided opportunities for the ambitious sons of the rural hinterland. A few came from a very long way away; one from Lathom in Lancashire, a gentleman's son from Sizergh in Westmorland, and William Barnes, the son of a husbandman of Down Hall in Cumberland, who followed his older brother Thomas, to whom he was apprenticed, into the craft. In these cases kinship may well have been an important factor in deciding on a craft, but there were relatively few sons following their fathers in business: only six cases were recorded and in two of these the father had already died by the time the son was apprenticed. Nor did tailors apprentice their sons to other masters of the company, the only case being that of Thomas Richardson, son of a York draper, who was apprenticed to Thomas Stapleton, tailor, on 22 September 1622.[23] The great majority of those who were apprenticed to the company in the 1620s were newcomers to the craft and trade, and came from a wide range of social and occupational backgrounds to judge from their fathers' occupations. There were four sons of drapers and four of tailors, but these were matched or exceeded by sons of rural workers, five husbandmen, four yeomen and four labourers, and by innholders, both from York and from country villages, who provided five apprentices. The status of the company can be gauged from the fact that three gentlemen and two clergymen apprenticed their sons, as did a York merchant and three millers, those well known aristocrats of pre-industrial rural society. Two grassmen from the vale of York also apprenticed sons to the company and the remaining places were provided by other craftsmen, a tanner, a carpenter, a haberdasher, and a basket-maker from Clifton in the suburbs of the city.[24] Recruitment was essentially local, but most of the apprentices were not only new to tailoring but came from a non-craft background in the rural hinterland, where the status of the craft was sufficient to attract the sons of yeomen and the occasional professional.

Having gained an apprenticeship the next stage was to be made a full member, or master, of the company. The average period of time which elapsed between the start of apprenticeship and becoming a member of the company for this cohort was ten years and seven months, with over half of them achieving this between eight and a half and thirteen years. There were exceptional cases: like that of Nathaniel Buck, whose progression may have been disturbed by service during the Civil Wars and who only took his freedom in 1662, twenty seven years after entering his apprenticeship, or, at the other extreme, the unaccountable case of Thomas Creeton, son of a York labourer who, having entered an eight year apprenticeship in 1625 was made free of the company three years and nine months later, in June 1629.[25] Disregarding these intriguing, but exceptional, cases what the evidence of the registers suggests is that drapers, being generally from better off backgrounds (one was the son of a cleric and another a son of a gentleman) or else following in the family business, progressed rapidly from apprentice to master. All five drapers apprenticed in this decade became masters in less than the average time taken by the cohort, the longest gap being the ten years and six months taken by Philip Smithson who, exceptionally, was apprenticed to his mother Helen in March 1622.[26] The tailors exhibited a much more diverse pattern, but within that it was clearly an advantage to have local knowledge: sons of York freemen, like Thomas Pickard, an innholder's son, usually gained their freedom from the company more quickly than apprentices from outside, even when, as sometimes was the case, these outsiders were, like Richard Smith of Hunmanby, apprenticed to a kinsman.[27] It seems that progress to the status of master craftsman was dependent on individual circumstances and was mostly influenced by local contacts and the social and financial standing of individuals. There is little evidence from this decade of the company itself restricting access to its crafts beyond the limitation of three apprentices to one craftsman at any one time.

If the company could allow supply and demand to find its own equilibrium in the 1620s this was certainly not the case in the first decade of the seventeenth century when in 1604–5 the city was ravaged by plague which, in the space of nine months, killed about 3,000 inhabitants, almost a third of the population, rich and poor alike, scattered throughout the parishes.[28] Devastation on this scale caused massive dislocation to the economic well-being of the city, and on 21 February 1605, when the worst had passed, the corporation insisted that any traders who had removed themselves and their households from the city were to return immediately or pay a substantial fine of £5 a week towards the maintenance of the poor for every week of continued absence.[29]

The tailors and drapers were affected as much as any other group in the city. Indeed leading members of the company were in the forefront of York's political and economic concerns at this time: William Greenbury, was master of the company in both 1604 and 1605, the crisis being responsible for the unusual step of having the same man serve in consecutive years, and was also Lord Mayor in 1605 when the city was engaged in dealing with the effects of the plague; Robert Askwith, who had been master of the company in 1594, although not facing the plague in the city itself, was representing it at King James I's first Parliament where he was active in promoting a new charter and in campaigning for improvements to the River Ouse. Both Greenbury and Askwith were drapers, and the sons of drapers who had themselves filled important civic office, and they were in regular official correspondence throughout these difficult months: indeed in 1606 Askwith was to succeed Greenbury both as Lord Mayor and as master of the company, also serving two consecutive terms in that office.[30]

It was following the ravages of 1604 that the company sought new ordinances, to be added to those approved in 1552, which received the corporation's approval on 7 June 1605. The new ordinances, four in number, represented a tightening of control over the tailoring craft in particular, in an attempt to prevent unfree or "foreign", that is to say non-York, craftsmen or traders from working in the city. Non-free tailors were forbidden to work in the city or in its suburbs, and only freemen were to retail cloth in the same area, and any freemen permitting unfree tailors or drapers to set up business in the city was to be subjected to a fine of 40s. by the corporation. A similar fine was to be levied on any freeman who put out any tailoring work to an unfree tailor, or allowed them to undertake work of that sort on their premises. In order to enforce these orders the powers of the searchers and beadle of the company were extended to include the searching of any suspect houses and anyone impeding such searches were liable to a fine of 6s. 8d. The impact of these ordinances was stiffened by that which empowered the mayor and corporation to imprison in the Kidcote any who failed to pay their fines within six days of being summoned. The final ordinance related to apprentices, tightening the regulations and requiring that all apprentices who left their masters without licence before their allotted term should be reported to the company so that they could not subsequently claim any credit for the years accrued.[31] The tailors and drapers were not alone in asking for some reconsideration of their regulations in this period: both the coopers and the vintners made representations to the corporation, though they did not register new ordinances.[32] These requests indicate the dislocation caused by the deaths of so many tradesmen in the plague months; the resulting skill shortage was both a problem for those needing to have work done and an opportunity for workers both in the city and from elsewhere to fill the gaps. In such circumstances control of the workforce was less easy to sustain and these ordinances can be seen as a direct attempt to ensure that the guilds retained control of their own crafts in such a volatile labour market.

If the new ordinances can be construed as a defensive response to a crisis the records of the company reveal a more positive attitude, and in view of the new ordinance regulating apprenticeship it is no surprise that a new register was started at this time. The first priority, however, was to fill the immediate skill shortage, and here the register of abled masters is revealing. Not only did the numbers of craftsmen admitted increase by about 50% in the first two decades of the century, the majority of those being in the years between 1605 and 1615, but also a new form of words was introduced from 1605 in many cases, and continued with decreasing regularity for about ten years. The traditional way of noting an individual's entry to the company, applied universally up to this date, was with the phrase "was abled a master" and this was usually followed by a note of the particular branch of the trade to be pursued, whether tailor or draper, but a new category emerged at this time, of individuals who were "admitted to the freedom of the company" with no reference to any particular craft. As can be seen from the table above these were a significant proportion of the new entrants, representing about a third of those admitted between 1605 and 1615, and the implication is that these men had not progressed through apprenticeship in the same way as had those referred to as "abled masters", but had either been advanced more rapidly through the system, before their indentures had been completed, or were allowed to enter without any formal training in the craft or had acquired any such training somewhere other than York. It is not clear from the surviving evidence whether these men entered the company on the same terms as former apprentices, or exercised the full rights of masters. Their subsequent careers in the company are interesting, however. Only two of them subsequently served office as searcher; one of these, Christopher Hudles was probably related to a former Master of the company and was sufficiently well connected to find two masters to stand surety for him, and the other Henry Petty may have been an exceptional case as he paid the high fee of 20s. on admittance, plus the gift of a silver spoon. The rest do not figure in the company's history and the suggestion that they may have been lesser craftsmen drafted in to cover a crisis is reinforced by the emergence of another small group of individuals who make an appearance between 1605 and 1608 and then disappear, the free sewers. Five men were admitted in this category, which was presumably linked to the new ordinance regulating the putting out of work by masters. These were presumably individuals who, though not full members of the company were licensed to undertake work on behalf of the masters during the shortage of skilled labour, and it is possible that some of those admitted simply to the freedom of the company also fell into that category. The company, therefore, relaxed its rules a little in these years in order to ensure the continuation of its business, and it is also worth noting that one of only two women recorded as taking on apprentices, Ursula Callam, the widow of William Callam, draper, who had been Master of the company in 1586 and sheriff of York in 1590-91, did so in March 1609.[33]

The impact of the plague was not only in its immediate aftermath, for just as it decimated the ranks of existing craftsmen it also cut off the supply of potential recruits through apprenticeship. We have already shown that, in normal circumstances, the city itself was likely to produce about a third of the new apprentices recorded, but in the years after 1605 this could not be guaranteed, thus the medium term future of trade was also at risk, and to ensure a sufficient supply of new apprentices it had to widen its recruitment field. If we compare the apprentices recruited in the years 1606-10 with those recruited in the period 1620-4 noted above, we might get some indication of the impact of the plague on the company. The first thing to notice, and perhaps the most important, is that in the five years from 1606 there were 41 more apprentices recruited than in the years 1620-4 and that the proportion of York residents among them was significantly less, 24% compared to 32% of the total in the 1620s. As in this later period there was a healthy representation from the villages on the edge of the city, bolstered by four recruits from Heslington, and from the parishes in the southern vale of York, but there were fewer recruits from the market towns of the county, which may themselves have suffered from the plague. The shortfall had to be made up from elsewhere and, interestingly, a significant number came from the rural hinterland of the East Riding, which hardly figured in the 1620s. Among these were men from Catton, Scagglethorpe, Kirby Underdale, Sledmere, Wressle, Fangfoss and Wetwang. These were not parishes which normally figured in the register at this period, and there were also a few recruits from parishes at the very extremities of the county, Bainbridge in Wensleydale, Hockerside and Marske in Swaledale, Scargill in Arkengarthdale. Compared with the later period the out-county recruits were also more numerous, three from Westmorland, two from Durham, one each from Lancashire, Northumberland and Cumberland, four from Lincolnshire and one from Derbyshire.[34] Although the overall numbers are small there are enough indicators to suggest that the opportunities available in the city after the plague of 1604–5 resulted in apprentices to the company being recruited from a more geographically dispersed and slightly extended field than was usually the case.

Finally we will consider those apprentices between 1606 and 1610 who subsequently became masters. We can identify 34 of these with certainty, and compared with the cohort from the 1620s they progressed to the freedom of the company in a slightly shorter period of time, the average length of time from signing indentures to becoming a master was exactly ten years for this group compared with ten years and seven months for those in the 1620s. Though modest this is a measurable difference between the two cohorts, the impact of which is underlined by the fact that over two-thirds of the masters in the years after 1605 achieved that status within ten years whilst only two-fifths of the 1620s cohort did so.[35]

The dramatic events which overtook the city and the region in 1604-5 brought terrible suffering to individuals, households and businesses but the company, like the city, weathered the storm.[36] The crafts continued to attract apprentices from around the county in sufficient numbers to supply any want; and by 1615 the company , having tightened its ordinances and loosened its qualifications for full membership, had returned to the level of activity which had been the case before the onset of plague, with its members continuing to play an important role in civic affairs.

We have already stated that the drapers and tailors were the second most important group represented on the common council at the beginning of our period, someway behind the merchants and mercers but also considerably more significant than any other crafts, and the important offices held by Robert Askwith and William Greenbury in 1604 and 1605 are evidence of that continuing importance. The overall influence of the tailors and drapers in the city can be illustrated best statistically: all but five Masters of the company between 1560 and 1660 held civic office in some capacity, whether as chamberlain, sheriff, alderman, Lord Mayor, or MP, and drapers and tailors, most usually the former, were the second biggest craft group represented in civic government between 1551 and the granting of the Royal Charter. The most junior of these civic offices was that of chamberlain, six being appointed yearly to oversee the city's finances, and it was usual for members of the company to fill this office before becoming Master: of the ninety-one tailors who acted as city chamberlain twenty-seven never became Master of the company, some like Vincent Busfield (d. by 1610), chamberlain in 1606, because they died young, but others like George Watson, chamberlain in 1622 and from a well-established York trading family, because of political or religious loyalties. Watson was described as "an obstinate recusant" (meaning Roman Catholic) in 1623.[37] Political and religious loyalties were especially important during the Civil War period and the removal of dissenters from the Corporation after 1665 curtailed some potentially promising civic careers, like that of Christopher Hewley, chamberlain in 1647, sheriff in 1654-5 and a benefactor to the city, but who never progressed further in office, removing himself to Wistow in the 1660s.[38] The city sheriffs, of whom there were two annually, held their own courts, and it was more usual for men to serve in this capacity after they had been Master of the company, though three men, William Brogden (sheriff in 1558), Peter Mann (sheriff in 1649-50) and John Robinson (sheriff in 1602-3), never headed the company. In Brogden's case religion may have been the reason: holding civic office under the Catholic Mary he subsequently had business links with recusant gentry such as the Vavasours of Hazlewood, to whom he lent money. In the cases of Mann and Robinson they each died within a few years of serving as sheriff, though Mann may also have got caught up in political events; having served as chamberlain in 1631 it was not until 1649–50, at the end of the Civil War and with Parliament in control of the city, that he became sheriff.[39] In all thirty-four members of the company served as sheriff in these years and, as with the chamberlain's office, it was filled by both tailors and drapers.

The aldermanic bench and the mayoralty were at the apex of civic office and were firmly in the hands of the drapers, though some of them described themselves as tailors and drapers, especially in the earlier part of the period. The only alderman who was described simply as "tailor" occurred at the beginning of the period; he was William Coupland, alderman from 1549, Lord Mayor in 1553 and 1568, and MP in the Parliament of 1554.[40] The company boasted fifteen aldermen between 1551 and 1662, fourteen of whom also served as Lord Mayor, two of them after 1662.[41] The involvement of leading members of the company in the highest civic offices continued throughout the period and beyond, and two of them, William Allanson and Robert Askwith, received knighthoods in the early seventeenth century by virtue of the fact that each happened to be Lord Mayor in the year of a royal visit: Askwith in 1617 when James I came to the city and was entertained by the mayor at his house in Hosier Lane, and Allanson in 1633 when Charles I stayed in York en route to his coronation in Edinburgh as King of Scotland.[42] Both Askwith and Allanson served the city as MP, Askwith in James' first three Parliaments and Allanson in the Long Parliament of 1640, in which he was a staunch supporter of Parliament against the king during the Civil War. Askwith's father, another Robert, had also been elected MP for the city at a by-election in 1581 and again in 1588, and the company had provided two MPs for the city at the very beginning of the period in the reign of the catholic Mary Tudor. William Coupland was MP in Mary's third parliament of 1554, and was a committed Catholic who, after the accession of Elizabeth I was described as "no favourer of religion". He attracted the attention of the authorities when militant Catholic opinions were expressed by gentlemen at his dining table in 1562, and during his second mayoralty in 1568 he unsuccessfully tried to restore performances of the Creed play and the Corpus Christi cycle. His will reflected his traditional religious beliefs and, at his death in 1569 he asked for pennies and halfpennies to be distributed to 1600 old people and children in the city. Richard White, one of the wealthiest laymen in York in the mid sixteenth century, lived in a house in Minster Gates when elected MP in spring 1554. At parliament he secured the renewal of the city's charter and stricter regulation of those who tried to evade the city's trading privileges. He held a lease of half of the Merchant Taylors' Hall in addition to owning ten other properties in the city at his death in 1558, when he left money for masses for his soul and for a lamp to be lit before the sacrament.[43]

The wills of both Coupland and White remind us that these men were not just craftsman or traders, but held opinions on a wide range of issues, and at the end of our period the conflict between king and parliament could not be ignored in a city which had the King and court present during the summer of 1642 and which was subject to one of the most decisive encounters of the war, the siege of the city and the ensuing battle of Marston Moor in July 1644.[44] We have already noted Allanson's strong support for Parliament at this time and this was balanced by the other leading member of the company, alderman Robert Hemsworth who, because of his royalist sympathies, was removed from the bench after the parliamentary victories of 1644 and remained excluded from civic government until the return of the monarchy when, in September 1662, he was restored once again to his aldermanic dignity.[45]

The company and its membership were not immune from the great changes and divisions which characterised English religion and politics between the Reformation and the Civil Wars and, in addition to those concerns which members of a craft held in common, these divisions of opinion on such matters must have impinged on the running of the company's affairs. It is on this issue that the surviving records of our period are most deficient, and we can only catch glimpses of the routine business. One routine matter was the disciplining of wayward members of the company. We have very little surviving evidence for transgressions of the ordinances governing the conduct of the craft, though this must have occupied a good deal of the searchers' time. In 1656 the corporation extended the rights of the company's searchers and beadle so that they could sue for warrants to enter the houses and distrain the goods of any members of the company who had refused to pay fines imposed by them. Much of the evidence we do have comes from this time and relates to one case of employing an apprentice without proper indentures and a couple of cases of masters putting work out to "strangers" without the permission of the Master, in these latter cases discipline was referred to the Lord Mayor as the offenders refused to accept the company's penalty.[46] Other disciplinary matters had more to do with the honour of the company and its officials than with the regulation of trade. Individuals were fined for speaking opprobrious words to the Master or searchers of the company, possibly as a consequence of earlier correction for breach of craft regulations, and occasionally disputes between members came before the company's officers. The few cases of which we have notice were usually settled by a promise to amend or by a modest fine but in one case, that of John Harper, his offences, whatever they were, resulted in temporary expulsion from the company before re-admittance, on pain of good behaviour, in November 1579.[47] The honour of the company was also reflected in the annual midsummer feast, which with the decline and abolition of the plays, became the chief festive occasion: regulations were frequently passed governing the expenses allowed at and the provision of food and drink for this event, and in 1581 the company appointed John Fell as the company's cook, to cater for this and any other dinners in the hall at the annual fee of 10s. These dinners could be lavish affairs, as no doubt was that provided for the whole company by Lancelot Turner, gentleman, on his admission in 1608 and which cost him £20.[48]

Turner's case was a rare one and, unlike the Merchant Adventurers, the Taylors did not attract many "social" members to its ranks: only one other figure in this category was noted in the register during this period, Paul Dawney, esquire, of the family based at Sessay. Other non-craft admissions almost certainly refer to individuals who had provided some service to the company; a clergyman Thomas Hinkston, vicar choral at the Minster, was admitted in 1601 on payment of a bottle of wine, and in 1648 a lawyer, George Prince, who donated a silver bowl.[49] The only official employed by the company on a regular basis was a clerk, the post being filled in both 1569 and 1579 by John Jackson, and in the 1650s, perhaps reflecting the puritan culture of the city at that time, the company appointed a "reader", presumably of Holy Scripture.[50]

It was no doubt the clerk's responsibility to maintain the registers which have formed the main sources for this chapter, and he was probably responsible also for keeping the records of the company's properties in Walmgate, Fishergate, the Havergarths, and the house in Micklegate with the Pageant House in Barker Row attached, from which, according to the surviving notes, it drew a modest annual income from letting, mostly for periods of 21 years.[51]

If the clerk maintained a register of the company's business it has not survived, but from time to time the house books of the corporation provide us with glimpses of the comapny and its members. The national market for the drapers was the source of the company's economic strength at this time, and the scale on which the leading drapers were involved can be measured from the fact that one of them, Christopher Maltby, was said to owe London merchants £1700 in 1585.[52] At the beginning of the period Richard White leased half of the Taylors' Hall from the company, presumably for business purposes. A few years later, in 1563, the hall was used for rather different purposes when a number of drapers, attending Stourbridge Fair near Cambridge, were caught up in the plague precautions and confined to the hall on their return to the city, having failed to comply with earlier orders to shut their shops and refrain from business.[53] When the city, along with other corporations at that time, sought to put its poor to work in 1569, weaving was the chosen employment and it was leading drapers such as William Beckwith, William Allen and Richard Calame who were put in charge of purchasing wool and finding suitable premises. The scheme did not prove successful and two years later the residue of the unsold cloth was sold by the city on the advice of some drapers, possibly at some benefit to themselves as it was reported that the city's cloth was not as valuable as first thought![54]

In 1574, the Hall itself was considered, among other places, as a possible location for settling the city's poor, whose numbers were increased by the relative decline of the city's trade compared to neighbouring towns.[55] Two of the leading members of the company, Christopher Myers and Robert Askwith, were sent to London in 1576 to complain about the tolls which were exacted of them by their competitors at Wakefield and Bradford, and rivalry between the city and the emerging clothing towns of the West Riding was a regular source of complaint, and occasionally of litigation, throughout the period.[56] Whilst the leading members of the company shared in the general prosperity of the city during this period, it is clear that, in comparative terms, the city was losing ground to some of its rivals in the region and, to some extent, the control which the company was able to exercise over the recruitment and the business activities of its members, contributed to that relative decline. The control of business was supported and enforced through the civic institutions, the mayor's and sheriffs' courts, in which the leading members of the company played an important part, through the imposition of fines, withdrawal of freedom, and occasionally imprisonment.

Not surprisingly, therefore, in such circumstances little work was done on the Hall itself, at least in the earlier years of the period when parts of it were sometimes leased out to members or to the corporation for purposes other than business. It is possible that the hall was re-roofed in 1567 when Alderman Hughes gave 40 shillings and four trees to the company, but this seems to be the sum total of activity prior to the seventeenth century when some new windows on the north east, the large chimney breast, and some panelling were added to the building, possibly on the occasion of one or other of the royal visits of 1617 or 1633 when, as it happened, the mayoralty was held by a member of the company.[57] However it was not until the Restoration, and in anticipation of the Royal Charter of 1662, that any major refit of the building was undertaken.

If the building was left to languish for much of this period we do know that, by the 1650s, the company had received a number of gifts of plate, and it might be fitting to end our account of the company during these years, when its members played a significant part in the economic and political life of the city, with the inventory of "all the things about the Taylors' Hall", compiled on 3 December 1649. It expressed that sense of clubbable solidarity of which the company's members were so proud and itemised those items which, no doubt, appeared at the annual dinners to confirm and celebrate their continuing existence:

> One long diaper table cloth and one little one of the same
> One diaper napkin
> Two great brass pots

Item, 16 green cushions
One dozen and a half of high stools
Two green carpet cloths in the Counting House
One marking iron to mark the pewter
One pair of rachets
Two great flagons
Eight dozen pewter dribblers, great and small

In Plate

One high silver bare bowl, given by Alderman Robert Askwith
One shallow bare bowl, of the gift of Henry Lyons
One shallow bare bowl, of the gift of Thomas Askwith, gent.
One high wine bowl, of the gift of Richard Jackson, tailor
One high wine bowl, of the gift of John Smith, cook
One high bare bowl given by Richard Atkinson, tailor
One silver can
One great high bare bowl, of the gift of James Brearey
One high bare bowl, of the gift of Mr George Prince
One great silver can, of the gift of Owen Hughes, price £6 17s. 6d.
One little can of silver, of the gift of John Shillito, tailor, cost £3
One high bare bowl, of the gift of Mr John Smith, £10 11s. 8d.[58]

Although York was no longer as dominant in the clothing trades as it had been at the beginning of our period, and had lost business to the burgeoning towns of the West Riding, it had begun to diversify and create a new source of prosperity for itself as a centre for fashionable consumption. In this the company had a continuing role to play, but whether it could sustain its role in the economic and political life of the city is the subject of the next chapter. Looking back on the history recounted above, and with this collection of tableware in its Hall, the members of the company in the 1650s might justifiably have come to the same conclusion about their contribution to the city in these years as that which one of its most illustrious members, Robert Askwith MP (d.1597), had had placed on his monument in St. Crux church, "for good hospitality, and other laudable parts, a credit and ornament to this city".[59]

NOTES

1 D. Palliser, *Tudor York* (Oxford, 1970), pp.223-5.

2 Ibid. pp.163-4; B. Johnson, *The Acts and ordinances of the Company of Merchant Taylors in the City of York* (York, 1949), pp.46-7; BI, MTA 5/1, ff.2-10.

3 *York Civic Records*, v, pp.57-62, also printed in Johnson, pp.128-31.

4 Johnson, p.47.

5 BI, MTA 5/4; printed in Johnson, pp.131-2.

6 See above pp.32, 45.

7 Table at C. Galley, *The Demography of early modern towns: York in the 16th and 17th centuries* (Liverpool, 1998), p.35; *York Freemen's Register*, I, pp.270-9, II, pp.1-45.

8 *VCH York*, p.167.

9 Galley, *York*, pp.33-40; *VCH York*, p.166-71.

10 BI, MTA 5/1, 9/1.

11 D. M. Smith, *The Company of Merchant Taylors in the City of York: Register of Admissions 1560-1835* (Borthwick List and Index 16, York, 1996) includes all those who became masters, for apprentices not admitted see MTA 9/1.

12 *VCH York*, p.167; *York Freemen's Registers*, II, pp.95-125.

13 BI, MTA 9/1. This was noted most frequently in the 1640s, for examples see ff. 104 (Bernard Dodsworth, "ran away"), 108 (Robert Hutchinson, "dead"), 110 (John Darling, "gone for a soldier"), 118 (Richard Burton, "now a barber").

14 Smith, *Admissions*, p.14.

15 York Reference Library, R. H. Skaife, "Civic Officials and Parliamentary Representatives of York", p.27; BI, MTA 9/1, f. 52v.

16 J. Patten, "Patterns of migration and movement of labour in three pre-industrial East Anglian towns" in P. Clark and D. Souden eds., *Migration in early modern England* (1987), pp.77-106.

17 BI, MTA 9/1, ff. 47-58, for the out-county entries see Bland, f.48v, Blanshard, f.49, Sewill, f.49v, Chapman, f.50, Allinson, f.54, Barnes, f.57, Hutton, f.57v.

18 BI, MTA 5/1; Smith, *Admissions*, pp.16, 39, 87; Skaife, "Civic Officials", p.699.

19 BI, MTA 6/1, f.43.

20 Smith, *Admissions*, pp.42, 50.

21 Ibid. p.32.

22 W. J. Sheils, "York in the 17th century" in P Nuttgens ed, *A History of York from Roman Times to 2000* (York 2001), pp.277-311.

23 Smith, *Admissions*, passim, esp. pp.6, 78.

24 BI, MTA 9/1, ff.47-69.

25 Smith, *Admissions*, pp.14, 23.

26 Ibid. p.86.

27 Ibid. pp.74, 86.

28 D. M. Palliser, "Epidemics in Tudor York", *Northern History*, 8 (1973), pp.45-63; Galley, *York*, pp.76-83.

29 YCA, House Books, B32, f. 345v.

30 Skaife, "Civic officials", pp.27, 321; YCA, House books, B32, ff. 331v-2.

31 Ibid. ff. 363v-5v, printed in Johnson, pp.136-8.

32 YCA, B32, f. 354-v.

33 Smith, *Admissions*, pp.50, 60 (John Lovell), 74; Skaife, "Civic Officials", p.141.

34 BI, MTA ff.1-20v.

35 Figures derived from Smith, *Admissions*.

36 Sheils, "York in the 17th century", pp.179-80.

37 Figures derived from Skaife, "Civic officials", for Watson see pp.813-4; there were a number of tailors with Catholic connections, see J. Aveling, *Catholic recusancy in the City of York, 1558-1790* (Catholic Record Society, monograph 2, 1970), see for example William Dyneley at pp.7,12, 52-3, 69, 176-81.

38 Skaife, "Civic officials" p.368; *VCH York*, p.199.

39 Skaife, "Civic officials", pp.117, 478, 618; Aveling, *Recusancy*, pp.36-7, 53, 66.

40 S. T. Bindoff, ed, *The History of Parliament, 1509-1558* 3 vols (1983) I, pp.715-16; Skaife, "Civic Officials", p.82.

41 The mayors were William Allanson (1633, 1655) Robert Askwith (1580, 1589), Robert Askwith (1606, 1617), Richard Calame (1570), William Coupland (1553, 1568), John Dyneley (1577), William Greenbury (1605, 1616), Robert Hemsworth (1631), Christopher Maltby (1583), William Metcalfe (1652), William Richardson (1671), Henry Tireman (1668), Andrew Trew (1585), Richard White (1552), see Skaife, *passim*.

42 *VCH York*, p.179; Skaife, "Civic Officials", pp.12, 27.

43 Bindoff, *History of Parliament*, I, pp.715-16; II, p.605.

44 L. P. Wenham, *The Great and Close Siege of York, 1644* (1970).

45 Skaife, "Civic officials", p.359; *VCH York*, p.176.

46 BI, MTA 5/1, f.11; 6/1, ff.25, 44; 4/1, pp.21-3;

47 *York Civic Records 1570-78*, vii. p.115; BI, MTA 5/1, f. 11.

48 BI, MTA 6/1, f.45; Smith, *Admissions*, p.97.

49 Ibid. pp.26, 47, 76.

50 Ibid. p.52, BI, MTA 4/1, p.22.

51 BI, MTA 5/2, f.13.

52 Palliser, *Tudor York*, p.193.

53 *York Civic Records 1558-1570*, vi, pp.62-5.

54 Ibid. pp.143-4; vii, pp.24, 32-3.

55 Ibid. p.86.

56 Ibid. p.121.

57 RCHM, *The City of York, V, The Central Area* (1981), pp.88-90.

58 BI, MTA 4/1, p.1.

59 Skaife, "Civic Officials", p.24; inscription in St. Crux church.

Plate 9 Richard Evers, Master of the Company in 1835 and 1850.

Plate 10   The Little Hall roof.

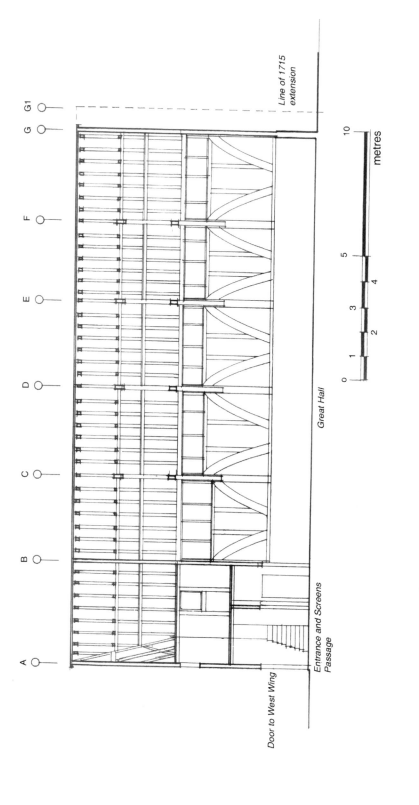

Plate 11 Long section of the Taylors' Hall looking to the north. The wall of the Great Hall is based on a reconstruction by Giles.

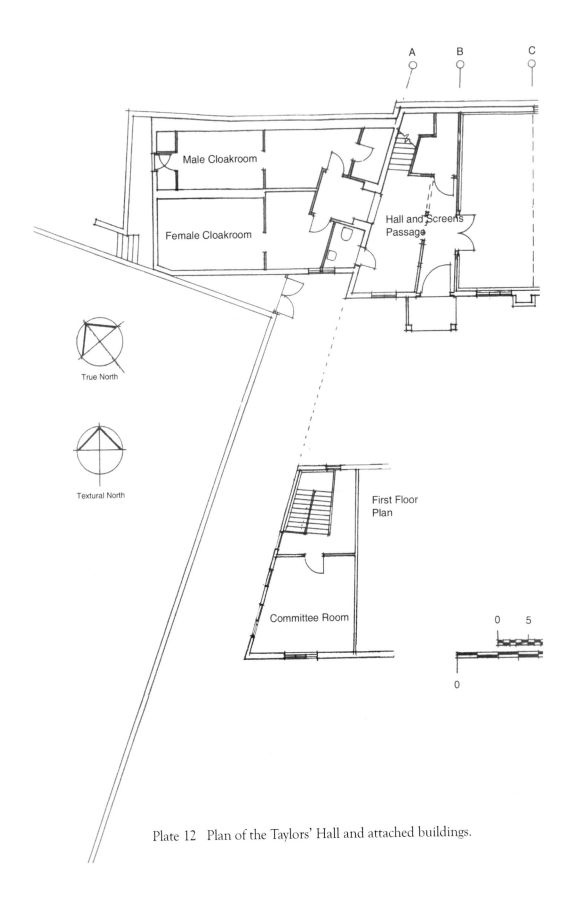

A   B   C

Male Cloakroom

Female Cloakroom

Hall and Screens Passage

True North

Textural North

First Floor Plan

Committee Room

0   5

0

Plate 12   Plan of the Taylors' Hall and attached buildings.

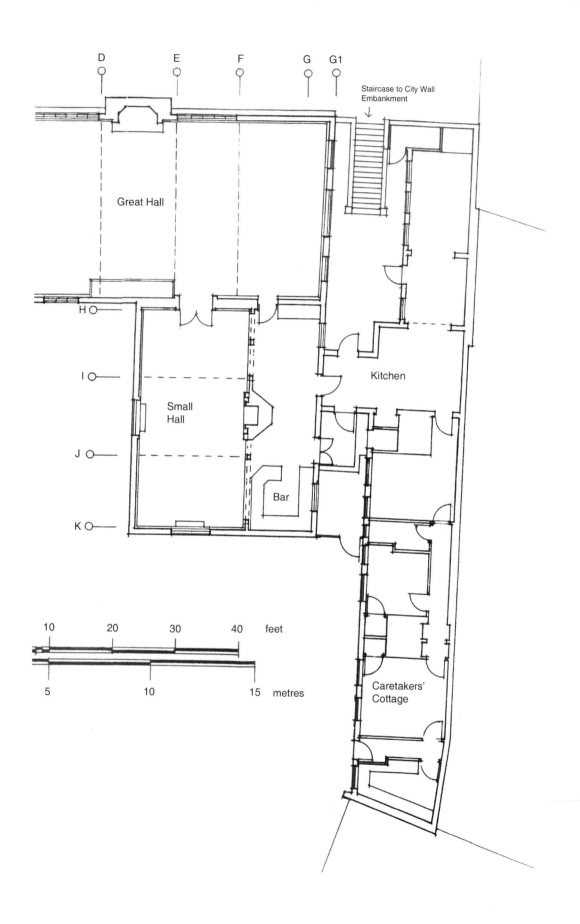

D   E   F   G   G1

Staircase to City Wall
Embankment

Great Hall

Kitchen

H

I

Small
Hall

J

Bar

K

| 10 | 20 | 30 | 40 | feet |

| 5 | 10 | 15 | metres |

Caretakers'
Cottage

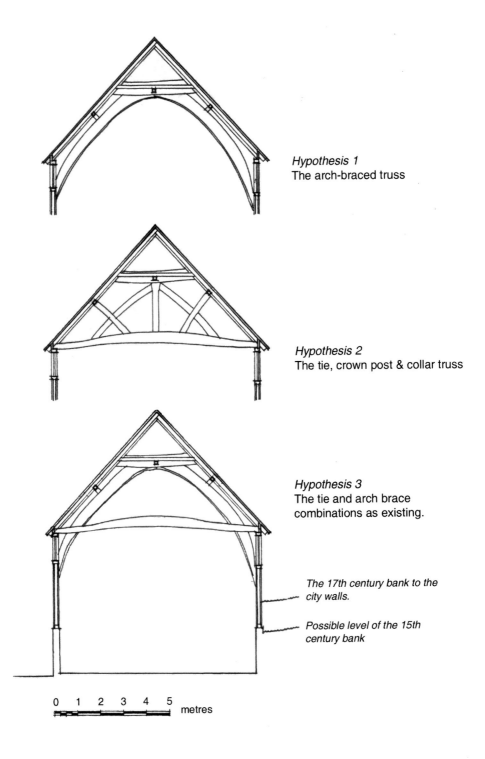

Hypothesis 1
The arch-braced truss

Hypothesis 2
The tie, crown post & collar truss

Hypothesis 3
The tie and arch brace
combinations as existing.

*The 17th century bank to the
city walls.*

*Possible level of the 15th
century bank*

0 1 2 3 4 5 metres

Plate 13   The Great Hall section looking to the west, showing three
alternative forms of the original construction.

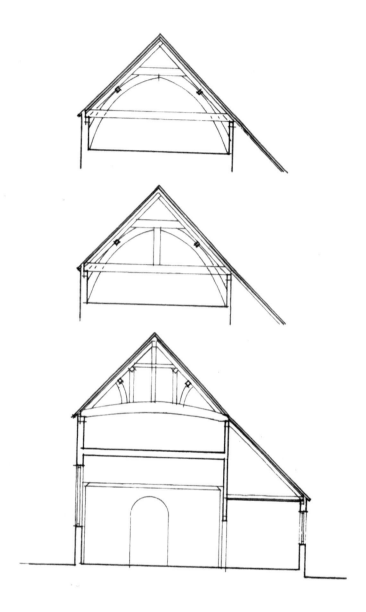

Plate 14 Section of the Little Hall, looking to the north, showing the
variations in the existing trusses. The ties run past the arch-braces.

Plate 15 The east side of the Hall and Almshouses as exposed by excavation of the previously lost church and cemetery of St Helen-on-the-Walls, Aldwark, in 1973-74.

Inexorable Decline or Successful Adaptation? The York Merchant Taylors' Company, 1662–1776[1]

S.D. Smith

I. Approaches to the Study of Early Modern Craft Guilds

The emergence of York's guilds, largely unscathed, from the turbulence of the Civil War and Commonwealth periods, has frequently been cited as a factor in the city's relative stagnation during the later seventeenth century.[2] Francis Drake, the best known commentator, bemoaned *Eboracum's* archaic corporatism, resulting in governance by officials 'who'locked themselves up from the world'. According to Drake, by the early eighteenth century the service sector had become 'the chief support of the city', owing to the decay of manufactures. By services, Drake referred to trades that catered for the needs and families of the country gentry, who came to York in order to transact business in the law courts and to enjoy the pleasures of the race course, and later the assembly rooms.[3] A pessimistic appraisal of manufacturing was likewise advanced in 1779 by York's MP, Charles Turner, who dismissed the guilds as backward-looking monopolies that prevented the city from reaping the benefits of Yorkshire's expanding textile economy.[4]

The hypothesis of 'Augustan decline' is largely accepted in three modern studies of the city. According to Allison, the main concern of the corporation throughout the eighteenth century was to enforce ancient regulations, rather than to encourage trade by attracting new manufacturers to the city.[5] In Malden's eyes, York's guilds functioned as local monopolists, shielded from competition by inadequate transport links. Intent only on their own survival, he argues that the guilds discouraged the corporation from improving road and river communications, to the detriment of the city's wider prosperity.[6] Galley's study is also critical of guild companies, extending the thesis of industrial decay further back in time by citing evidence of admissions to the civic freedom. Whereas textiles accounted for 7.4 percent of admissions during the third quarter of the seventeenth century, Galley points out that during the fourth quarter their share had slipped to 5.7 percent. The apparent decline in textile manufacturing in York is attributed to two causes. Firstly, Galley argues that the urban economy became more service orientated, resulting in a fall in manufacturing employment owing to economic restructuring. Secondly, Galley attributes the specific contraction of the clothing trades to the granting of the Merchant Taylors' 1662 charter, which he suggests strengthened the new company's grip on the manufacture and distribution of textiles within the city.[7]

While both contemporary commentators and historians have advanced plausible arguments that the guilds contributed to York's decline, there is little evidence currently available that can be cited in support of these hypotheses. Virtually nothing is known about the course of economic growth in York during the period under discussion and trends in the wealth of the city's inhabitants have yet to be estimated. Even the size of the York's population cannot be ascertained with certainty prior to the first census of 1801.[8] Nor have York's post-medieval guilds (the purported villains of the piece) been subjected to close study. The hypotheses associating them with stagnation, in consequence, betray the influences of an assortment of intellectual contexts rather than exhibiting the results of empirical research. Drake's questioning of whether an economy built on services could ever be prosperous, for example, exhibits the mercantilist prejudice that only the production of goods created true wealth; it also articulates anti-corporatist attitudes that feature in the works of Daniel Defoe and other contemporary authors.[9] Similarly, Turner's condemnation of guilds appeared at a time when liberal theories of political economy (particularly Adam Smith's criticism of apprenticeship) were gaining currency.

The verdicts passed by Allison, Maulden, and Galley, in their turn, are related to an older historical literature which portrays the demise of the guilds as a necessary precondition for Britain's transition to industrialisation. Unwin, Kramer, and Tawney's general surveys of early modern economic transformation, published at the beginning of the twentieth century, have exercised great influence on subsequent scholars. Collectively, the famous triumvirate criticised the restrictions that guild companies placed on the labour market, while simultaneously retaining a nostalgia for institutions that sought to regulate the economy in order to achieve social objectives.[10] The tendency to equate town guilds with economic stagnation received a second wind during the 1960s and 1970s owing to the popularity of the proto-industrialisation thesis. This development model emphasises the expansion of rural manufacturing during the early stages of industrialisation, frequently contrasting proto-industry's dynamism with urban malaise.[11]

Only recently have post-medieval guilds been subject to detailed reappraisal by economic historians of early modern Europe. Examples have been unearthed of guilds that were either revived or newly formed during the later seventeenth and early eighteenth centuries. In addition, it is now recognised that in some regions of Europe urban guilds succeeded in gaining a rural membership. Such evidence does not fit very comfortably with rural-urban, tradi-tional-modern, or stagnant-dynamic dichotomies.[12] Indeed, revisionist histori-ans have argued that the adaptability and survival of guilds undermines tradi-tional portrayals of these institutions as opponents of technological change and the defenders of traditional working practices.

The emerging 'new historiography of guilds' consists of both an economic and a social branch. New economic approaches style guild regulations as 'mar-ket correcting' rather than 'market distorting'. The assumption on which this analysis is based is that, in an imperfect market, guilds provided the best avail-able assurance of product quality, the most effective safeguards for investment in human capital, and the surest protection to innovators in the absence of a viable patent system.[13] New social histories of guilds argue that formal associa-tions of merchants and artisans generated 'social capital' through mutual net-working that took the form of shared values and community solidarity, collec-tive bargaining, and more efficient mechanisms for the settlement of disputes. Such bold reinterpretations of the persistence of European guilds have not gone unchallenged. Critics object that the evidence presented by revisionists is insuf-ficient to establish whether positive interpretations of guild survival are supe-rior to older explanations, emphasising the protection afforded to guilds by poor communications and the high costs associated with mobilising opposition to their privileges.[14]

To date, the lively and on-going debate surrounding European guilds has exercised only a limited impact on the study of their British equivalents. In consequence, the thesis that guilds steadily declined during the seventeenth and eighteenth centuries has only rarely been questioned.[15] An important rea-son for the acceptance of the decline hypothesis lies in the assumption that Britain's exceptional status, as the world's first industrial nation, rested on the achievements of individual entrepreneurs rather than corporate institutions. So compelling is the modernising paradigm in British history that the limited amount of empirical work that exists on guilds has struggled to make an impression, despite the fact that research has unearthed important findings that contradict the decline thesis. Urban historians, for example, have demonstrated that guilds did not decay uniformly across the country and that local factors were of signifi-cance in determining their survival or extinction.[16]

The fact that the decline model appears to fit the experiences of some high-profile guilds added to its credibility. While London's Merchant Taylors recovered from the disasters of the great plague and fire in 1665 and 1666, the court minutes make plain that by the Glorious Revolution 'the seam between the Company and its craft had been unravelled'; by this date, the company functioned primarily as a charitable fraternity.[17] The London example, however, is by no means typical of guild experience. The most wide-ranging survey of English guilds to date (an unpublished study by Walker) is based on an analysis of the registers of guilds located in six towns and includes the records of no fewer than forty London companies. Walker's study concludes that guild recruitment re-vived generally after 1660, with membership reaching a peak between 1700 and 1720.[18] Moreover, Walker differentiates between *merchant* guilds (many of which had abandoned guild controls by the early eighteenth century), *craft* guilds (most of which persisted until the 1740s), and *service* oriented guilds (the long-est surviving institutions). Walker's findings deserve to be better known and investigated further. A perceptive essay by Barry, however, takes up the theme of guild vitality and argues that, even after older corporate institutions had fallen into decay, middling groups in towns (the 'urban bourgeoisie') replicated collec-tivism in the form of new group associations modelled on the principles of guild fellowship.[19]

Renewed interest in post-medieval guilds suggests that the time is ripe for England's urban guilds to be subject to closer inspection. To this end, the present chapter presents the results of some preliminary research into the archive of York's Merchant Taylors', coupled with an analysis of civic records and other local sources. In view of the state of current knowledge of English guilds and liveried companies, the findings detailed below can be considered novel. The analysis, however, is restricted by the existence of so few secondary authorities addressing the history of York itself during this period. Extending the scope of the conclusions is also rendered difficult by the absence of comparable studies of companies located in other urban centres. Nevertheless, close examination of the activities of even a single craft guild is sufficient to question many assump-tions of an existing historical literature constructed largely from generalisations. It is to be hoped that the evidence of York's Merchant Taylors will provoke researchers into undertaking similar projects in the near future.

II. Membership Trends

In 1662, York's Merchant Taylors' guild received a new charter from Charles II – one of a series of grants made during the 1660s and 1670s, enabling both ancient and more recently established guild fraternities in England to gain the privileges of incorporation. The restored Stuart monarchy's issue of charters was motivated, in part, by a desire to revive economic regulations that had fallen into abeyance during the Civil War in some regions of the country. York was one of a number of towns, however, where continuity rather than disruption largely characterised corporate control of the local economy during the Interregnum.[20] At the Restoration, the pre-conflict structure of civic governance was still largely intact, notwithstanding York's capture and occupation in 1644 by parliamentary forces.[21] The Merchant Taylors' guild remained in existence despite the political upheavals; in consequence, the society's new charter essentially confirmed longstanding rights and privileges rather than granting new powers.

No complete list of merchant taylors survives for any year during the period under study.[22] The estimates of membership presented in Table 1 are, therefore, conjectural and have been teased out of the company's brogue book and a series of poll books recording votes cast by tailors and drapers in parliamentary elections. It must be repeated that these totals represent only best guesses in the absence of any comprehensive listing. If the data are correct, however, the company increased in size from between 170 and 190 members at the beginning of the century, peaking at between 250 and 260 merchant taylors around the year 1740. While the membership totals can only be inferred, annual data do exist of the number of persons 'enabled' or admitted to the company. This information (presented in Table 2) supports the hypothesis that recruitment into the guild remained strong until well into the eighteenth century.

The decade with the highest number of new entrants was 1660-9 when ninety-seven members were enabled. The total during these years was inflated, however, by tailors and drapers who had postponed entry until after the new charter was secured.[23] Thereafter, enabling fluctuated around a stable trend, averaging 74 admittances per decade (with a peak of 84 during the 1690s) until 1730-9, after which a moderate falling-off in entries is detectable.

It has been suggested that aggregate membership is a poor guide to guild recruitment if admissions by purchase replaced admissions by apprenticeship, resulting in a dilution of a guild's occupational base.[24] In Table 3, trends in apprenticeship and the mode of entry into the company are presented. It is clear from these data that the York Merchant Taylors did not experience a decline in apprenticeship and that service remained the dominant entry route during the later seventeenth and eighteenth centuries. The company did, however, rely more heavily on the city as a source of apprentices. After 1710, it is also clear that women formed an increasingly important source of new entrants (table 1).

A shift towards urban self-recruitment has been detected in guild admissions in other towns and has been interpreted as a symptom of guild decline. Brooks, for example, argues that by the later seventeenth century the geographical narrowing of the apprenticeship catchment area generated dynastic and social 'in-breeding', as urban guilds exhibited high rates of patrimony and were infiltrated by disproportionate numbers of gentry and other elite families.[25] Yet there are few signs of these tendencies at work in the case of York's Merchant Taylors'. An increased level of recruitment from within the city was related instead to the guild's flexible response to changes in working practices, particularly its attitude towards female tailors.[26]

Drawing meaningful comparisons between membership of the York Merchant Taylors' and other guilds is difficult. Judging from the tallies of various mercantile societies that have been assembled by historians, it appears that the company ranked among the largest private corporate bodies outside of London.[27] It is instructive to compare York with Oxford's mercers and drapers' company, whose membership can be tracked more accurately. Like York's guild, the Oxford tailors experienced expansion between the later seventeenth and early eighteenth centuries. Total membership was between 110 and 120 members during the mid-seventeenth century, rising to peak at around 150 tailors during the years 1710 to 1720, before declining after the 1730s.[28] Admissions to the York and Oxford companies, therefore, were comparable in size and followed a similar trend.

In order to relate the data of new entrants to total membership of York's Merchant Taylors, it is necessary to know something about the rate of exit from the company. Unfortunately, while detailed accounts of admittances were kept, no records exist of members leaving as the result of death, retirement from trade, or departure from the city. Some information about exit rates, however, can be inferred from the company's brogue book (which names tailors fined for non-attendance at hall between 1707 and 1714), and from four parliamentary poll books compiled during the York elections of 1741, 1758, 1774, and 1784.

Eighteenth-century poll books are enigmatic documents: they purport to state the occupation and address of voters, but the accuracy of their construction is not known and the exclusion of an individual from the poll record could result from a number of reasons other than death or out-migration.[29] A voter might not appear due to ill-health, temporary absence from York, or the abrupt closure of the contest by the withdrawal of a candidate before all eligible electors had cast their votes (as happened in the election of 1774). Nevertheless, by linking the names appearing in the brogue book and electoral polls with the details of enabled merchant taylors entered into a database, the sources can provide a crude indication of survivorship for male members of the company.[30] The results of this exercise are collated in Table 4.

Despite the fact that the listings were compiled for the purposes of fining absent members and recording the votes of electors, the evidence provides a consistent and plausible indication of survivorship among different cohorts of members admitted to the company, particularly if the subset of members who also appear in the freemen's register (and who thereby enjoyed the franchise at the time of the elections) is used as the basis of comparison with the lists of voters. When the survivorship rates are plotted on a logarithmic scale graph, they trace out S-shaped curves that can be divided into three sections (Figure 2). Over the first section of the S-curves (a period of typically between ten and fifteen years), most new entrants continued in business. Over the second section of the curves (spanning approximately two decades), the rates of exit from the company accelerated as brothers died, migrated from York, or left off trade. Over the final section of the S-curves, the exit rates decelerate until only a few members of the original cohort entering the society remain alive.[31]

The decennial totals of new enablings can be compared with the numbers of individuals described as tailors or drapers admitted to the civic freedom. It was possible to become a freeman of York in one of three ways: by order of the corporation (usually in return for a fee), by patrimony (through having a father who was a freeman), or by servitude (the successful completion of an apprenticeship). Referring back to Table 2, in columns 1 and 3 the raw decennial totals of company enablings and admittances are juxtaposed. It is possible, however, to make a more interesting comparison. In column 2, the number of company members enabled in each decade who *also* gained their civic freedom at some point is recorded; conversely, column 4 states the number of freemen admitted each decade who at some point in their careers were enabled as merchant taylors.

When columns 1 and 2 of Table 2 are compared, it is evident that the proportion of enabled members who gained the civic freedom diminished after 1710. This decline largely reflects the admission of women into the company in larger numbers, only eight of whom were made free of the city.[32] If analysis is confined to the brother merchant taylors (Table 5), it is clear that after 1710 male enabled members were *more* likely to appear in the freemen's register than previously.[33] Specifically, between 1670 and 1709 some seventy-seven percent of merchant taylors can be found in the freemen's register, whereas between 1710 and 1759 the proportion rises to eighty-eight percent. The increase in the total of freedoms was preceded by a court minute of 1705 stating that no person should be admitted a member until after they were made free of the city, a condition restated in a further ordinance of 1707.[34] These resolutions may have been prompted by the civic corporation's attempts to enforce the privileges of freemen more rigorously during the early eighteenth century in response to the undermining of freemen's rights in other towns.[35] Two council minutes of 1720 and 1738 reaffirmed the corporation's right to restrict the entitlement to trade in York to persons free of the city; Table 5 indicates that this policy enjoyed a measure of success in the case of male merchant taylors.[36]

Returning to Table 2, columns 3 and 4 reveal a striking fall in the proportion of freemen enabled by the company during the eighteenth century. Whereas between eighty-four and ninety-six percent of freemen tailors prior to the 1700–9 cohort were admitted to the company, thereafter the percentage consistently declined, until only slightly more than half of the freemen were also enabled merchant taylors. A similar discrepancy (based on a comparison of the raw totals of admissions and freemen) is highlighted by Johnson in his study of the company. Johnson interpreted the surplus of freedoms over enablings as evidence of a deterioration in relations with the corporation: a sign that the company was 'beginning to lose its hold over the Tailors, Drapers and Hosiers working in York, and abdicating, as far as men were concerned, its economic role.'[37] This is clearly an important thesis and Johnson's argument must be carefully evaluated. The Statute of Artificers of 1563 permitted anyone outside of London and Norwich, who had served an apprenticeship and who was admitted as a freedman, to practice his trade regardless of whether he was a member of a guild company. In theory, therefore, the continued survival of the Merchant Taylors as a trading organisation (even armed with its new charter of 1662), depended on the continuing good will of the corporation. It is Johnson's contention that cooperation between the guild and the civic authorities broke down gradaually during the eighteenth century.

Unwin and Kramer's general thesis of steady guild decline during the later seventeenth and eighteenth centuries is consistent with Johnson's interpretation of the freemen's register. Indeed, the descriptors applied by Johnson to the Merchant Taylors ('arterio-sclerosis', 'paralysing influences of an increasing old age', 'inability to change with the times', 'lack of vitality') evoke these two historians' conception of slow ossification.[38] Yet York's Merchant Taylors appear to have experienced an expansion in membership between 1660 and 1740, in common with other guilds. Moreover, it is difficult to substantiate the claim that the company lost the support and good will of the corporation during the eighteenth century. Aside from the freemen's roll itself, there is a lack of supporting evidence in either the company's court minute books or the council's house books. On the contrary, the sources suggest that the corporation and the merchant tailors maintained a good working relationship. The society's 1705 order that only freemen be admitted to membership, for example, continued to be observed and the database records that in most cases enablings took place only after the civic freedom had been attained.[39] Master tailors and drapers also do not figure prominently on the surviving lists of traders whom the council targeted for not being freemen in its campaign of 1775.[40]

The argument that the demise of guilds was linked to a restructuring of civic governance is worth pursuing a little further. Stuart assaults on civic liberties, gentry interference in borough affairs, Whig-Tory party rivalry, and the replacement of ruling city oligarchies of tradesmen with new mercantile and retail interests have all been evoked by historians of the seventeenth and eighteenth centuries as creating conditions inimical to guilds.[41] These arguments, in theory, can be applied to York since the city faced *quo warranto* proceedings in 1661 and 1684, while during the eighteenth century the freemen's list was susceptible to electoral manipulation as gentry candidates contested a series of parliamentary polls.[42] Nevertheless, the occupational basis of guild membership and entitlement to the civic freedom remained strong in the city. Though the numbers of freemen bulged before contested parliamentary elections (particularly the polls of 1741 and 1758, which featured multiple candidates), the database suggests that the impact of the contests on company membership was slight.[43] Table 6 presents an analysis of the voting behaviour of the 154 individuals in the database who were free of the city but not of the company. During the relevant period (the years after 1709), though two-thirds of the suspected 'imposters' cast a vote, the overwhelming majority of these had served an apprenticeship with a master tailor or draper. It can also be added that only eighteen of the freemen merchant tailors admitted during these years were *not* former apprentices.

The contradictions inherent in the thesis of gradual decline require that alternative explanations for the failure of company admissions to keep pace with the numbers of freemen be considered. Growth in the numbers of freemen who were not also free of the company could, firstly, reflect a proliferation of tailors in the city's liberties lying outside of the jurisdiction of the company.[44] The Merchant Taylors certainly regarded the liberties as a threat and took action against tailors operating in Minster Yard and St. Peter's during the 1690s.[45] This interpretation must, however, be rejected since the database reveals that no fewer than sixty-three percent of individuals enumerated in column 3 of Table 5 appear in the company's registers of apprentices, while the York addresses of those voting in parliamentary elections between 1741 and 1784 demonstrates that the distribution of the non-company tailors was similar to the locations of the enabled brothers. A second doubtful interpretation is that the data records an increasing number of freemen residing outside of York. Yet the proportion of freemen merchant tailors with non-York addresses remained constant at around twelve percent during each of the parliamentary elections held in 1741, 1758, and 1774.[46] It is also striking that just twenty-one individuals in the database appear in the 1742 county poll book, for which the voting qualification was possession of a freehold *outside* of York. And of these twenty-one voters, only two were freemen of the city but not enabled company members.[47]

A third plausible explanation is that the factors responsible for the admission of women may also have led to a reduction in the proportion of freemen merchant tailors who were also enabled brothers. If the functions of the tailors and drapers are split into a manufacturing side and a marketing side, it is possible that from the early decades of the eighteenth century the occupational base of the merchant tailors shifted towards masters operating workshops that produced garments, many of whom were female. In contrast, masters primarily engaged in marketing and distribution could have opted to join York's Merchant Adventurers' company, hardly any of whom were women.[48] Close connections existed between the merchant tailors and the merchant adventurers among some of the more affluent tailors and drapers. George Barnatt, John Hay, Richard Hobson, and Thomas Spooner (senior and junior) are all examples of masters of the Merchant Taylors' company who were also admitted to the society of Merchant Adventurers. In four out of these five cases, the individuals concerned served as governors of the Adventurers' company.[49] In all, thirty-seven merchant tailors can be positively identified as having been members of the Merchant Adventurers' between 1660 and 1776. Another six individuals are suspected of having been merchants (on the basis of occupational descriptions employed in the freemen's register, poll books, and other records), but are absent from the register of merchant adventurers.[50] Yet despite this evidence of overlapping guild membership, the database delivers a damaging blow to the mercantile side of this explanation. Of the forty-three actual or suspected merchant adventurers identified, there are only two cases of persons listed as freemen merchant tailors who were not also enabled of the company.

Apprenticeship practices provide a fourth reason why the proportion of freemen tailors and merchant tailors appearing in the masters' enabling books declined during the eighteenth century. Two sources exist documenting the apprenticeship of merchant tailors in York: the company's own registers and the civic registers maintained by the corporation.[51] If the details of apprenticeship indentures during the first three quarters of the eighteenth-century are examined, a curious anomaly is revealed. The corporation's registers not only document a smaller number of indentures than the company accounts, but many of the indentures listed in the civic volumes are absent from the Merchant Taylors' registers. Moreover, the relationship between the two sources is not constant over time. Of the 140 indentures of merchant tailors or drapers dated in the civic registers between 1710 and 1739, a total of 43 (30.7 percent) are absent from the company's registers. In contrast, of the 130 indentures in the civic registers dated between 1740 and 1776, only 12 (9.2 percent) are *not* duplicated in the company's own records.[52]

The details of apprenticeship agreements were enrolled in the city's registers for two main purposes. Firstly, persons claiming the freedom as former apprentices (in order to exercise their trade in York, or claim exemption from tolls and other trading privileges, or to vote in a parliamentary election) were required to produce a copy of their indentures. Secondly, contract details were entered in the civic register in cases where the child being bound was a poor parish apprentice. Funds existed to sponsor the placement of poor children through the corporation and a number of trades were expected accept a quota of pauper apprentices.[53] During years of exceptional hardship, the council was empowered to suspend civic regulations in order to attract trade to the city, including the formal requirement that tradesmen be freemen. It is possible, therefore, that during the 1720s and early 1730s, the corporation bound a large number of parish apprentices in response to economic difficulties and that merchant tailors were among the masters taking them on.

Very few of the individuals entered in the civic apprenticeship registers, but missing from the company's own books, were prosecuted by the company's officers for carrying on trade without being members of the society.[54] One reason for this could be that the children who were bound did not receive training in return for a premium paid by their parents or guardians, but were rather servants who were set to work in their master's household for a set number of years. Such individuals would, after completing their indentures, duly appear on the freemen's list as having served apprenticeships with master merchant tailors, but these nominal apprentices would not be qualified to gain admission to the company.[55] It is also possible that children were bound to a merchant tailor but received training in a different trade.[56] The database provides limited support for these related hypotheses. When the names of the forty-three 'missing' apprentices between 1710 and 1739 were checked, twelve matches were found with freemen who were not also enabled members of the company. Repeating the search process for 'missing' apprentices bound between 1740 and 1759 unearthed a further two matches. It should be stressed that *only* indentures that specified the master was a merchant tailor or draper were examined and that a few more examples would, perhaps, be found if all civic indentures were analysed and a name search made for apprentices who, after their service ended, gained the freedom but did not become merchant tailors.

While each of the above hypotheses possess some merit, they collectively account for only a small part of the change in the relationship between freemen and enabled company members. The explanation most consistent with the findings of the database is that the rise of non-enabled freemen tailors was generated by growing numbers of journeymen working in the city. Johnson must be credited with drawing attention to this phenomenon in his study. Although it is difficult to quantify the number of journeymen accurately, his claim that their ranks increased during the eighteenth century is almost certainly correct. Figure

3 compares the percentage of freemen who were enabled with the percentage of apprentices gaining admittance to the company in each decade. It can be seen that both of these series fall to unprecedented levels after 1720-9. Studies of merchant tailor guilds in other urban centres have also found evidence of a rise in journeymen during the eighteenth century and an associated increase in 'tramping' from town to town by journeymen in search of employment.[57] In the case of York, the population of journeymen was swelled through the combined effects of an increase in the waiting time faced by apprentices after 1700-9, and by a rise in the mean age of admittance after 1710-19. A short-run peak in the number of apprentices enrolled between 1710-19 and 1730-9 also contributed to the trend.[58]

Did the greater numbers of journeymen alter relations between masters and workers in York, as Johnson suggests? The court minute books include references to two incidents that, if read in isolation, support Johnson's thesis. In 1721, the journeymen tailors took industrial action with the aim of reducing the length of their working day from fourteen to thirteen hours. The defiance of the company's regulation of journeymen's terms of hire was met head-on by the court of assistants, who coordinated the response of master tailors in an attempt to break the strike.[59] Evidence of further industrial unrest appears in a court minute of 1753 that bound all masters to observe common rules on the use of journeymen labour. These regulations specified the length of the working day (6am until 8pm), set a maximum wage of 8s. per week, and imposed restrictions on both the employment of former apprentices without the permission of their ex-master, and also on competition for the hire of journeymen.[60] It must be emphasised, however, that the two strikes were exceptional events; moreover, in both cases, the timing of the industrial unrest was influenced by events outside of the city, as well as conditions specific to York.

The 1721 and 1753 strikes coincided with industrial action taken by journeymen in other urban centres.[61] As a result of the strikes, concessions were granted to journeymen on working conditions and wages (at least after 1721, to judge from differences in the York regulations between the two dates). The mobility of the journeymen undoubtedly helped to communicate grievances between towns and assisted workers in coordinating action against the guilds as employers' organisations. Strike action also exploited divisions within the ranks of the master tailors. If sufficient numbers of masters were prepared to break regulations in order to increase output (by offering higher wages or better working conditions to poach journeymen), then the guild's ability to control the labour market was undermined. Walker's unpublished study suggests that, in the case of manufacturing guilds such as the tailors, a combination of a glutted labour market and rising demand for goods brought about precisely this scenario during the middle of the eighteenth century.[62] In York, as elsewhere, the company faced challenges to its authority in 1721 and 1753, but the demise of the guild's economic function occurred later than in other towns. Admittances and total membership both probably contracted after the 1730s, but the declines were relatively modest prior to the 1760s and 1770s. Company records also do not suggest that growing numbers of journeymen resulted in a significant rise in fines imposed on masters breaking rank.

The persistence of regulatory control by York's Merchant Taylors' company was assisted by both the nature of the tailoring trade and the specific characteristics of York itself. Unlike other forms of manufacturing, tailoring contains a strong bespoke element. Master tailors provided a measuring, fitting, and styling service when supplying garments. The willingness of customers to travel to tailors in London or other towns provided the main form of competition for York's tailors, since the market for ready-to-wear garments originating outside of the city was limited. Similarly, the characteristics of the trade and the high cost of transportation ensured that the bulk of output from tailors' workshops was sold locally.[63] While demand for bespoke clothing probably increased during the eighteenth century (as more gentry families resided in York, while the law courts and the Minster continued to supply a stream of orders to workshops for clerical and legal robes), York's static population placed limits on the expansion of the local market. In consequence, the pressures of competition and demand do not appear strong enough to have provoked an exodus of masters from the company until the 1760s and 1770s. The resilience of the York Merchant Taylors was also boosted by the company's grip on female tailors, who continued to work as members of the company, subject to its ordinances. Outside of York, the failure to regulate the women mantua-makers was a contributory cause of guild decline; within York, the eventual demise of the Merchant Taylors' trading privileges can also be linked to the decline of female admissions.[64]

The rise in the number of journeymen is the most convincing reason for the increase in the number of freemen tailors not also free of the company, though non-residence, civic apprenticeship, and the admission of women to the guild also contributed to the trend. Of the various alternatives considered, the journeymen hypothesis is most consistent with the timing of membership trends (Figure 3), while accounting for the similar distribution of freemen tailors and company tailors throughout the city recorded in the parliamentary poll books. Johnson's study correctly emphasises the importance of the journeymen, but his arguments that the Merchant Taylors suffered from a breakdown in relations with the corporation, and that the guild steadily ossified during the eighteenth century, are not compelling. The available data indicate that the demise of the guild's economic function occurred relatively late in the eighteenth century and that it also happened comparatively quickly. Decline appears to have resulted from the decision of masters to hire journeymen and women outside of the company's regulations.

III INDUSTRIAL PRODUCTIVITY AND SOCIAL WELFARE

If all that survived to document the activities of the Merchant Taylors is the charter and ordinances of 1662, it would be tempting to dismiss the company as a cartel that existed solely to place restraints on trade for the benefits of its members. The charter concerns itself almost exclusively with specifying the legal basis for incorporation, detailing the procedures for selecting the new company's officials, and setting out the terms of the company's local monopoly of trade. Within a two-mile radius of the city, the fraternity was granted the authority to regulate 'in all, and singular matters, causes and things, touching or concerning the said art or mistery of Taylors and Drapers'. No person was to be permitted to exercise either trade 'untill he or they be first made a member or ffreeman of the said societie of Merchant Taylors'. Restrictions were placed on the supply of labour through the regulation of apprenticeship, the employment of journeymen in workshops, and the ability of master tailors or drapers to work in any house but their own. The undercutting of one member by another to gain custom was outlawed and any tailor or draper found to 'begg or sue for the Custome of any man or woman' could expect to be fined.[65]

To enforce its monopoly privileges, the company's officials were given sweeping powers of search. Provided they first obtained the assistance of a constable, it was lawful for the searchers 'to enter into any shop house, sellar, warehouse, or other place or places, whatsoever', and to seek out 'all unlawful and unserviceable wares, touching the said respective Trades of Taylors and Drapers.' It was also lawful 'to distreyne any of the goods or chatells of any such Offender or Offenders', and to withhold them from their owners until any fine or other penalty levied by the justices was discharged.[66] The surviving court minutes and company account books record that these powers were employed by the society against offenders throughout the period under examination. In addition to exercising the power of search and prosecuting offenders in the courts, the guild could also seek to enforce discipline among its members by issuing a summons to appear at the hall, where grievances could be aired and complaints made against the behaviour of specific individuals.[67]

Very few of the formal rules and regulations governing the company can be interpreted as measures conducive to the public good. Indeed, the counter-argument that guilds existed primarily to serve the private interest of their members receives support from several incidents recorded in the minute books documenting vigorous responses to challenges to the company's authority. A typical example of internal regulation is the bye-law drafted in 1675 against the employment of foreign workers, 'that may bind the whole Company by Consent of themselves for working of the Mercht. Taylors traid'. The following year the guild defended its control of blanket trade from encroachment by the upholsterers, who had seized goods from the current master of the company, Richard Mason.[68]

The counter-argument that guild regulation might have beneficial economic outcomes is harder to document, but receives potential support from two ordinances. Any manufacturer of garments that, in the opinion of the master and the four wardens, 'shall seem not to be well wrought or as it ought to have been', could be summoned by the beadle to appear and ordered to remedy the defects within ten days on pain of a fine.[69] In theory, a system of quality control such as this was capable of boosting consumer confidence in products originating from York's Merchant Tailors'. The effectiveness of the measure, however, was blunted by the generally weak brand identity enjoyed by manufacturers during this period; moreover, the sale of goods outside of the city does not appear to have been substantial. It can also be noted that there is little in the surviving records to indicate that the company sought to develop quality assurance any further than this ordinance. Finally, is also unclear on what basis a garment might be rejected by officials; whether defectiveness was simply a matter of bad workmanship, or whether innovative departures from accepted product lines were also penalised.

The second ordinance with the potential to generate efficiency gains provided for the settlement of disputes among company members: 'for the better continuance of Brotherly love and charity between them.'[70] When evaluating the significance of this measure it must be emphasised that the public provision of commercial legislation, funding of law courts, and the legal enforcement of property rights all lagged behind the development of trade and industry during the seventeenth and eighteenth centuries. Private supply of some of these services, through associations of merchants and manufactures, provided an alternative to reliance on inadequate public institutions. Such arrangements had the potential to reduce risk and uncertainty by providing low-cost methods to resolve disputes and settle debts. Only one court minute, however, indicates that the company intervened actively to settle disputes among brothers. In November 1692, five members of the company involved in a lawsuit were ordered to make an end of their quarrel and to avoid future strife and trouble.[71] What is most striking about this isolated incident is that the disputants had already elected to go to law, rather than first seeking a resolution of their differences by means of an internal mechanism to settle grievances.

It is clear that the charter of 1662 was not designed primarily to promote productive efficiency within the textile trades in York. With the singular exception of a grant of two guineas to Hale Wyvill 'in order to engage the woollen Manufactory in York', there is nothing in the court minutes to indicate that the company's officials sought actively to promote innovation among members. The prime objective of even this solitary project was to establish a small factory to employ poor children in the city, rather than to promote the application of new industrial techniques.[72] To judge the company in terms of productive efficiency, however, may be misplaced if the Merchant Taylors' chief contribution to the local economy took the form of social welfare provision. Neither the charter nor the ordinances make any clear allusion to the supply of services of this nature, but there is a body of evidence that indicates that welfare was a core activity of the guild.

One of the basic functions of the Merchant Taylors was to act as a benefit club for members and their dependants. From 1719, entries in the court minute books regularly list the quarterly amounts given to support inmates of the 'Masendue' hospital (situated adjacent to the hall), and payments voted by the court of assistants to needy tailors or their widows.[73] Occasionally, the reason for the petition for assistance is stated. John Gardhouse, for example, was given 2s. 6d. in 1720 'towards his wifes funerall', whereas John Pindar in 1725 received 5s. because he was 'a prisoner' (presumably in a debtors' jail).[74] The sums expended by the assistants for these purposes, however, were modest. In 1718, a vote was held on the amount that should be given quarterly to support the residents of the Masendue: sixteen of the assistants voted to allow 20s. and five 10s. The minute books record that the quarterly sum of 7s. 6d. was paid until 1730, with an additional 2s. 6d. for the salary of the hospital porter (usually a retired or infirm brother). Annual charitable disbursements only ranged between £3 and £6 before 1730, even including discretionary payments to individuals.[75] To put these sums in context, the court agreed by a unanimous vote in 1713 to grant a largess of £3 towards the support of horse racing on Clifton Ings, and from 1711 until 1756 the yearly sum of between two and four guineas was donated for this purpose.

After 1730, the scale of philanthropy increased noticeably. The Merchant Taylors raised a total of £159 3s. 10d. between 1729 and 1730 to finance the demolition and reconstruction of the Masendue hospital. To support the four inhabitants of the almshouse, an endowment was also created consisting of the £10 yearly rental of properties owned by the society in Micklegate and Walmgate, along with the interest on the sum of £20 that John Napier had paid in return for an exemption from serving as an officer of the company. An additional £10 was bequeathed to the trustees of the hospital by Thomas Nevil in his will of 1756.[76] These donations enabled payments to support the hospital inmates to be raised from 30s. a year to £10, supplemented by a winter fuel allowance of £1. In total, annual disbursements agreed by the court of assistants approximately tripled between 1731 and 1775.[77]

Financing the Masendue and discretionary payments to tailors and their widows are the most conspicuous welfare entries in the company's records, but other less visible forms of support were extended by the guild. One of the rationales underpinning guild restriction of competition was the provision of security in old age. While small numbers of poor and infirm merchant taylors received monetary payments, many more were assisted by limitations placed on the entry of newcomers into trade, helping them continue in business for longer. The survivorship estimates presented in Table 4 and Figure 2 provide an indication of the guild's success in providing productive employment opportunities for older members. Apprenticeship was another device that could be used to assist merchant tailors and their dependants through difficult phases of the family life cycle.

Up until the end of the third decade of the eighteenth century, the clerks who compiled the apprenticeship register consistently recorded whether the father of the apprentice being bound was deceased. In Table 7, it can be seen that between 1660 and 1729 (after which the data become less reliable) the fatherless rate among apprentices was consistently more than thirty percent and at times it exceeded forty percent.[78] High rates of paternal mortality feature in the apprenticeship registers maintained by guild companies and corporations in other regions of the country. In the case of Bristol, for example, the fatherless rate among apprentices increased from 15 percent, 1642–65, to 19 percent, 1675–6, 24 percent 1695–6, and 34 percent 1706-06.[79]

Limited understanding of York's demographic history make it difficult to assess either the significance of a fatherless rate in excess of thirty percent and the relationship between paternal mortality and poverty. The absence of a pre-census listing for York make it impossible to estimate the proportion of children aged between twelve and sixteen belonging to households not headed by a father during the eighteenth century. Survivorship indices calculated by Galley (based on demographic data spanning the years from 1561 to 1700) provide, however, a rough guide to paternal mortality. Galley's study indicates that between 630 and 710 males out of 1,000 twenty-five-year-olds could expect to be alive at the age of fifty.[80] If the years from twenty-five to fifty are taken as representative of the age-span of fathers binding their children to service, then the proportion of fatherless children recorded in the apprenticeship registers must be regarded as significant (assuming that males fathered children and put them out to trade at consistent intervals).[81] Yet the absence of independent evidence that an apprentice or their family suffered from poverty makes it difficult to link paternal mortality directly with social welfare provision.

Research on female-headed households during the later eighteenth century has established that women with dependent children suffered from a greater incidence of poverty than the population as a whole.[82] Of the fatherless apprentices identified in the company registers, 81.3 percent of the indentures state simply that the father was deceased, whereas the remaining 18.7 percent of cases consist of apprentices bound by their mothers, nearly all of whom were described as 'widows'. This latter figure is higher than the 14.6 percent of female headed households contained in a survey of families in twenty English communities, and it is nearly double the 9.7 percent of households headed by lone mothers between 1787 and 1815 identified by the same source.[83] The *prima facie* case that fatherless children originated from poor families is weakened, however, by the fact that a high proportion of dependent children raised by lone mothers were put to work before the age of fourteen. The resources of these families were clearly sufficient to enable children to enter apprenticeships or receive similar forms of training.[84] A reasonable inference, therefore, is that apprenticeship into the Merchant Taylors' company provided families sufficiently well-off not to depend on immediate child earnings with a means of adjusting to difficulties in the family life-cycle. The assistance the guild provided to such families cannot, therefore, be regarded as 'social welfare' as the term is conventionally understood. The benefits conferred to middling families imposed costs on the wider community (including poorer households), by restricting local employment opportunities. Nevertheless, the prevalence of fatherless apprentices may provide an important explanation for the persistence of guilds in urban centres for precisely the same reason that educational and medical subsidies to middle England persist in the modern welfare state.

In the company's defence, some of the apprentices bound to master tailors were drawn from poor families. The re-establishment of guild and corporate privileges after the Restoration formed part of the response to social instability during the Civil War and Commonwealth periods by the governing authorities. Close links existed between urban poverty, incorporation, and guild regulation of apprenticeship. Indeed, the year that the company received its charter also saw the passage of the first Settlement Act, establishing residence qualifications for poor relief. How large a problem was poverty in York during the later seventeenth and eighteenth centuries? Accounts maintained by York's corporation reveal that between 350 and 400 individuals were in receipt of parish relief during the 1660s and 1670s, while 500 received assistance between 1722 and 1729. These figures almost certainly understate the incidence of poverty in the city because the numbers are restricted to those eligible to claim relief.[85]

The spectre of urban destitution and vice was an important motivation for the establishment of charity schools by the Society for the Propagation of Christian Knowledge (SPCK) during the early eighteenth century. Among the aims of the resulting 'blue coat' and 'grey coat' schools was the preparation of male and female children from low income families for entry into trade. Where such schemes were supported by the corporation and guilds, the schools proved sustainable financially, enabling them to place some of their pupils in apprenticeships.[86] Enthusiasm for charity schools and the use of apprenticeship to curb poverty was strong in York, where they supplemented existing apprenticeship charities. Several sermons written in support of the SPCK's proposals by York's clergy were published, while a blue coat school for boys on Peasholme Green and a grey coat school for girls in Marygate both opened in 1705.[87] Individual merchant tailors are known to have supported the charity school movement. A list of 202 subscribers to the boys' school in 1736 includes the names of at least ten members of the company, and possibly as many as eighteen of the brothers.[88] Admittedly, this is not a large proportion of members, but the source reports that the value of subscriptions had declined by £70 over the two preceding years; if the support of the trading community had dropped correspondingly, earlier lists may have included the names of more members of the company.

The records of the Merchant Taylors do not provide a complete account of the society's involvement with pauper apprentices, but they do document links between the company and parish administrators. Consistent recording of poor parish children who were exempted from payment of the King's duty on indentures was maintained between 1764 and 1776. During these years, a total of twenty exemptions were made out of 144 enrollments. The apprenticeship registers maintained by the corporation record two additional indentures that do not appear in the company registers during these years that may also have bound poor children.[89] A further thirty-three poor children also appear in the company registers between 1721 and 1749: a period when the clerks appear to have paid close attention to distinguishing parish apprentices. Of these children, eleven were bound by the churchwardens of Holy Trinity in Goodramgate, two by St. Michael's in Spurriergate, one by St. Martin's in Micklegate, five came from charity schools, and the remainder from unspecified parishes. The civic apprenticeship register includes the details of a further twelve indentures not listed in the company's accounts during the same years, consisting of three blue coat children, one parish apprentice from Holy Trinity Goodramgate, and eight poor apprentices from other parishes.[90]

How effective was apprenticeship in addressing poverty? An assessment of the effectiveness of the transition from 'welfare to work' can be made by profiling the career paths of male apprentices according to their family origin.[91] The results of this exercise are presented in Table 8 which provides measures of career progression for four groups: A) fatherless apprentices; B) the sons of merchant tailors, C) a control group of apprentices, and D) apprentices described as 'poor'. The database reveals that having a merchant tailor as a parent boosted the chances of successful completion of apprenticeship (measured by admission into the company or the civic freedom). Over the period as a whole, fatherless apprentices did as well as the control group, reinforcing the view that they were not drawn primarily from poor backgrounds. Orphans were slightly less likely to become master tailors, but successful masters drawn from groups A, B, and C enrolled the same average number of apprentices, suggesting similar scales of operation.[92] The data on pauper apprentices is less extensive than for the other groups, but the comparison indicates that poor children were less likely to complete their apprenticeships and enter into trade. Only 15 percent of group D gained admission into the company: less than half the rate of control group C.

This section has attempted to assess whether guild restriction of competition conferred general social benefits, as opposed to protecting the interests of the narrow constituency of guild members and their families. Little direct evidence was found of productive efficiency likely to further economic growth in York. The claim that guilds provided welfare provision receives more support, but most of the benefits generated by guild regulation of the tailoring trade (particularly direct maintenance payments and employment protection for elderly tailors) were appropriated by the merchant tailors themselves, or their dependants. Only in the cases of orphaned or pauper apprentices, were outsiders able to share in the allocation of welfare provision. Fatherless apprentices, however, may have been drawn disproportionately from middling families, while the career profiles of pauper apprentices suggest that the company provided very few of them with a route to an independent livelihood. The finding that the company generated little in the way of unequivocal economic and social benefits, however, is not itself evidence that the guild damaged the development of York. The final section of this chapter, therefore, attempts to assess whether the wider influence of the guild was detrimental to the city.

IV The 'Influence' of the Company in York

At the beginning of the seventeenth century, York was home to between twenty-five and thirty guilds. A hundred years later, a similar number remained in existence; as late as 1800, around twenty guilds were still operating.[93] Aside from its specific trading privileges, however, what influence could a company exercise over the city's economic development? 'Influence' is a difficult concept to define or measure objectively, but if the Merchant Taylors (along with the other guild companies) did contribute to York's economic stagnation, it ought to be possible to discover evidence of the guild's leverage within local government from surviving records.

It has been suggested that the number of merchant taylors probably peaked at between 200 and 250 during the eighteenth century (Table 1). While the company was large for an organisation of its type, the size of its membership must be placed in the context of York's total population of around 12,000 inhabitants (or between 1,950 and 2,600 households).[94] The annual number of admittances to the civic freedom provides another benchmark by which the prominence of the company can be gauged. During the twenty years from 1690 to 1709, the number of merchant tailors enabled (male and female) was equivalent to approximately ten percent of those admitted to the freedom in York. Over the next sixty years (1700–59), the nominal proportion dropped to between six and eight percent, though if the freemen tailors (the majority of whom were probably journeymen working in company workshops) are added to company admissions, the ratio of tailors to all freemen remained roughly constant at between eight and nine percent.[95] If political and commercial influence was a function of numerical strength, it does not appear, therefore, that the leverage of the Merchant Taylors increased during the period that York's economy is believed to have stagnated. Moreover, the increase in both admissions to the freedom and the company, coupled with the admission of women after 1710, contradicts the conventional assumption that guilds contributed to urban stagnation by erecting entry barriers to newcomers.

An organisation's wealth can be disproportionate to its size and deployed in ways that secure corporate objectives. The Merchant Taylors' company, however, was not a particularly affluent organisation during the period under review. The most complete series of accounts that survive are the statements of income and expenditure prepared by the successive masters of the company which were audited every August. Summary details of income and expenditure are presented in Table 9. The Merchant Taylors' accounts can be compared with the budget of the civic corporation. In 1750, the council's income was £1,828 (including a balance of £333 carried over from 1749), while expenditure amounted to £1,765. These figures are approximately eighteen times greater than the Merchant Taylors' income and expenditure.[96] Neither the size of the company's budget, nor the stated purposes for which funds were spent, suggest that money was used to buy influence. Yet though the resources of the company were comparatively modest, it is important to note that there is no suggestion that the Merchant Taylors were at any time seriously indebted or that the guild faced a mounting financial crisis during the eighteenth century that contributed to its demise. By the same token, however, it also appears doubtful that the survival of the Merchant Taylors (after it ceased to be a trading organisation) was a consequence of the guild's wealth or ownership of property.[97]

The company's revenue was derived from a small amount of rental property which supplemented the annual fees raised from new admissions, the enrollment of apprentices, and fines levied on existing members. Expenses included a commitment to support the Masendue and needy merchant tailors, but the most chargeable items were the sums spent in repairing the hall and the houses rented out by the company. Periodically, income was boosted by a cash injection as a master raised a loan (or lent money himself), secured on the society's collection of silver plate, to finance building work. When the loan was repaid, the payment was recorded as an item of expenditure.

A further guide to the degree of local political influence enjoyed by the company is the number of merchant tailors who held civic office. According to the database, only twenty-one of the 671 males enabled between 1660 and 1793 held the office of sheriff or chamberlain. Of these individuals, a mere half dozen achieved the higher office of alderman, while a company member was chosen lord mayor on just six occasions.[98] The Merchant Taylors' grip on the corporation appears even weaker when it is considered that fourteen of the twenty-one civic office holders are described as drapers or mercers in either company records, the freemen's list, or the parliamentary poll books. Seven of these men were also members of the Merchant Adventurers' and held office in that company. The disproportionate representation of drapers and mercers is also a feature of office holding within the Merchant Taylors' company itself, since these trades accounted for just under a quarter of searchers, wardens, and assistants (about two-and-a-half times more than their share of the society's membership).

York's corporation consisted of an upper house, that met on Ouse Bridge, and a common council that assembled in the Guildhall. The upper chamber comprised the lord mayor, two sheriffs, twelve aldermen, and the 'twenty-four' (former office holders whose numbers varied in practice). Common councilmen were referred to as the 'forty-eight'.[99] On the basis of these figures, it is clear that merchant tailors at no time dominated either the upper house or the common council. It must also be stressed that the impression gained from studying lists of office holders is biased in favour of the company's influence because it automatically excludes from consideration candidates who sought office but were rejected. By no means all members of the company with aspirations to gain civic status were successful. To cite a few examples, Edward Addison and John Layland failed in their attempts to be elected commoner for Monkgate in 1748; the same fate also befell William Dalton, Thomas Bilton, James Clifton, and Archibald Creighton in the selections for Walmgate in 1748, 1751, 1754, and 1755. John Etherington failed to be appointed sheriff in two successive elections of 1743 and 1744, while John Greggs and William Bilton also failed in 1750 and 1756.[100]

The company's authority within York appears to have been confined to the specific areas of exemption from civic control outlined in its charter. Guild and council evidently cooperated in enforcing the civic freedom and company membership qualifications on traders. Court assistants and councillors probably also worked together in seeking to use apprenticeship as a means of reducing the numbers of poor children supported by the parish rates. On occasion, the Merchant Taylors were able to make their voice heard in the council chamber and the company's records contain sporadic references to lobbying activity. In 1711, the company petitioned the council against the incorporation of York's guild of brewers. Another example of lobbying occurred in 1764 when it was voted to give five guineas 'to Oppose the turnpike intended to be set at Grimston Smithy.'[101] Activities such as these, however, were isolated events and there is insufficient material in either the company records or the council's house books to sustain the thesis that the guild was able to shape the corporation's policies on transportation or the admittance of strangers to the freedom. On particular issues, such as the Grimston turnpike, the Merchant Taylors voiced concerns, but evidence that the company furthered its own interests at the expense of the community in any systematic fashion is lacking.[102]

Merchant tailors who were freemen of the city possessed the right to vote in parliamentary elections. There was an abrupt end to quarterly business at the hall in March 1685 when Sir Metcalf Robinson and his supporters called 'to perswaid the Company for voats for them to serve in parliament for the Citty.'[103] Notwithstanding this comment, when the elections themselves are analysed there is little indication that the tailors coordinated their votes in favour of a preferred candidate. The poll books for 1741, 1758, 1774, and 1784 permit analysis of electoral behaviour. Electors had a single vote if the seat was contested by two candidates, but could opt to vote twice if there were more than two contenders up for the count. While merchant tailors accounted for only a small proportion of the electorate, it is theoretically possible for a minority block-vote to exercise a disproportionate influence on the outcome of a first-past-the-post election.

Close scrutiny of the voting records reveals, however, that even in the case of closely contested polls, company members split their votes evenly among the candidates (Table 10), thereby dissipating their collective electoral influence. Among the poll findings, the most ironic result occurred in contest held in 1774. At this election, the thirty-six votes that Charles Turner received from company members helped this outspoken critic of York's guilds to secure victory.

Descriptive accounts of eighteenth-century York, beginning with Drake's *Eboracum*, emphasise how the city increasingly came to be regarded as a centre of fashionable society. The creation of new or augmented public places is one symptom of this transition. Lord Mayor's Walk acquired a new line of trees in 1719; in 1732, work on a promenade along the river called the New Walk was begun. York's extensive Georgian building programme included the construction of Burlington's Assembly Rooms (1731-2) and the Mansion House (1725-32). Lavish private residences were also built in the city and a number of these are illustrated in John Cossin's 1727 map of York. In addition to new buildings, some older residences were also beautified by facades and other embellishments.[104]

Evidence of cultural change impacting on the Merchant Taylors appears in the court minute books and accounts. The hall was rented by a variety of public entertainers, including theatre companies from the 1690s. Thomas Kerrigan's players performed there nearly every year between 1720 and 1744, after which Kerrigan's widow moved the company to the new theatre in Mint Yard that had opened in 1736.[105] Mention has already been made of the society's sponsorship of horse racing through the corporation during the early part of the eighteenth century. Another interesting minute is the decision taken in February 1726 to 'Indempnify any one that Alderman Charles Rodman shall Molest by bringing any Carryages up the lane leading to the Hall.'[106] Increased traffic levels, particularly of coaches and carriages, was a feature of York's gentrification and obliged the corporation to finance badly needed road improvements. It is not clear from the source whether company members or theatre patrons had taken to arriving by carriage, but the repeated references to coaches raises the question of the Merchant Taylors' social status.

Conclusions regarding the social origins of apprentices and master tailors must be qualified by the fact that the occupation of fathers is unknown in between a fifth and a third of cases, and also because the accuracy of the descriptors applied to parents cannot be appraised. Bearing in mind these caveats, no fewer than 7.7 percent of boys bound between 1660 and 1759 were sons of gentlemen (among apprentices whose parental occupations are stated). The participation of gentry sons was not, however, constant and declined on trend.

Whereas between 1669 and 1689 between ten and sixteen percent of male apprentices came from gentry families, during the years 1690 to 1759 the ratio ranged from just three to nine percent. Gentility was higher among female apprentices: between ten and sixteen percent of girls possessed gentry parents between 1710 and 1759.[107] The reasons for the emergence of a gender differential may possibly reflect the fact that the daughters of gentlemen were able to bring into the dress-making trades valuable social contacts and familiarity with fashion; it is also conceivable that the presence of women in the company acted as a deterrent to the enrolment of gentlemen's sons.

These estimates of gentry participation in the York Merchant Taylors are consistent with studies of other companies that have also discovered that the offspring of gentry families are over-represented in early modern guilds.[108] Enrolment of gentry offspring into the Merchant Taylors was less common than into the Merchant Adventurers, but still remained significant.[109] While generating some interesting data, however, the examination of the family origins of new entrants merely constitutes one side of the equation of social mobility. What can be said of enabled company *members* who laid claim to the title of gentility? An examination of the parliamentary poll books and other sources identified a total of fifteen merchant tailors described as 'gentleman' or 'Esq.' Nearly all of these individuals were either the sons of gentry (four cases), or had held civic office (eight cases), or were merchant drapers (nine cases, of whom seven were also members of the Merchant Adventurers'). Membership of the merchant tailors' company itself does not appear to have offered a promising avenue for social advancement.[110] This finding, coupled with the fact that male gentry apprentices declined during the eighteenth century, implies that the company probably suffered a diminution in its social standing during the decades after 1700 as York itself became more gentrified.

Much work remains to be done on the cultural and social influence of the Merchant Taylors within the city, but the approaches pursued in this section all suggest that the guild was not in a strong position, politically or socially, to encroach on the governance of York. The potential sources of influence examined suggest that, on the balance of probability, the ability of the guild to shape civic policies declined. The company was successful, however, in defending its right to regulate trade according to its charter. Court minutes and entries in the accounts reveal that searches and prosecutions continued to be mounted and that fines for infringements of bye-laws were collected. There is also no indication that the company's membership was diluted by non-participants in trade (due to an attempt, for example, by gentry families to subvert the corporation) prior to its eventual economic decline.

The findings presented in this section question the contemporary claims voiced by Drake and Turner that a crude inverse relationship existed between the strength of York's guilds and the economic development of the city. This conclusion may be compared with Corfield's finding that no simple correlation between the form of town governance (particularly the distinction between 'open' and 'closed' corporations) and the economic performance of towns and cities. In the case of guilds, instances can be cited of expanding urban centres that contained significant numbers of guild companies (Bristol and Coventry, for example) that must be offset against case studies of stagnation.[111]

V CONCLUSIONS

In this chapter, a largely quantitative survey of the Merchant Taylors' company during the century after incorporation has been presented. The analysis does not claim to be comprehensive and it is accepted that alternative approaches to studying the guild's activities are possible and indeed desirable. Gadd and Wallis' comment that 'even the most nuanced investigation of those named as freemen in company minute books can only produce a pallid and disjointed impression of the urban economy' is taken in good part. The sources consulted, for example, provide little information about the conditions of work experienced by servants, journeymen, or 'foreign' (non-free) workers who laboured, in large numbers, in the workshops of tailors and drapers. Yet it is contended that the present study is a necessary step towards understanding how the York Merchant Taylors' guild responded to the challenges faced by all urban craft and merchant guilds during the later seventeenth and eighteenth centuries.

'What were the salient features of the 18th Century with regard to the Merchant Taylors?' Johnson answered his own question by emphasising three core themes: the admission of women, 'the rise of a working class manifesting itself at intervals', and the steady erosion of the company's power to regulate the trades of drapery and tailoring.[112] There can be no disagreement about the importance of female membership. Women sustained the Merchant Taylors after 1710 and their admission differentiates York from London's livery companies and other provincial guilds.[113] Johnson's second conclusion is more controversial, but it is clear that an increase in the numbers of journeymen was a significant development that ultimately contributed to the economic demise of the guild during the later eighteenth century. In 1660, the Merchant Taylors constituted a three-tiered institution that consisted of assistants, wardens, and common members. Presiding over the organisation was an executive officer, or master, who served a single year term, while searchers were elected to enforce guild regulations. Compared with London's guilds, York's tripartite hierarchy was relatively flat. In London, additional distinctions were commonly made between liverymen, householders, and journeymen's election to the livery was more than twice was difficult as progression to the York Merchant Taylors' higher offices.[114] During the eighteenth century, however, York's company hierarchy became more elongated as journeymen numbers increased and women were also admitted as a distinct category of members.

Given the knowledge that the Merchant Taylors would soon enter into irrevocable decline, it is tempting to seize on areas of concern and concur with Johnson's third suggestion that the eighteenth century saw the company succumb to 'the paralysing influences of an increasing old age and inability to change with the times.'[115] The power of hindsight, however, often obscures more than it reveals. Arguably, the most salient feature of the Merchant Taylors during the first half of the eighteenth century is how little indication there is of company decline. In aggregate terms, membership was sustained, at least until the 1740s, with no detectable dilution of the company's occupational basis. Dis-aggregating the membership data reveals that significant numbers of parish apprentices and females were admitted between 1650 and 1750. Neither feature, however, provides compelling evidence that the tailor's trade was becoming pauperised. Poor children had long been apprenticed to trade in York; indeed, the increased emphasis in the accounts on parish apprentices is more a reflection of the charity school movement's strength in York than the guild's weakness. Similarly, while the number of female merchant tailors rose dramatically, the existing evidence does not suggest that they represented a cheap source of low-skilled labour.[116] The notion that the company was becoming stigmatised by pauperism is also questioned by the fact that gentlemen, professionals, and merchant tailors continued to enroll their children as apprentices.

If the historian is predisposed to find them, there are signs during the second half of the eighteenth century that cast doubt on the Merchant Taylors' future viability. The fragile estimates of company size presented in Table 1, coupled with the more reliable admissions data, suggest that recruitment had begun to slacken by the 1740s, though whether this represented more than a cyclical dip is less clear. In 1766, the regular keeping of the brogue book was revived, but in contrast to previous periods the entries are sketchy and, perhaps, indicative of a weakening resolve to maintain hall rituals and to collect fines. It is also the case that between 1766 and 1778 indentures enrolled in the civic register record generally low premiums paid for children bound into the tailoring trades (in cases where they were paid at all).[117] By the later 1760s, there is also evidence that the company was beginning to feel vulnerable as guild corporations were subject to legal challenge in Norwich and other towns.

Possibly in response to these latter developments, the company sought legal opinions in 1765 and 1768 from James Wallace and Thomas Walker, barristers of Middle Temple and Lincoln's Inn. Both lawyers advised that the company's charter was valid since it preceded the civic charter of 1664 (which had confirmed existing grants and franchises). Nevertheless, they counselled that two legal cases (Wagoners' Case and the case of the Tailors of Ipswich) had established the crown did not have the right to grant corporate trading monopolies. Walker concluded that the charters and bye-laws that regulated entry to the tailoring trades within York, constituted a 'restraint of Trade [that] has been Universally deemed illegal contrary to the natural Rights of Mankind before they enter into civil Society and of their civil rights and those of the Community after they have enter'd into Society which no Person can take from them or abridge but the Power of the Ligislature or some Custom presumed Coeval with the Constitution of the Kingdom.'[118]

Yet if the company was disheartened by the learned pronouncements of such lawyers, little sign of it appears in the surviving records. Searches, prosecutions, and fines continued without interruption and no reference was made to the legal opinions in the court minute books. Within York, the corporation continued to enforce apprenticeship and freedom regulations; as late as 1775, it compelled a number of traders either to pay admittance fees or to provide an account of why they should be exempted from redemption fees or license charges. Much the same pattern can be detected in the records of London's livery companies where, as in York, the law was regarded as a legitimate instrument to be exploited in tactical battles, rather than a supreme authority to be obeyed without question.[119] Notwithstanding solicitor Walker's smooth eloquence, the common law judgements of Coke did *not* establish a clear legal precedent that guild monopoly privileges were illegal. Defending their charter rights could involve guilds in court battles, but it required a series of test cases in higher courts late in the eighteenth century, followed by specific acts of parliament, before the regulatory authority of the guilds were finally consigned to the dustbin of history.[120]

Table 1

Conjectural Estimates of the Membership of the Merchant Taylors' Company at Four Bench-mark Dates

Benchmark Date	Males	Females	Total
1707–14	168–186	4	172–190
1741	191	67	258
1758	153	78	231
1774	144	64	208

Sources: BI, MTA 13/1, Brogue Book; *The Poll for the Election of Members to Serve a Parliament for the City of York* (York, 1741); *The Poll for a Member of Parliament to Represent the City of York* (York, 1758); *The Poll for Members in Parliament to Represent the City of York* (York, 1774); *The State of the Poll for Members of Parliament to Represent the City of York* (York, 1784).

Notes: See the Appendix for details of the calculation.

Table 2

Merchant Taylors Enabled of the Company
and Made Free of the City, 1660-1759

	(1) Enabled	(2) Enabled and Free	(3) Made Free [a]	(4) Free and Enabled
1660–9	97	66	66	63
1670–9	78	60	82	71
1680–9	70	58	57	48
1690–9	84	60	60	56
1700–9	68	53	64	58
1710–9	71	43	54	39
1720–9	71	39	56	46
1730–9	55	29	68	41
1740–9	66	49	82	46
1750–9	61	32	58	31
Totals	721	489	647	499

Sources: BI, MTA12/1, Accounts 1665–1712, MTA 12/2, Accounts 1713–1826; *The Company of Merchant Taylors in the City of York: Register of Admissions 1560–1835* ed. David M. Smith (Borthwick List and Index 16, York, 1996); *Register of the Freemen of the City of York from the City Records; vol. II, 1559–1759* ed. F. Collins (Surtees Society 102, 1900).

Notes: [a] Qualifications for inclusion in freemen's column: *either* 1) trade listed as 'merchant tailor', *or* 2) trade listed as 'draper', *and/or* 3) trade listed as 'tailor', 'mercer'/'mercator scissoris', 'draper' and positive identification with an individual appearing in the abled masters' books (normally by parentage).

Table 3

Methods of Admission into the Company and Sources of Apprentices, 1660–1769 (decadal averages)

	Admittances	Apprenticeship	Redemption	Patrimony (estimate) [a]	Unknown
1660–99	82.25[b]	43.00	3.00	5.25	31.00 [c]
1700–39	66.25	39.00	8.00	9.00	10.25
1740–69	58.33	38.00	6.00	4.33	10.00

	All Apprentices	York Apprentices	Non-York Apprentices	Unknown Apprentices
1660–99	118.25	32.00	70.00	16.25
1700–39	154.75	76.00	64.00	14.75
1740–69	133.00	79.33	44.00	9.67

Sources: BI, MTA 9/1 and MTA 9/2, Apprenticeship Registers, 1606–1751 and 1751–1862; MTA12/1, Accounts 1665-1712, MTA 12/2, Accounts 1713–1826; *The Company of Merchant Taylors in the City of York: Register of Admissions 1560–1835* ed. David M. Smith (Borthwick List and Index 16, York, 1996).

Notes: [a] Estimate based on stated occupation of parents in the master's abling books or apprenticeship register. [b] Excluding the exceptional 1660–9 decade (see text), the average between 1670 and 1699 is 77.67 per decade. [c] Since the database only records apprenticeship indentures from 1660, many of these 'unknowns' are likely to have gained entry through service.

Table 4

Estimates of Survivorship Among Male Merchant Taylors, 1660–1769

Cohort	Males enabled N	Brogues 1707–14 Nᵃ	Brogues 1707–14 Survivorship	1741 Poll Nᵇ	1741 Poll Survivorship (I)	1741 Poll (II)	1758 Poll Nᵇ	1758 Poll Survivorship (I)	1758 Poll (II)	1774 Poll Nᵇ	1774 Poll Survivorship (I)	1774 Poll (II)	1784 Poll Nᵇ	1784 Poll Survivorship (I)	1784 Poll (II)
1660–9	97	13	.13	1	.01	.02	0	0	0	0	0	0	0	0	0
1670–9	78	17	.22	2	.03	.03	0	0	0	0	0	0	0	0	0
1680–9	70	28	.40	3	.04	.05	1	.01	.02	0	0	0	0	0	0
1690–9	82	51	.62	11	.13	.19	2	.02	.04	0	0	0	0	0	0
1700–9	65	54	.83	18	.28	.35	2	.03	.04	0	0	0	0	0	0
1710–9	50	-	-	21	.42	.53	8	.16	.20	3	.06	.08	0	0	0
1720–9	40	-	-	19	.48	.49	10	.25	.26	2	.05	.05	0	0	0
1730–9	35	-	-	18	.51	.64	13	.37	.46	3	.09	.11	0	0	0
1740–9	53	-	-	-	-	-	27	.51	.55	13	.25	.27	4	.08	.08
1750–9	39	-	-	-	-	-	25	.64	.78	18	.46	.56	12	.31	.38
1760–9	28	-	-	-	-	-	-	-	-	13	.46	.68	10	.36	.50

TABLE 4 NOTES

Sources: BI, MTA 12/1, Accounts 1665-1712, MTA 12/2, Accounts 1713–1826 *The Company of Merchant Taylors in the City of York: Register of Admissions 1560–1835* ed. David M. Smith (Borthwick List and Index 16, York, 1996); BI, MTA 13/1, Brogue Book; *The Poll for the Election of Members to Serve a Parliament for the City of York* (York, 1741); *The Poll for a Member of Parliament to Represent the City of York* (York, 1758); *The Poll for Members in Parliament to Represent the City of York* (York, 1774); *The State of the Poll for Members of Parliament to Represent the City of York* (York, 1784).

Notes: [a] The total number of individuals recorded in this column is fewer than the 191 names listed in the brogue book because it excludes four duplicated names, three individuals enabled before 1660, and nineteen individuals enabled after 1710. Two individuals appear in the brogue book and the apprenticeship registers who are absent from the abling books (these were assigned abling dates by taking the mean interval between apprenticeship and enablement for their year group). [b] The qualification for voter inclusion is a name match (first name and surname) with the database of abled merchant tailors *and* an occupational designation of 'taylor', 'draper', or 'mercer', *and* residence in York (note: very few 'mercers' were recorded and the omission of this category would, therefore, leave the results barely affected). [c] In the case of the poll books, column (I) gives the proportion of voters to enabled members in each respective cohort and column (II) the proportion of voters to enabled members who were also freemen. The number of merchant tailors whose votes were accepted at the polls, but are not recorded as being freemen, was as follows: 1741 poll five, 1758 poll one, 1774 poll five, 1784 poll three (these figures include non-resident voters).

Table 5

Male Merchant Taylors Enabled of the Company
and Made Free of the City, 1660–1759

	Enabled (1)	Enabled and Free (2)	Free (3)	Free and Enabled (4)
1660–9	97	66	66	63
1670–9	78	60	82	71
1680–9	70	58	57	48
1690–9	82	58	58	54
1700–9	65	51	62	56
1710–9	50	42	53	38
1720–9	40	38	54	44
1730–9	35	29	68	41
1740–9	53	49	82	46
1750–9	39	32	58	31
Totals	609	483	640	492

Sources: As for Table 2.

Table 6

Voting Record of Freemen Taylors
(not also Free of the Company) in Parliamentary Elections
(1741, 1758, 1774, and 1784 polls)

Category	whole period	Made Free 1660–1709	Made Free 1709–69
Former Apprentices and Voters	64	1	63
Non-Apprentices and Voters	18	0	18
Former Apprentices and Non-Voters	35	10	25
Non-Apprentices and Non-Voters	37	22	15
Totals	154	33	121

Sources: BI, MTA 9/1 and MTA 9/2, Apprenticeship Registers, 1606–1751 and 1751–1862; *The Poll for the Election of Members to Serve a Parliament for the City of York* (York, 1741); *The Poll for a Member of Parliament to Represent the City of York* (York, 1758); *The Poll for Members in Parliament to Represent the City of York* (York, 1774); *The State of the Poll for Members of Parliament to Represent the City of York* (York, 1784); *Register of the Freemen of the City of York from the City Records; vol. II, 1559–1759* ed. F. Collins (Surtees Society 102, 1900).

Note: Voter qualification is the casting of a ballot in at least one of the parliamentary polls held in 1741, 1758, 1774, and 1784.

Table 7

Fatherless Apprentices Bound to Members of the Company, 1660–1729

	All Apprentices		York Only		Yorkshire Only	
	(a)	(b)	(a)	(b)	(a)	(b)
1660–9	53	.35	12	.27	36	.41
1670–9	17	.24	6	.35	8	.18
1680–9	38	.33	10	.30	20	.32
1690–9	46	.40	8	.24	12	.30
1700–9	45	.36	14	.30	17	.35
1710–9	38	.33	13	.21	17	.44
1720–9	63	.41	33	.43	22	.37

Source: BI, MTA 9/1, Apprenticeship Registers, 1606–1751.

Notes: (a) Decennial total of apprentices bound without living fathers; (b) Fatherless apprentices as a proportion of total apprentices bound during the decade. The data excludes indentures where neither parent is specified (zero cases 1660–9, 1 case 1670–9, 4 cases 1680–9, 14 cases 1690–9, 4 cases 1700–9, 6 cases 1710–9, 12 cases 1720–9).

Table 8

Career Progression of Male Apprentices, 1660–1759

A) Fatherless Apprentices

cohort	sample size	mean age when bound (years)	enabled	waiting time (years)[a]	freemen	company officers[b]	civic officers[c]	master tailors	apprentices
1660-9	53	17.30 (3)	14	11.86	13	7	1	10	28
1670-9	17	17.05 (5)	6	11.83	4	3	0	1	6
1680-9	38	16.31 (5)	10	9.20	7	3	0	4	5
1690-9	47	14.04 (6)	20	11.65	16	3	0	9	29
1700-9	36	14.45 (6)	12	12.25	15	3	0	5	20
1710-9	20	16.46 (4)	7	16.14	8	0	0	4	17
1720-9	21	17.67 (5)	4	17.50	7	2	0	3	10
1730-9	23	14.58 (4)	5	14.20	12	1	0	1	2
1740-9	12	12.55 (3)	5	9.80	5	4	0	3	6
1750-9	8		3	17.00	3	3	0	2	3
Totals	275		86		90	29	1	42	126

B) Sons of Tailors/Drapers [a]

cohort	sample size	age when bound (years)	enabled	Waiting time[a] years	freemen	company officers[b]	civic officers[c]	master tailors	apprentices
1660–9	19	15.96 (5)	7	13.43	5	1	0	2	2
1670–9	11	14.88 (3)	7	9.43	6	1	0	3	11
1680–9	18	15.12 (4)	8	11.38	10	1	0	5	15
1690–9	14	14.78 (4)	8	9.13	8	3	0	5	16
1700–9	24	15.52 (7)	9	12.33	11	5	0	5	23
1710–9	6	15.08 (1)	3	30.67	3	0	0	1	1
1720–9	12	21.57 (5)	4	13.40	7	1	0	2	2
1730–9	10	14.81 (5)	4	10.75	9	2	1	0	0
1740–9	10	17.85 (4)	5	13.60	5	2	1	3	7
1750–9	7	14.48 (4)	0	-	2	0	0	0	0
Totals	131		55		66	16	2	26	77

C) Control Group[a]

cohort	sample size	age when bound (years)	enabled	waiting time[a] (years)	freemen	company officer[b]	civic officer[x]	master tailors	apprentices
1660–9	82	15.26 (8)	28	8.43	25	10	0	16	48
1670–9	48	16.04 (5)	20	10.95	20	8	0	12	30
1680–9	69	14.48 (9)	24	11.38	16	8	0	17	75
1690–9	71	15.30 (9)	23	9.74	24	11	4	16	64
1700–9	59	13.73 (5)	12	11.00	20	6	1	9	45
1710–9	37	14.83 (6)	15	12.87	20	8	1	13	38
1720–9	37	13.60 (4)	17	16.12	26	8	0	14	44
1730–9	69	14.17 (14)	19	14.68	33	2	0	5	12
1740–9	63	13.80 (19)	16	12.81	23	9	1	8	12
1750–9	57	14.89 (16)	11	11.91	10	7	7	7	17
Totals	592		185		217	77	14	117	385

D) Poor Apprentices and Comparative Analysis

cohort	sample size	age when bound (years)	enabled	waiting time (years)[a]	freemen	company officers[b]	civic officers[c]	master tailors[d]	apprentices[d]
Poor Apprentices (D)									
1720–49	23	15.12 (2)	4	16.00	9	2	0	2	3
1764–76	16	12.22 (6)	2	15.50	6	0	0	-	-
Totals	39		6		15	2	0	-	-
Fatherless Apprentices (A)									
1720–49	56	15.36 (12)	14	13.57	24	7	0	7	18
1764–76	8	15.43 (1)	3	9.67	3	2	1	-	-
Totals	64		17	.	27	9	1	-	-
Sons of Tailors/Drapers (B)									
1720–49	32	17.82 (15)	14	12.71	14	5	2	5	9
1764–76	8	13.59 (6)	1	17.00	2	0	0	-	-
Totals	40		15		16	5	2	-	-
Control Group (C)									
1720–49	169	13.84 (38)	52	14.77	83	19	1	27	68
1764–76	34	13.21 (9)	7	10.71	7	3	1	-	-
Totals	203		59		90	22	2	-	-

Sources: As for Tables 2 and 4 plus BI, MTA 9/1 and 9/1, Apprenticeship Registers, 1606–1751 and 1751–1862; YML, Add. Ms 149, R.H. Skaife, York Civic Officials (compiled 1859). For details of the sources and methods used to calculate mean age at admission, see S.D. Smith, 'Women's Admission to Guilds in Early Modern England: the Case of the York Merchant Tailors, 1693-1776' (see footnote 1).

Notes: [a] Mean interval between the signing of apprenticeship indentures and admission to the company by successful former apprentices. [b] Numbers the holding offices of either master, warden, or searcher. [c] Numbers holding the offices of either chamberlain, sheriff, alderman, or Lord Mayor. [d] Details of masters and apprentices bound after 1776 are not included in the database.

Table 9

Income and Expenditure of the Merchant Taylors' Company
(five yearly averages, 1666–1775)

	Income (£)	Expenditure (£)	Balance (£)	Commodity Price Index (1666–70 = 100)
1666–70	32.9	39.7	–6.8	100.0
1671–75	22.5	28.1	–5.6	102.2
1676–80	28.4	20.4	8.0	101.8
1681–85	41.0	26.3	14.7	99.1
1686–90	28.5	23.7	4.8	91.3
1691–95	46.1	39.1	7.0	100.9
1696–1700	39.7	44.0	–4.3	119.7
1701–05	44.8	50.2	–5.4	95.2
1706–10	51.6	55.4	–3.8	105.2
1711–15	115.9	91.8	24.1	113.1
1716–20	73.5	35.4	38.1	101.8
1721–25	127.6	58.7	68.9	95.6
1726–30	128.8	75.0	53.8	104.8
1731–35	85.6	53.4	32.2	89.1
1736–40	101.6	42.6	59.0	95.6
1741–45	105.1	49.9	55.2	98.3
1746–50	69.6	46.1	23.5	98.7
1751–55	137.9	110.5	27.4	98.7
1756–60	91.6	70.1	21.5	112.7
1761–65	82.0	51.9	30.1	111.8
1766–70	101.2	86.1	15.1	124.5
1771–75	72.4	63.5	8.9	138.4

Source: BI, MTA 12/1, Accounts 1665–1712, MTA 12/2, Accounts 1713–1826. The price index is derived from the Phelps-Brown and Hopkins and the Gilboy and Schumpeter commodity price indexes. The index is not designed to measure changes in the cost of living in York and merely provides an indication of the purchasing power of money between 1660 and 1775.

Table 10

Votes Cast in the Parliamentary Elections of 1741, 1758, 1774, and 1784

Candidates	1741 All Ballots	1741 MT Ballots	1758 All Ballots	1758 MT Ballots	1774 All Ballots	1774 MT Ballots	1784 All Ballots	1784 MT Ballots
Edward Thompson	1,447	66	–	–	–	–	–	–
Geoffrey Wentworth	1,325	92	–	–	–	–	–	–
Sir John Lister Kaye	1,315	83	–	–	–	–	–	–
Sir William Milner	1,115	40	–	–	–	–	812	28
William Thornton	–	–	1,239	54	–	–	–	–
Robert Lane	–	–	994	52	–	–	–	–
Charles Turner	–	–	–	–	828	36	–	–
Lord John Cavendish	–	–	–	–	807	33	–	–
Martin Bladen Hawke	–	–	–	–	647	35	–	–
Viscount Galway	–	–	–	–	–	–	1,083	4
Richard Slater Milnes	–	–	–	–	–	–	1,024	24
Lord John Cavendish	–	–	–	–	–	–	913	33
TOTALS	5,232	281	2,233	106	2,282	104	3,832	89

Source: As for Table 4.

Note: MT = votes from enabled merchant tailors.

Figure 1: Decennial Admissions to the York Merchant Tailors', 1660-1769

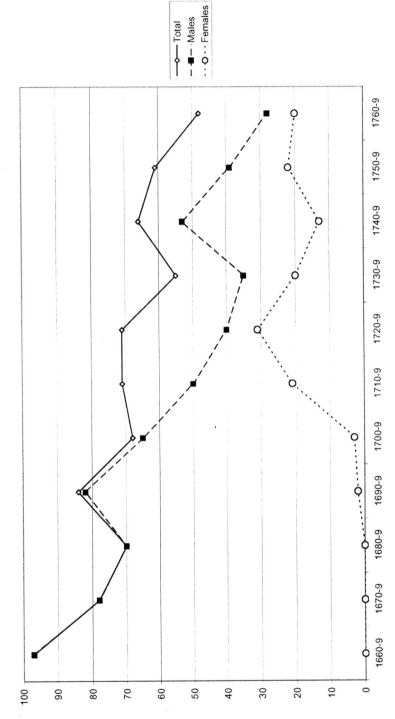

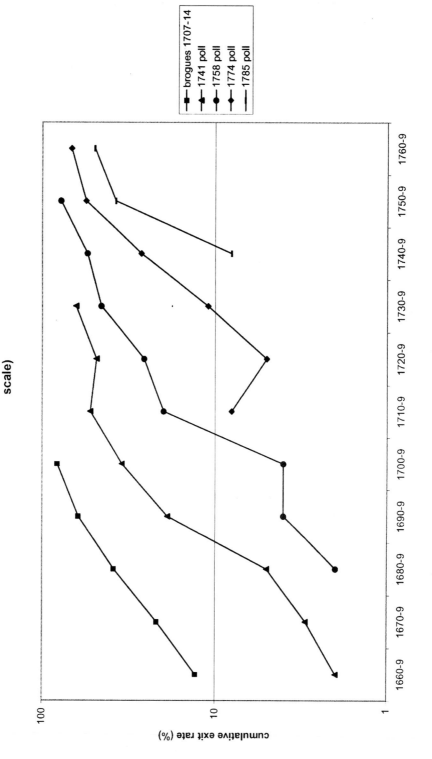

Figure 2: Estimated Exit Rates from the Merchant Tailors' by Entry Cohort, 1660-1769 (logarithmic scale)

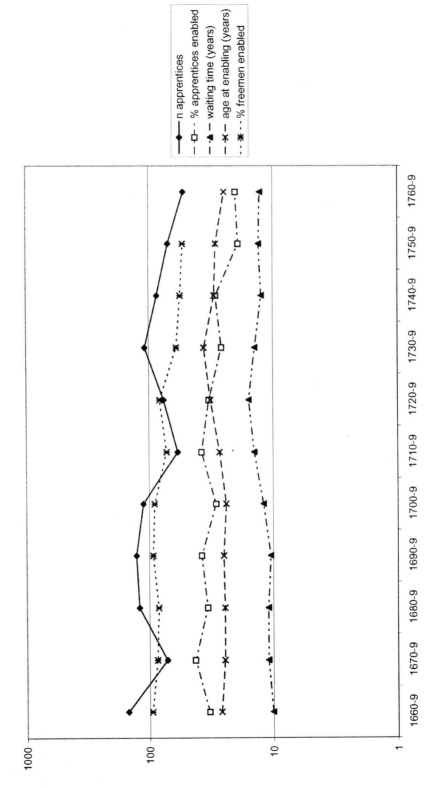

Figure 3: Indicators of Male Journeymen Numbers, 1660-1769 (logarithmic scale)

(1)   **Calculation of Benchmark Estimates of Membership Size from the Brogue Book and the Parliamentary Poll Books**

At a meeting of the general court in August 1707, it was ordered 'that the Brogue book be made use on for the use of the Company', and that 'absent brothers' names be entered into the Brogue book & no apprentices be taken on until Brogues discharged.'[121] The brogue book was maintained for the next seven years and records a total of 187 different names. Its pages also record that, between 1707 and 1714, twenty-eight members died and one other tailor left the city owing brogues.[122] If every member missed at least one hall during these seven years and was fined, the average size of the membership would be 158 brothers. The most recently enabled members, however, are less well represented in the brogue book than longer established merchant tailors. Of the fifty-seven new members recorded in the abled masters' book between 1707 and 1714, only thirty-three are named in the brogue book.[123] In contrast, during the previous seven year period (1699–1706), of the fifty-three admissions, no fewer than forty-one names appear in the brogue book. The principal reason for the disparity in attendance between the two seven year intervals lies in the growing importance of female members of the company. Only three women were admitted between 1699 and 1706, whereas fifteen gained membership between 1707 and 1714. No female names are recorded in the brogue book at any of the periods during the eighteenth century when it was maintained, indicating that women were either excluded from meetings and functions held at the hall or, not subjected to the same assembly requirement. Adjusting for female members, 82 percent of brothers enabled during the seven years preceding 1707 appear in the book compared with 79 percent of brothers admitted during the seven years after 1707.[124]

The information contained within the brogue book can be used to estimate the size of the company if it is assumed that the *survivors* of earlier cohorts admitted as brothers were represented in the same proportion as those admitted between 1699 and 1714; in other words, if the names occurring in the brogue book accounted for about eighty percent of company members. The calculation is as follows:

$$1.266 \times (187 - 54) + 54 - (1.266 \times 29) = 185.7 = 186 \text{ male merchant tailors.}$$

In the above calculation, the multiplier 1.266 is assumed ratio of names in the brogue book to enabled members, the figure 187 is the number of names appearing in the brogue book, the figure 54 is the number of male tailors and drapers known to have been enabled between 1707 and 1714, and the figure 29 is the number of enabled brothers dying or leaving the city.[125] The estimate of 186 members makes no allowance for female members admitted before 1707, but the earliest recorded female admission during the period under discussion occurred in 1693 and only four women in total were enabled before 1707. If it is assumed that all four were still alive in 1714, the implied number of company members rises to 190.

It must be stressed that the figure of 186 to 190 merchant tailors is only an estimate and a fragile one at that. The brogue book does not provide any information about the status of each member; it is not clear, therefore, whether the whole membership was active in trade or even resided within the city. It must also be emphasised that the key feature of the brogue book that permits an estimate of membership to be generated is the *exit* rate (the number of members leaving the company during the years under consideration). Did the compiler of the brogue book record the deaths or departures from York of every member who had outstanding brogues between 1707 and 1714? If he did, then the estimate of membership is probably secure, but it is difficult to accept that during these years the company's new members outnumbered deaths and departures by nearly two to one. If exits are understated and were equivalent to the number of enablings, then the size of the company during the early eighteenth-century would only be 168 brothers plus four women. For this reason, in Table 1 a membership range of between 172 and 190 merchant tailors is suggested.

The parliamentary poll books of 1741, 1748, and 1774 list the names, addresses, and occupations of voters at a specific moment in time. In consequence, it is not necessary to know the exit rate from the company in order to estimate the size of the membership for each of these years. It is, however, necessary to infer by some method what proportion of eligible male merchant taylors voted at each poll and an adjustment must also be made to allow for non-franchised female members of the company. The first stage of the calculation was to enumerate voters appearing in the polls described as merchant tailors (including related trade descriptors) who are also in the database.

Table A1

Voting 1741 poll only	Voting 1758 poll only	Voting in 1741 and 1758 polls
73	43	57
Voting 1758 poll only	Voting 1774 poll only	Voting in 1758 and 1774 polls
43	23	37

Sources: *The Poll for the Election of Members to serve a Parliament for the City of York* (York, 1741); *The Poll for a Member of Parliament to Represent the City of York* (York, 1758); *The Poll for Members in Parliament to Represent the City of York* (York, 1774).[126]

Multipliers were used to estimate the proportion of merchant tailors voting in each election. The multipliers were derived by calculating the proportion of members enabled during the five years preceding each poll who voted in that election. For 1741 the multiplier used was 1.47, for 1758 it was 1.53, and for 1774 it was 2.60.

The estimate of the number of female merchant tailors at each benchmark was obtained in two stages. Firstly, it was assumed that the proportion of male and female members was equal to the proportion of male and female admittances. Secondly, it was assumed that the male rates of survivorship derived from the poll books (see Table 4) were also applicable to females. The cohorts of female enabled members were multiplied by the survivorship ratio and summed to generate the estimates of female membership in 1741, 1758, and 1774 presented in Table 1.

The caution expressed in the text regarding the accuracy of Table 1 is repeated here: the estimates presented are conjectural only and represent best guesses in the absence of any complete listing of company members.

(2)   The Accuracy of the Membership and Apprenticeship records of the Merchant Taylors' Company

The abled masters' book was tested for accuracy by cross-checking entries in the company's account books, the brogue book, and the apprenticeship registers. The account books include a record of 'abling money' received from new entrants and an examination of these entries resulted in the discovery of forty-one merchant taylors between who are not listed in the abled masters' book. Of these forty-one omissions, seven occurred during the years 1667–8 and a further thirteen between the years 1679 and 1681. Inspection of the abled masters' book indicates that the most likely cause of the omissions are damage to the manuscript prior to conservation work being carried out by staff at the Borthwick Institute.

A further check of the accuracy of the abled masters' book was made for the years 1707 to 1714 by comparing the list of names in the brogue book (excluding duplicates and persons enabled before 1660) with the record of enablings. Of the 187 individuals identified in the brogue book, all but four appear in the database. Two of the missing persons appear in the apprenticeship records as indentured apprentices and a third also appears in this source as a master.

The account books also record the amounts paid for the enrolment of apprenticeship indentures under the heading 'incomes'. Unfortunately, prior to 1705 the accounts do not name the apprentice being bound in a clear and consistent manner. A random sample was taken of every third apprentice bound each year between 1705 and 1776. Of the 71 apprentices selected, all but one was found in the database compiled from the company's apprenticeship registers.

The company's apprenticeship registers were subsequently checked against the registers maintained by the corporation. The findings of this exercise are discussed in the main body of the text where the reasons why this comparison cannot be used as a test of accuracy are explained.

Table A2

date of indentures	MT or drapers' indentures company registers	civic indentures appearing in civic registers	% appearing in in company registers
1710–19	23	16	69.57
1720–29	59	39	66.10
1730–39	58	42	72.41
1740–49	26	22	84.62
1750–59	34	30	88.23
1760–69	48	44	91.67
1770–76	22	22	100.00
Totals	270	215	79.63

Sources: YCA, D13 and D14, Register of Apprentices 1721–56 and 1756–86.

In addition, the names of first masters appearing in the apprenticeship registers were compared with the database. Unfortunately, it was only possible to check for consistency of male entries because of the problem of women changing their names after marriage, preventing accurate record linkage in the majority of cases. Of the 370 male masters identified during the period 1660–1776 (a total that excludes masters who became enabled before 1660 and masters to whom apprentices were turned over during their term), all but nineteen appear in the database. Fifteen of the omissions occurred during the years between

1700 and 1749, assuming that the individual concerned took on an apprentice shortly after being enabled.

The conclusion of this investigation is that the records of the Merchant Taylors' company were maintained to a high standard, as measured by tests of internal consistency. Of the sources examined, the apprenticeship registers appear to have been kept most accurately whereas the abled masters' book contains the greatest number of errors. Damage to the original manuscript is one reason for the inaccuracy of the latter source. The best test of accuracy for the membership data is probably the comparison of first masters with enabled members of the company, since the charter and ordinances forbade non-enabled merchant tailors from taking apprentices. This test implies that the error rate of the database is five percent overall, but that during the first half of the eighteenth century the omission rate could be as high as eleven percent. The reasons why both the abled masters' book and the company's account books appear to understate admittances during these years are not known.

Direct comparisons with the records of other guilds has not been attempted, but the general accuracy of guild registration of apprenticeship and admittance has been remarked on by historians.[127] It should be recognised that the binding of apprentices and the abling of tailors and drapers represented important stages in the lives of the individuals concerned. In the case of company admission, an element of ritual was preserved throughout the period being surveyed, the minute books making reference to the admission of redemptioners before the whole company and of other members before the court of assistants. Attention to detail on the part of the clerks, therefore, reflects the importance of the event being recorded.

An earlier investigation of the Merchant Taylors' company by Johnson resulted in the compilation statistics of admittances, the enrolment of apprentices, and the numbers of freemen who were merchant tailors or drapers. A comparison of Johnson's data with those of the present study is made in the table below.

Table A3

	Freedoms		Company Admissions		Apprentices	
	Johnson	present study	Johnson	present study	Johnson	present study
1676–1700	179	157	175	206	296	282
1701–1725	206	153	169	178	361	343
1726–1750	186	172	142	146	428	402

Source: B. P. Johnson, 'The Gilds of York' in *The Noble City of York* ed. Alberic Stacpoole (York: Ceralis Press, 1972), pp.577–8.

In comparison with the database, Johnson gives a consistently higher figure for freedoms, a consistently lower figure for admissions, and a consistently higher figure for the number of apprentices. In the case of freedoms, the divergence arises partly because Johnson counts all of the clothing trades in his total (not just tailors and drapers) and partly because of a difference in methodology. Rather than enumerating freemen solely by occupational classification, the present study links individuals appearing in the freemen's list with lists of enabled brothers of the company. In the case of company admissions, the divergence results partly because Johnson used the abled masters' book as the sole source for enablings (it has been demonstrated above that this source understates admissions). The discrepancy is too great, however, to be accounted for by this circumstance alone. In the case of the numbers of bound apprentices, the difference probably arises as a result of the apprenticeship registers listing the same apprentice more than once, either through the apprentice being turned over to a new master or because of duplicate entries in the original manuscript.

(3)   Incorporation and the Decline of Textile Manufacturing in York

A decline in the proportion of freedoms accounted for by the textile trades is one of the main evidential supports for the thesis that guilds contributed to the decline of York's manufacturing base. For example, Galley cites this as evidence that the new charter of 1662 contributed to de-industrialisation in York by reviving guild control of the distribution of clothing.[128] It is not safe, however, to base conclusions solely on the freemen's register without attempting to link records that provide information about the occupation and paternity of individuals. The freeman's register contains examples of persons described as 'merchant tailors', 'mercers', and 'drapers' who do not appear in the masters' abling book. Conversely, not all persons admitted to company membership appear on the freemen's register. The apprenticeship details entered in the database reveal that other individuals, who do appear in the register, gained their freedom by patrimony *before* they became enabled merchant tailors and drapers. In consequence, a notional reduction in the number of textile related freedoms is not, by itself, evidence that a decline occurred in the textile trades. The reason for this is that a change in the mode by which an individual became free, or an alteration in the relationship between the corporation and the guild companies, could generate the same result.[129] Two factors render the freemen's register an unsatisfactory guide to the numbers of tailors in York. Firstly, the growth of female manufacturers is badly understated (only eight of the 145 women enabled also obtained their freedom). Secondly, the database reveals that during the five decades from 1660-9 to 1700-9, apprentices originating from York enrolled by the Merchant Taylors' accounted for 36.4 percent of servants whose origin is known. During the five succeeding decades (from 1710-19 until 1750-9), however, York apprentices accounted for 58.4 percent of the total. It is conjectured that as the geographical field of apprentices narrowed, the proportion of freemen tailors qualifying by patrimony as the sons of merchant tailors increased, thereby reducing the number of 'visible' tailors in the freemen's register.[130]

NOTES

1. It is a pleasure to thank the librarian and archivists of the Borthwick Institute for
   Archives, the York City Archives, and the York Minster Library for their assistance
   during the course of research. An early draft of this chapter benefited from the
   comments of Natasha Glaisyer and Sheilagh Ogilvie. A companion article to this
   chapter is 'Women's Admission to Guilds in Early Modern England: the Case of
   the York Merchant Tailors', 1693–1776', *Gender and History*, 17 (2005), pp.99–126.

2. 'Past and present local historians have paid scant attention to the beginnings of
   modern industrial activity in York partly because the City was clearly not a leading
   industrial centre in pre-Victorian times and partly because of the personal interests
   and backgrounds of the same historians', W.B. Taylor, 'The workshops and
   Manufactories of York in the second half of the Eighteenth Century', Sheldon
   Memorial Trust Essay Competition, 1990 [typescript, York City Archives]. For the
   eighteenth-century, there are no surveys of the city's economy and population
   comparable to D.M. Palliser's *Tudor York* (Oxford, 1979), Chris Galley's *The Demography of Early Modern Towns: York in the Sixteenth and Seventeenth Centuries* (Liverpool,
   1998), or (for the nineteenth century) W.A. Armstong's *Stability and Change in an
   English County Town* (Cambridge, 1974). Some aspects of the cultural and literary life
   of the city are, however, covered in *Eighteenth-Century York: Culture, Space and Society*,
   ed. Mark Hallett and Jane Rendall (Borthwick Text and Calendar 30, York, 2003).
   For a sketch of York's early eighteenth-century mercantile community, see also
   Perry Gauci, *The Politics of Trade: The Overseas Merchant in State and Society, 1660–1720*
   (Oxford, 2001), pp.48–55, 95–9, 144–50.

3. Francis Drake, *Eboracum: Or, the History and Antiquities of the City of York* (London,
   1736), pp.239–40.

4. R.J. Malden, 'Freemen and Apprentices of York, 1720–1820', unpub. M. Phil.
   dissertation (University of York, 1984), p.20. By 1760, Leeds and Hull had both
   surpassed York's population, E.A. Wrigley, 'Urban Growth and Agricultural
   Change: England and the Continent in the Early Modern Period', in *Population
   and History from the Traditional to the Modern World* ed. Robert I. Rotberg and
   Theodore K. Rabb (Cambridge, 1986), p.126.

5. K.J. Allison and P.M. Tillott, 'York in the 18th Century' in *VCH York*, pp.215–20,
   225.

6. Malden, 'Freemen and Apprentices', pp.14–15, 18–20. On guilds and communications generally, see Barry Supple, 'The Nature of Enterprise', *Cambridge Economic
   History of Europe, vol. V: The Economic Organisation of Early Modern Europe* (Cambridge,
   1977), 437.

7. Galley, *Demography of Early Modern Towns*, pp.34–6. The first of these explanations
   echoes the observations of Collins, whose preface to his edition of the register
   comments that the years 1559 to 1759 witnessed a 'very marked addition to the
   number of trades, arising from the prosperity of the country and the increase in
   the wealth of the inhabitants of the city, bringing with them the greater demand

for the comforts as well as, what were then considered, the luxuries of life', *Register of the Freemen of the City of York from the City Records; vol. II, 1559–1759* ed. F. Collins (Surtees Society 102, 1900). See Appendix 3 for a criticism of the use of the freemen's register as evidence for a decline in manufacturing.

8. For estimates of population see Galley, *Demography of Early Modern Towns*, pp.43–4. Galley argues that York's population remained static at around 12,000 inhabitants between 1660 and 1760.

9. Rosemary Sweet, *The English Town, 1680–1840: Government, Society, and Culture* (Pearson Education, 1999), p.39.

10. George Unwin, *Industrial Organisation in the Sixteenth and Seventeenth Centuries* (Oxford, 1904); R.H. Tawney, *The Acquisitive Society* (London, 1921); Stella Kramer, *The English Craft Guilds* (New York, 1927). See also T.H. Marshall, 'Capitalism and the Decline of the English Gilds', *Cambridge Historical Journal*, 3 (1929), pp.23–33.

11. Franklin F. Mendels, 'Proto-Industrialization: The First Phase of the Industrialization Process,' *Journal of Economic History*, 32 (1972), pp.241–61; Peter Kriedte, Hans Medick, and Jurgen Schlumbohm, *Industrialisation before Industrialisation: Rural Industry in the Genesis of Capitalism* (Cambridge, 1981); Sheilagh Ogilvie and Markus Cerman, eds., *European Proto-Industrialisation* (Cambridge, 1996). On the growth of English rural industry, see Joan Thirsk, 'Industries in the Countryside' in *Essays in the Economic and Social History of Tudor and Stuart England* ed. F.J. Fisher (Cambridge, 1961), pp.70–88. Examples exist, however, of rural and urban industries that complemented rather than competed against one another; moreover, there are instances of rural and urban manufacturers producing the same goods where the urban product was superior in terms of quality and possibly also cost. See C.B. Phillips, 'Town and Country: Economic Change in Kendal, *c.*1500–1700' in *The Transformation of English Provincial Towns, 1600–1800* ed. Peter Clark (London, 1984), pp.116–17, 123; Walker, 'Extent of Guild Control', pp.6, 69.

12. Sheilagh Ogilvie, *State Corporatism and Proto-Industry: the Württemberg Black Forest, 1580–1797* (Cambridge, 1997), pp.339–66, 431ff; Ulrich Pfister, 'Craft Guilds and Proto-industrialisation in Europe, 16th to 18th Centuries' in *Guilds, Economy, and Society* ed. S.R. Epstein, H.G. Haupt, Carlo Poni, Hugo Soly (Seville: International Economic History Conference, 1998), pp.11–24; Laura Van Aert and IIIlja Van Damme, 'Retail Dynamics and a City in Crisis: The Mercer Guild in Pre-Industrial Antwerp (ca.1648–ca.1748), paper presented at the 7th International Conference for Urban History: The European City in Comparative Perspective, Panteion University, Athens (2004); Erik Lindberg, 'The Revival of Guilds: A Preface to a Study of Institutions and Trade in the Baltic Area, c.1650–1880', working paper, Department of Economic History, Uppsala University (2002) www.tcd.ie/iiis/pdf/lindberg.pdf

13. S.R. Epstein, 'Craft Guilds, Apprenticeship, and Technological Change in Pre-industrial Europe', *Journal of Economic History*, 58 (1998), pp.684–713.

14. Sheilagh Ogilvie, 'Guilds, Efficiency, and Social Capital: Evidence from German Proto-industry', *Economic History Review*, 57 (2004), pp.286–333.

15. Very little space, for example, is devoted to guilds in *The Cambridge Urban History of Britain, vol. ii, 1540–1840* ed. Peter Clark (Cambridge, 2000). The only previous

book-length study dealing with the York merchant tailors is written by a former master of the company: Bernard Johnson, *The Acts and Ordinances of the Company of the Merchant Taylors, in the City of York* (York, 1949).

16. P.J. Corfield, *The Impact of English Towns, 1700–1800* (Oxford, 1982), pp.86–90; *Guilds, Society and Economy in London 1450–1800* ed. Ian Anders Gadd and Patrick Wallis (London, 2002), pp.2–3; Sweet, *The English Town*, p.38.

17. Matthew Davies and Ann Saunders, *The History of the Merchant Taylors' Company* (Leeds, 2004), pp.221, 227.

18. M.J. Walker, 'The Extent of Guild Control of Trades in England, c.1660–1820: A Study Based on a Sample of Provincial Towns and London Companies', unpub. Ph.D thesis (University of Cambridge, 1985). Walker examined guilds in Oxford, Shrewsbury, Coventry, Exeter, Newcastle, and Bristol.

19. Christopher Brooks, 'Apprenticeship, Social Mobility and the Middling Sort, 1550-1800' and Jonathan Barry, 'Bourgeois Collectivism? Urban Association and the Middling Sort', in *The Middling Sort of People: Culture, Society and Politics in England, 1550–1800* (Basingstoke and London, 1994), pp.65, 98–100.

20. G.D. Ramsay, 'Industrial Laissez-faire and the Policy of Cromwell', *Economic History Review*, 16 (1946); J.P. Cooper, 'Social and Economic Policies under the Commonwealth' in *The Interregnum: the Quest for Settlement, 1646–1660* (London, 1973); John Elliott, 'Revolution and Continuity in Early Modern Europe' in *The General Crisis of the Seventeenth Century* eds. Geoffrey Parker and Lesley M. Smith (London, 1978).

21. G.C.F. Forster, 'York in the 17th Century' in *VCH York*, pp.174–5; Johnson, pp.59–61. See also the chapter by W.J. Sheils in the present volume.

22. The reason for this omission is that the Merchant Taylors did not raise income by imposing quarterage. In consequence, there are no lists of members who had either paid quarterage or were arrears, and no series of quarterage receipts from which membership can be inferred. The company instead relied on fines for income, supplemented by a periodic cess on city property (which was paid by the more affluent members) to raise money for repairs. On quarterage payments, see Walker, 'Extent of Guild Control', pp.31–3. For an example of the process by which cess was levied, see BI, MTA 2/1, f.89.

23. While, therefore, re-incorporation may not have been necessary to restore the guild's authority, the surge in admissions after 1662 indicates that the gaining of a new charter was still regarded as significant event by York's trading community.

24. Brooks, 'Apprenticeship and Social Mobility', p.63.

25. Brooks, 'Apprenticeship and Social Mobility', pp.63–6.

26. For more detailed discussion of the admission of women, see Smith, 'Women's Admission', pp.103–6.

27. Richard Grassby, *The Business Community of Seventeenth-Century England* (Cambridge, 1995), pp.54–60.

28. Soren Johnson, 'An Oxford Mercer's Life', unpub. Stanford History Department Honour's Thesis (1998), p.47; Walker, 'Extent of Guild Control', p.131. Walker estimates that the tailors' guilds at Oxford and York were much larger than those

of Coventry (25 to 30 members during the years 1660-80 and 1730-40) and Bristol (70 members in 1700). See also Ronald M. Berger, *The Most Necessary Luxuries: The Mercers' Company of Coventry, 1550-1680* (Pennsylvania State University Press, 1993), pp.115-17. The Oxford guild was dis-established in 1576, but was revived in 1648. It has been suggested that the mercers and tailors were able to control trade without a guild during the later sixteenth century because of their dominant position within Oxford's corporation, but that Civil War disturbances, coupled with growth in the urban economy, necessitated the revival of guild regulation, Victoria County History, *A History of the County of Oxford*, vol. IV, *The City of Oxford* ed. Alan Crossley (Oxford1979), p.117.

29. R. Hall, 'Profiling the Yorkshire County Elector of the Early Eighteenth Century: New Materials and Methods', *Historical Research*, 74 (2001), p.173.

30. Unfortunately, it is not possible to analyse survivorship in business among female merchant tailors because women were excluded from the franchise and the brogue book.

31. Unexpectedly few entrants belonging to the 1700-9 cohort appear in the 1758 poll, while the representation of the 1720-9 cohort is poor in the 1741, 1774, and (to a lesser extent) 1758 elections. Given the long intervals between the voting lists and entry cohorts, however, it is not easy to draw conclusions from this data. Regarding the 1720-9 cohort, however, see S.D. Smith, '"The City Itself is but Poor": Evidence for the Depressed State of York's Economy During the 1720s', *York Historian*, 21 (2004), pp.21-5.

32. For details, see Smith, 'Women's Admission', p.103.

33. This result holds true even if the first decade is excluded from consideration on the grounds that individuals belonging to this cohorts may have gained their freedom some time before electing to join the company after the charter was secured (and who are, therefore, absent from the database).

34. BI, MTA 2/2, f.119; 2/3, f.7; Johnson, p.82.

35 It should be noted that even if all regulations were enforced, the share of enabled merchant tailors who were also freemen would always be less than 100 percent if some of the traders resided in the liberties of St. Peter and St. Mary or were exempted from the requirement of being free because of militia service.

36. Malden, 'Freemen and Apprentices', pp.59-60. Though the data suggests that the company cooperated with the Council on this issue, it was still considered necessary to indemnify the master in 1731 from prosecution 'for admitting any person free of the Company without being first made free of the City', BI, MTA 2/3 f.107.

37. Johnson, pp.50-1, 55, 66, 70, 82.

38. Johnson, pp.89, 94.

39. BI, MTA 2/2, f.119.

40. YCA, House Book, vol. 44, 1756-1780, ff.389-406. The list of persons who 'when called upon to take their freedom...have been admitted' included Thomas Richardson, tailor, of Skeldergate. An individual of the same name, trade, and address voted in the 1784 election. The freemens' roll, states that a Thomas

Richardson (merchant tailor) was admitted in 1766 and so there is some ambiguity about this case. Four other tailors appear on the lists. John Exelby, formerly of Spurriergate, 'Removed into the Minster Yard' (a liberty) following the Council committee's enquiries. Having paid a redemption fee of £15 to become a merchant tailor in 1775, he probably found the prospect of a expending a further £25 to become a freeman daunting. John Lowther of Peter Lane is described as having 'Given Over' trade in response to the committee's investigation; he does not appear in the database as either being enabled or having served an apprentice. John Brown of Micklegate claimed exemption from being a freeman 'By serving in the militia.' An individual of this name began an apprenticeship in 1742, but is not listed among the members of the company. Finally, James Wood, of Micklegate was included in a list of licensed retail tradesman of limited means whose presence in the city should be indulged in return for an annual payment of 10s. No person of this name appears in the database.

41. Walker, 'Extent of Guild Control', pp.20-1.

42. Forster, 'York in the 17th Century', pp.174-5; Malden, 'Freemen and Apprentices', pp.48-50.

43. This finding is consistent with Walker's conclusion that electoral interference diluted membership only after a guild had lost its economic function, Walker, 'Extent of Guild Control', p.268.

44. Appendix 2 to this chapter demonstrates that defective record keeping does not provide an explanation of the trend because the accounts kept by the company were internally consistent and that their accuracy improved rather than deteriorated over time.

45. William Cammidge, *The Guilds of York: the inception, growth, purpose and influence of the two surviving guilds, Merchant Adventures and Merchant Taylors* (York, 1905), p.30; Johnson, p.79.

46. The proportion of non-York freemen merchant tailors voting only rose significantly in the 1784 election when it reached 22.6 percent in a reduced poll. It should be noted that the compiler of the 1741 poll book took special pains to identify place men, non-resident voters, and voters not appearing in the freemen's roll. The author of the 1758 poll book was similarly motivated by a desire to correct inaccuracies in a rival account of the election and to expose electoral malpractice.

47. *The Poll for the County of York* (York, 1742). Two editions of this work are preserved at York Minster Library published by John Jackson and the partnership of Ward and Chandler. Minor variations exist between the editions. The Ward and Chandler publication was used to check names in the database because of its convenient alphabetical listing of voters. Jackson's edition includes an appendix 'Containing a List of the Persons who offered to Poll, and were rejected'.

48. Johnson reports only one example of a woman admitted as a merchant adventurer during this period, Johnson, 'The Gilds of York', p.577.

49. YML, R.H. Skaife, 'York Civic Officials (1859)'.

50. D.M. Smith ed., *The Company of Merchant Adventurers in the City of York: Register of Admissions, 1581-1835* (Borthwick List and Index 18, York, 1996).

51. BI, MTA 9/1 and MTA 9/2; YCA, D13 and D14, Register of Apprentices, 1721–56 and 1756–86. An earlier register also survives (D12) recording the details of apprenticeship indentures between 1574 and 1688. It should be noted that the civic register volumes are organised according to the date at which the indenture was entered in the register. D13, therefore, includes many indentures dated before 1721 but which were not enrolled until some years after the parties had signed them.

52. The Appendix provides a further breakdown of the results of this comparison.

53. Allison and Tillott, 'York in the 18th Century', p.226.

54. The Merchant Taylors' minute books and account books contain the names of individuals singled out for prosecution by the company's officials. The database reveals few examples of matches with the names of freemen who were not enabled members.

55. They would not have been capable of producing a masterpiece and would have no incentive to subject themselves to company controls if not operating a workshop.

56. For examples of this practice, see Giorgio Riello, 'The Shaping of a Family Trade: The Cordwainers' Company in Eighteenth-Century London' in *Guilds, Society, and Economy in London* ed. Gadd and Wallis, pp.145–6.

57. Walker, 'Extent of Guild Control', pp.330–1. It should be noted that 'tramping' journeymen were not a new phenomenon and that both European and English craft guilds shared this characteristic.

58. The difference of means test indicates that both the rise in the waiting time and mean age of male admittance during the years 1660–1719 and 1720–76 is significant at 95% confidence. Additional research to improve understanding of the demography and economy of York is required in order to determine causes of the increased number of journeymen further.

59. BI, MTA 2/3, f.71; Johnson, pp.89–90.

60. BI, MTA 2/4, f.80; Johnson, p.91. The amount of the bond was set at £10 per offence. The 1753 minute indicates, however, that the fine of 40s proposed in 1721 had failed to deter masters from acceding to the journeymen's demand to leave off work at 8pm rather than 9pm.

61. Walker, 'Extent of Guild Control', pp.330–1, 337–8, 342; Madeleine Ginsburg, 'The Tailoring and Dressmaking Trades, 1700–1850', *Costume*, 6 (1972), p.66.

62. Walker, 'Extent of Guild Control', iii, pp.337–8.

63. Ginsburg, 'Tailoring and Dressmaking Trades, pp.67–72, 64–5, 68–9.

64. Walker, 'Extent of Guild Control', pp.235–8, 301; Johnson, 'Comparative Table of Clothing Trade Freedoms' between pp.114 and 115.

65. Johnson, pp.145–6, 151–2; BI, MTA 2/1, f.153v.

66. Johnson, pp.146–7, 151. The Lord Mayor (in accordance with the charter) granted a warrant in 1662 authorising officers of the company to conduct searches, Cammidge, *Guilds of York*, p.29.

67. The brogue book is a particularly interesting source since it records fines levied for non-attendance. The years when the brogue book was actively maintained or

revived (1707-14, 1739-49, and 1766) direct attention to periods when the guild attempted to enforce its ordinances.

68. BI, MTA 2/1, ff.142-3.

69. Johnson, p.152.

70. Johnson, p.150.

71. BI, MTA 2/2, f.60v.

72. BI, MTA 2/4, f.152v; Malden, 'Freemen and Apprentices', pp.93-5.

73. The name is derived from 'maison dieu'. In June 1745, the court of assistants voted to expel Elinor Fleming from the hospital and the following November it was ordered that no married person should be admitted, BI, MTA 2/4, ff.44, 45.

74. BI, MTA 2/3 ff.66, 85.

75. BI, MTA 2/3, ff.36v, 55.

76. BI, MTA 12/2, f.44; 2/3, ff.61-4, 83-6, 103-6, 116-7; 2/4, f.92; Cammidge, Guilds of York, pp. 33-4. In his pamphlet, Cammidge draws attention to the engraved stone mounted on the front of one of the cottage buildings constructed for inmates dated 1730.

77. BI, MTA 2/4, ff.3-6, 19-22, 41-4, 63-5, 87-90 (sample years taken at five yearly intervals). It should be noted that even these higher amounts were much less than the charitable sums expended by London livery companies, Ian Archer, 'The Livery Companies and Charity in the Sixteenth and Seventeenth Centuries', in Guilds, Society and Economy in London ed. Gadd and Wallis, pp.15-28. Moreover, unlike their metropolitan counterparts, there is no indication that the Merchant Taylors provided scholarships or bursaries for school or university education.

78. After the third decade of the eighteenth century, the incidence of fatherless apprentices drops away rapidly in the merchant taylors' register: during the decades 1730-9 and 1740-9 the rate is less than twenty percent; during the decades 1750-9 and 1760-9, it is less than ten percent. It is not clear whether the fall represents a real change or an alteration in the practices of the clerks.

79. Grassby, Business Community, p.159. Not all regions shared in this trend and the proportion of fatherless apprentices also varied between trades: see Joan Lane, Apprenticeship in England, 1600-1914 (London, 1996), pp.62-3.

80. Galley, Demography of Early Modern Towns, p.173. A national life table, spanning the years from 1838 until 1854, similarly reveals that a population of 1,000 twenty-five year olds would be reduced to 730 by the time the survivors celebrated their fiftieth birthdays, E.A. Wrigley and R.S. Schofield, The Population History of England, 1541-1871: A Reconstruction (Cambridge, 1981), p.709.

81. There is no method of ascertaining whether nominally 'fatherless' apprentices were illegitimate or children who had been abandoned by their fathers. Some European guilds placed restrictions on the binding of illegitimate children as apprentices, see Ogilvie, 'Guilds, Efficiency, and Social Capital', p.15.

82. Sara Horrell, Jane Humphries, and Hans-Joachim Voth', 'Stature and Relative Deprivation: Fatherless Children in Early Industrial Britain', Continuity and Change, 13 (1998), pp.75-6.

83. Sheilagh Ogilvie and Jeremy Edwards, 'Women and the "Second Serfdom": Evidence from Early Modern Bohemia', *Journal of Economic History*, 60 (2000), p.971; Jane Humphries, 'Female-headed Households in Early Industrial Britain: the Vanguard of the Proletariat?', *Labour History Review*, 63 (1998), p.58. The original data was collected by the Cambridge Group for the History of Population and Social Structure. It is possible that some of the women referred to as 'widows' in the merchant tailors' apprenticeship registers had remarried and that the children concerned had stepfathers, but it is also likely that numbers of apprentices described simply as having deceased fathers were presented by widows.

84. Humphries, 'Female-headed Households', pp.40-4.

85. Forster, 'York in the 17ᵗʰ Century' and Allison and Tillott, 'York in the 18ᵗʰ Century' in *VCH York*, pp.171, 226.

86. Kendal provides one provincial example of charity schools supported by the towns merchants and aldermen: see 'An Exact and Industrious Tradesman' ed. Smith, pp.lxxix-lxxxi, cii-cv.

87. 'An Exact and Industrious Tradesman' ed. Smith, p. civ; W.B. Taylor, *Blue Coat: Grey Coat* (York, 1997), pp.1-4, 47; Robert William Unwin, *Charity schools and the defence of Anglicanism: James Talbot, rector of Spofforth, 1700–09* (Borthwick Paper 65, York, 1984); Malden, 'Freemen and Apprentices', pp.94-5.

88. Francis Drake, *Eboracum*, Appendix, pp.liii-lvi. The individuals positively identified are: George Barnatt, William Dawson, Jacques Priestley, Thomas Norfolk, John Greenup, John Etherington, Thomas Siddall, Thomas Spooner, Thomas Agar, and Isaac Robinson. Considered likely company members are: William Hutchinson, James Jenkinson, Samuel Smith, Robert Waite, John Raper, William Thompson, Thomas Wilson, and possibly also Mr. [Malby?] Beckwith.

89. YCA, D14. See the Appendix for a discussion of discrepancies between the company and the civic registers. After 1710, a duty was levied on apprentices set at the rate of 6d. per £1 for premiums up to £50 and 12d. per £1 on premiums above this rate. Masters were responsible for paying this tax, known as the King's duty; the original returns are preserved at the National Archives (TNA, IR, 1/6).

90. BI, MTA 9/2; YCA, D13. See the Appendix for further discussion of the civic apprenticeship indentures.

91. Unfortunately, problems of record linkage restrict analysis to male apprentices due to female surname changes on marriage.

92. The database reveals that only 33 percent of the 131 apprentices between 1660 and 1759 whose father was a tailor or draper were bound to a parent. Paternal mortality, however, influences this result. During the years for which data is available (1660-1720), one-third of apprentices were bound to a parent but a quarter of the apprentices born to fathers in the trade had experienced paternal mortality by the time their indentures were drawn up. The corrected share of apprentices bound to fathers in the trade, allowing for parental mortality, is 41.8 percent. The finding that less than half of apprentices were bound to their fathers suggests that a family strategy may have operated by which sons were sent to the workshops of others in order to gain experience and additional skills.

93. Walker, 'Extent of Guild Control', p.123. When the size of the York's population is considered, the number of guilds in the city was not excessive in comparison with other provincial centres, but the survival of so many of them to 1800 was exceptional. One of the few studies to take issue with the Drake/Turner view of corporate control is Taylor, 'Workshops and Manufactories', pp.20-2. See also W.B. Taylor, 'York in the Second Half of the Eighteenth Century – Expanding, Stagnant, or in Decline?', unpub. M.Sc. dissertation (University of York, 1988).

94. The mean size of households in York is not known but is thought to lie in the range of 4.5 to 6.1 during the later seventeenth century, Galley, *Demography of Early Modern Towns*, p. 46. If merchant tailors each belonged to separate households, at their peak c.1740 they probably accounted for between 7.5 and 12.7 percent of all households in the city.

95. Data for admissions to the freedom from Forster, 'York in the 17th Century', p.167; Allison and Tillott, 'York in the 18th Century', p.217.

96. Allison and Tillott, 'York in the 18th Century', p.232.

97. Compare Corfield, *Impact of English Towns*, p.88. For details of the company's rent roll, see BI, MTA 2/1 f.161, 'A Rentall of all the Lands belonging to the societye of merchant Taylors of the Citty of York' [1671], which itemises rents worth in total £17 13s. 8d. A list of plate is also given on f.164 and, though it is not valued, it was pawned in 1661-2 to help pay for the cost of obtaining the charter (which in total amounted to £186 18s. 7d.) and again in 1702 to borrow £25, BI, MTA 2/1, ff.82-3, 160-1; 2/2, f.105.

98. The source of this information is R.H. Skaife, 'York Civic Officials' [compiled 1859], YML, Add. Ms 149. Six individuals described as merchant tailors or drapers also held the ceremonial offices of macebearer and sword-bearer between 1662 and 1795, but of these only Robert Drake (appointed macebearer 1750) and Thomas Stephenson (sword-bearer, date of appointment not stated but after mid-eighteenth century) were enabled during the period under examination, Hugh Murray, 'The Mayor's Esquires', Sheldon Memorial Trust Essay Prize, 1984 [typescript, York Civic Archives], pp.31-3.

99. Maulden, 'Freemen and Apprentices', pp.23-5.

100. YCA, B43, ff.109, 138, 284, 288, 316, 372, 477, 484. John Etherington was later successful in becoming commoner for Walmgate.

101. BI, MTA 2/3 f.23, 2/4, f.124.

102. Taylor, 'Workshops and Manufactories', pp.20-1. For an examination of the declining ability of guilds to determine the social and economic policies of corporations in general, see J.R. Kellett, 'The Breakdown of Gild and Corporation Control over the Handicraft and Retail Trades in London', *Economic History Review*, 10 (1957-8), pp.381-94 and Walker, 'Guild Control'.

103. BI, MTA 2/2, f.24.

104. Allison and Tillott, 'York in the 18th Century', pp.207-8; Hugh Murray, *Scarborough, York and Leeds: The Town Plans of John Cossins, 1697-1743* (York, 1997), pp.17-56.

105. Johnson, pp.110-11. A playbill survives describing a production put on by

Kerrigan's company: *For the Benefit of Mr. Craig. At Merchant Taylors Hall in old Work, on Saturday next being the 7th, 1739, will be perform'd a comedy, call'd, The twin rivals... To which will be added, a ballad, call'd Flora:, or, Hob in the Well* (York: Thomas Gent [1739]).

106. BI, MTA 2/3, f.88. A court minute of 1730 renewed indemnification, MTA 2/3, f.105.

107. For boys the sample size is 1,132 with 302 cases where the parental occupation is unknown; for girls, it is 497 with 179 unknowns. The ratio of apprentices whose parental occupation is stated to those whose parental occupation is unknown remained roughly constant between the two dates. The percentage of men admitted to the company with gentry parents was seven percent (in line with apprentices), but only three women from gentry families are recorded as being enabled. Female gentility among company members, however, is understated due to the problem of record linkage (see Appendix for details).

108. Barry, 'Apprenticeship and Social Mobility', pp.56-9; Grassby, *Business Community*, pp.144-50.

109. A comparison of apprenticeship indentures enrolled between 1680 and 1720 (excluding cases where parental details or place of origin are not stated) produces the following results:

| | Merchant Tailors | | | Merchant Adventurers | | |
	All	Esq	Gent	All	Esq	Gent
York	135	1	5	38	0	11
Yorkshire	181	1	12	70	4	39
Others	30	0	4	9	3	3
Totals	346	2 (.01)	21 (.06)	117	7 (.06)	53 (.45)

Merchant adventurer data from Gauci, *Politics of Trade*, p. 97. Gentry admission rates into the York Merchant Adventurers' are high by national standards, judging from the evidence presented in Barry, 'Apprenticeship and Social Mobility', pp.144-50. The data implies, therefore, that the Merchant Adventurers' (a merchant's guild) experienced gentry encroachment and a decline in the guild's occupational base to a greater extent than the Merchant Tailors' (a craft guild).

110. Sources such as the poll books document only upwards social mobility; they are silent about the extent of downward mobility.

111. Corfield, *Impact of English Towns*.

112. Johnson, pp.93-4.

113. See Smith, 'Women's Admission'.

114. Steven Rappaport, *Worlds Within Worlds: Structures of Life in Sixteenth-Century London* (Cambridge, 1989), pp.217-20. Rappaport suggests approximately one-fifth of guild members obtained liveried status compared with fifty percent of enabled members 1660-99 in Table 8, C.

115. Johnson, p.94.

116. See Smith, 'Women's Admission', pp.103–6.

117. BI, MTA 2/4, f.133; 13/1; YCA, D14. Of the thirteen indentures examined binding an apprentice to a merchant tailor, 20 stipulated no premium but service (including two parental apprenticeships), 2 did not state the premium, 11 set a premium of between £1 and £5, 3 between £5 and £10, and 3 between £10 and £20.

118. BL, Add. MS 8,935, 'Case, In a Charter granted to the Master, Wardens, Assistants and Fellowship of the Company of Merchant Taylors in the City of York.'

119. YCA, B44, House Book, 1756–1780, ff.389–406.

120. Walker, 'Extent of Guild Control', pp.67–8, 244–61; Kellett, 'Breakdown of Gild and Corporation Control', pp.381–94.

121. BI, MTA 2/3, Court Minute Book 1706–1734, f.7v. Absent wardens were to pay 12d. for each absence from the Hall or failure to attend wearing a gown, assistants 6d., and other members 4d (f.8v). A record of brogues and other fines also exists in the company's Account Books (MTA 12/1 and 12/1), but it is less comprehensive. Entries in the accounts often group fines together, as for example in 1683 when a sample entry reads: 'Received of 3 several Persons then theire fines [£] 0.1.6.'

122. The Brogue Book lists 191 names but four names are duplicated.

123. BI, MT 13/1, Brogue Book. An account of brogues was also maintained for the years 1739–49 and 1754–60, but coverage is less complete. A summary of the entries in the original Abled Masters' Books is provided by *The Company of Merchant Taylors in the City of York: Register of Admissions 1560–1835* ed. David M. Smith (Borthwick List and Index 16, York, 1996). .

124. The attendance rate was probably slightly higher among members admitted between 1699 and 1707; there may also have been less propensity to fine the most recently admitted (and probably poorer) abled merchant tailors.

125. This multiplier (1.0/0.79 = 1.266) assumes that the attendance rate recorded for members enabled averaged over 1699 and 1714 (79 percent) applied across the membership as a whole.

126. The number of persons describing themselves as 'tailors' or 'drapers' voting in each poll closely followed electoral turnout:

Election	All Electors	Company Members Only	All Resident York Voters	All 'Merchant Tailors'
1741	2,601 (100)	130 (100)	171 (100)	195 (100)
1758	2,233 (86)	100 (77)	142 (83)	158 (81)
1774	1,141 (44)	60 (46)	85 (50)	92 (47)

127. Walker, 'Extent of Guild Control', p.34.

128. Palliser, *Tudor York*, pp.154-9; Galley, *Demography of Early Modern Towns*, pp.33-6; Malden, 'Freemen and Apprentices'.

129. On freeman's lists generally, see D.M. Woodward, 'Freemen Rolls', *Local History*, 9 (1970); J.H.C. Patten, 'Freemen and Apprentices', *Local History*, 4 (1971); J.F. Pound, 'The Validity of the Freemen's Lists: some Norwich Evidence', *Economic History Review*, 34 (1981), pp.48-59.

130. This criticism can be extended to other trades. Gauci, for example, states that 'York's post-1660 decline is clear...with dwindling numbers of freemen declaring themselves merchants.' Yet he also reports a statistically significant rise in the percentage of admissions to the freedom by patrimony from an average of 31.2%, 1640/9-1680/9, to 57.0%, 1690/9-1730/9, Gauci, *Politics of Trade*, pp.49-50.

The Merchant Taylors in the Nineteenth Century

E. Royle

When the Royal Commissioners on Municipal Corporations visited York in 1833, they concluded that "the [Merchant Taylors'] Company and its influence are comparatively gone". Yet the Company continued to meet quarterly, with property to look after and charitable doles to administer, and though by 1833 "they had ceased to enforce their most obnoxious power of compelling those tailors carrying on their business in the city, to take up their freedom of the company", at the beginning of the nineteenth century they still had a residual role in the regulation of trade.[1] This chapter will consider the activities of the Company under three broad headings: its relationship to tailoring and drapery businesses in the city; the administration of property and charitable payments to the poor; and the meetings, rituals and networks of sociability which the members enjoyed.

The Company and the Trade

At the end of the eighteenth century the Company still sought to exercise the right established in its Charter of 1662 of regulating the tailoring and drapery trades in the city, but with diminishing success. The last instance of the Company resolving to maintain standards was in December 1780 when the Court agreed to prosecute any person or persons found cutting woollen cloths contrary to the Charter;[2] and the last instance of the Company acting as a Masters' guild was in 1789 when the Court resolved to support the masters in their refusal of a demand from the journeymen tailors for an advance of wages.[3] After this they still continued their claim to regulate who should practise their trade in the city, issuing indentures of apprenticeship, requiring masters to take their freedoms of the Company, and levying the requisite fees.[4] The Court was also concerned about in-comers, setting up a committee in 1799 "to enquire concerning Hawkers and Venders [sic] of Cloth and take such Measures to prevent them in this City as in their judgment may appear the most effectual".[5] In fact they seem to have accepted that it was legitimate for anyone to sell cloth in the Thursday Market on market day, and that their jurisdiction over vendors of materials other than woollens was at best unclear.[6] The prevailing direction of public opinion was against all restraints on trade. A change in the law on the registering of apprentices also undermined the Company, removing the need for the clerk to fill up the indentures.[7]

The attempt to compel masters to take their freedom could indeed seem "most obnoxious". Although those claiming their freedom by apprenticeship or patrimony had to pay only the customary entrance fine of 13s. 4d. plus fees to the officers of 8s. 4d., tailors seeking their freedom by Order of the Court had to pay £15 and drapers £30, while female mantua makers paid £5.[8] This was a lot of money and most did all they could to avoid it. Notices were periodically issued against men and women plying their trade contrary to the Company's charter, and sometimes the pressure worked. Of eight notices served in November 1806, three resulted in those summoned taking up their freedoms, two of them becoming future Masters of the Company. When Lucy Anderson and Joseph Dalby were issued with writs in November 1802, the former eventually agreed and was admitted in February 1803, but no more was heard of Dalby.[9] Ann Boddy was the last woman to be admitted as a master, in May 1805.[10]

The practice of requiring all masters to take their freedom finally came to an end following notices issued on John Mason, Frederick Kauter, John Nicholson and George Whiteley in May 1814. All were summoned to attend at the Hall on 20 June. Mason, who was a Linen Draper, and Whiteley did not do so, Nicholson came and took his freedom but Kauter, having promised he would take it in August then went back on his word.[11] In November the Company's solicitor was instructed "to write to those who do not attend to take their Freedoms according to their Notices"[12] and on 7 October 1816 it was decided to bring the case again Frederick Kauter to trial.[13] Why the Company chose to take their stand with Kauter is not clear, but perhaps it was because he had for eleven years been foreman to John Wade (Master in 1808) before setting up his own business in the same street in February 1814.[14] When the judgment went against the Company in April 1818 they decided against further proceedings, but in so doing they forfeited their claim to compel any tailors or drapers in the city to take their freedoms of the Company.[15]

The Company was now a voluntary association with no legal powers to compel membership, but this was not the end of its relationship with the trade. The persistence of family firms in the city meant a continuing tradition of links between the leading members of the trade and the Company. Recruitment, however, was narrowly based and numbers small. Between 1816 and 1830 only one master took his freedom, and between 1830 and 1844 only thirteen more masters were admitted, all but one paying the minimum rate. The exception was William Catton, a draper who paid the full £30 in March 1840, the last man so to do.[16] Total membership of the Company at the time of the Royal Commission in 1833 was about 25; in May 1844, the number was around 27.[17] The company had shrunk to its leading members and none was a woman.[18] Whereas there had previously been "Assistants" in addition to an elite of members who had held the office of Searcher at least twice and were eligible to attend meetings for elections and manage the affairs of the Company, there now in effect remained only the elite. Of the 27 members listed in May 1844, all but seven had held or were to hold the office of Master. Of these seven, four were numbered among the mainly elderly "poor and needy" brethren. Put another way, of the thirteen who gained their Freedoms between the Kauter case in 1818 and June 1844, all but three became Master of the Company and these three were the sons of Masters, fallen on hard times.[19]

The register of apprentices records just seventeen registrations between 1820 and the end of the record in 1862.[20] Even John Hollins, master in 1823, who earlier in that year had taken his son John as his indentured apprentice, failed to register him with the Company.[21] Most names added to the lists appear to have come from the same few families, their employees and their apprentices. Between 1851 and 1875, seventeen new masters were admitted, of whom seven took their Freedoms by apprenticeship and five by patrimony.[22] The last apprentice to be admitted a freeman was William Ward Wentworth, a former apprentice of Christopher Annakin, during his second Mastership in May 1870.[23] Albany Atkinson when Master in 1878 failed to get his former apprentice, John Thompson, admitted because the Court was not quorate.[24] Nothing could indicate more clearly the reluctance of the Court to admit members where once it had been only too eager to do so. After 1851 no fees were charged for admission other than those paid to the officers. In 1895 this amounted to a total of two guineas for admittance by patrimony or apprenticeship and four guineas for admittance by Order of the Court.[25] What had once been an importance source of income for the Company had dried up and been abandoned.

The remaining five admissions in the third quarter of the nineteenth century came in two groups, in 1853 and 1874, and were by Order. Invitations were offered to men who could be expected to bring new leadership to the Company and all were seen as potential future Masters. Of the three admitted in 1853 all were in early middle-age: Robert William Anderson was foreman to Richard Evers (Master in 1835 and 1850), who proposed him; the other two, Christopher Annakin and Albany Atkinson, were well established and respected in their trade.[26] The two admitted in 1874, George Nicholson junior and John Henry Anderson, were both the sons of leading members.[27] Thereafter, admission by Order was to be the normal means by which new members of the Company were recruited. Between 1875 and 1914, there were only three further admissions by patrimony.

By the end of the 1870s drastic action was clearly needed to ensure the survival of the Company, and so in February 1879 it was resolved

> That in the opinion of this Court it is desirable to strengthen the position and influence of the Company by the admission to the freedom of the Company of such Gentlemen resident in the city not being entitled to be admitted thereto by Patrimony or Servitude as may be willing to take up their freedom on payment of the usual Court fees and Stamp Duty and this Court do therefore order that such Gentlemen (not however exceeding six in number until further Order[)] be admitted to their freedom of the Company accordingly their names being previously submitted to and approved by this or some other Quarterly Court.[28]

In accordance with this resolution batches of new members were elected from time to time: six immediately in 1879, five in 1885 along with one by patrimony; five and one by patrimony in 1888, one (an employee of a leading member) in 1893, four in 1905 and four and one by patrimony in 1912.[29] Rather like the unreformed City Corporation before 1835, the Company preserved itself by nomination and patronage. Yet only one of these members was not connected with the tailoring or drapery trades – Joseph Wilkinson, Town Clerk to the City and clerk to the Company since 1864, admitted as a mark of appreciation in 1888.[30]

Though a few families and large businesses increasingly dominated this select membership, it would be unwise to suggest that the Company had become merely a rich man's club with a monolithic outlook. They shared a common interest in their trade and in public service but otherwise the members were very different and some were – or became – relatively poor. Their livelihoods had been made through trade and so were precarious in that their capital was tied up in stock, with quite large amounts of money at any one time owing to suppliers and owed by customers. Numbers of them went bankrupt, especially in the first half of the century; others fell on hard times in old age, or their widows and daughters did. Dispensers of charity, some of them became objects of charity.

Among the bankrupts was James Masser, tailor and draper at 36 Fossgate and Master in 1842. He was declared bankrupt in December 1848 and his finances never recovered. In February 1854 he was writing to the Court that he was behind with his rent and pressed by his creditors, asking for £5. Despite assurances that this would be his last application, in November of the same year he was begging for another £5 – "I have my wife laid up in an inflamation which has been attended with expence [sic] & loss of time to me". Again the Company helped and in March 1855 they offered him the post of Porter at the Hall and a payment of £10 a year. In May 1857 he received an additional one-off payment of £2 5s. 0d. to enable him to pay off his arrears of rent, and in June 1859 he was appointed Beadle as well as Porter, with pay of £12 a year plus fees and an additional £4 a year as a poor member. In 1864 he was given one of the Company's cottages rent free in exchange for lighting the fires and cleaning the rooms in the Halls, and this remained the situation until his death in 1868.[31]

Later in the nineteenth century the position of Master came to be dominated by a few families whose firms were among the largest and most durable in the city. Over half the 65 years between 1850 and 1915 saw one of the Wade, Anderson, Nicholson, Kirby or Whitehead families providing the Master of the Company. John Wade, father and son, between them held the Mastership ten times between 1808 and 1887.[32] The firm of R. W. Anderson dated back even further, incorporating the businesses of William Robinson established in 1762 and William Evers, 1802. Two generations of Everses and three of Andersons together with other men associated with the firm and its offshoots brought the total of Masterships connected to this one firm between 1815 and 1910 to eighteen.[33] Other similarly important firms were Kirby and Nicholson which provided nine Masterships,[34] and W. J. Whitehead, founded by William Whitehead, a leading early Methodist, in 1789. His sons, grandson and employees provided twelve Masters in a family business that lasted just over a hundred years.[35]

The presence of these important family firms along with several smaller concerns helped keep the Merchant Taylors in touch with the tailoring and drapery trades of the city but they no longer had a monopoly of the trade. One family business never associated with the Merchant Taylors was Leak and Thorp, founded in 1848 by William Leak whose personal and public profile was similar to that of several contemporary leading members of the Company.[36] Another sign that the Company was not always quite at the heart of things was the formation of a York branch of the Master Tailors' Association, founded in London in 1887. There was no apparent rivalry with the Merchant Taylors and when asked for a donation in February 1909 the Company sent two guineas. Maybe matters were helped by the fact that the local secretary was William P. C. Beckwith, admitted in 1905, grandson of William R. Beckwith, tailor of Colliergate, and eldest son of William Thomas Beckwith (Master in 1896, 1903, 1908 and 1913) who was Master when the first donation was made.[37]

CHARITABLE WORK

The administration of charitable funds and the properties which supported them remained a constant theme of the Company's work. There were four properties. The first was the Aldwark site, with its two halls (considered below), associated cottages and four almshouses or hospital, built in 1730. Secondly, there were two closes in Murton amounting to a little over eight acres.[38] Thirdly, off the Hull Road outside Walmgate Bar in the vicinity of what is now Lilac Avenue lay the Havergarths, a property of over six acres held partly by the Merchant Adventurers and partly the Merchant Taylors. The latter's portion amounted to a little over three acres, but half an acre was sold in 1825 to pay the costs of enclosure. These lands were charged with 10s. 0d. a year payable to the poor of the hospital.[39] Finally there was what turned out to be the most valuable property, a garden and orchard of just over two acres outside Micklegate Bar off Blossom Street, enclosed in 1822, which was charged with £10 a year for the support of the hospital. In the early 1830s this land was disposed of on long leases for the building of Park Street to yield an annual rental of £80 0s. 0d., and the £10 charge was transferred to the Havergarths.[40]

Begging letters were received at almost every Quarterly Court and grants were frequently made to deserving cases in addition to the doles paid to regular pensioners, who usually numbered about six, each receiving between £1 and £5 a year at the start of the century, rising to between £5 and £10 a year by the end.[41] Policy was determined by the condition of the Company's finances and its changing membership. As fewer ordinary working master tailors joined, once the needs of the Company's own poor had been met charity was extended to poor tailors not members of the Company but was refused to those connected with neither the Company nor the trade. Donations were also made to certain local institutions, notably the County Hospital and the Dispensary, of which several of the Company's leading members were governors, as this gave the Master tickets to enable the Company's poor to receive treatment. Each quarter far more money was disbursed in charitable gifts than was strictly required by the charitable endowments: in 1900 in response to an enquiry from the Crown Solicitor the Company was able to state that "in accordance with the directions contained in the several Bequests" the Merchant Taylors were obliged to distribute £15 10s. 0d. a year, "yet the sum actually distributed amounted to more than twice that sum".[42]

The operations of the Quarterly Court in considering charitable donations can be illustrated by a few examples across the century. Priority was given to freemen of the company, mostly in their old age, and their widows and just occasionally their other female dependants. Though the sums were small, the Court usually showed itself responsive to individual need. When Jane Bilton, for example, applied for a vacancy in the hospital in November 1791, she was admitted "on Condition she takes her Freedom of the Company" but in February 1792 she was then refunded 10s. 6d. of her 13s. 4d. freedom money, and when she left the hospital in 1807 to go and live with a relative she was allowed to keep her pension.[43] The Company could be generous to deserving cases and sometimes used positions as servants as a form of relief, as was the case with

James Masser (see above). John Gladdin, who already lived in the hospital with his wife, was made porter at the Hall in February 1795. A year later he was granted an extra guinea "being very ill" and a few months later his widow was appointed to continue as nominal porter and to enjoy the emoluments of her late husband while a deputy porter was appointed to assist her. She was still in receipt of payments in 1813.[44]

However, as wartime inflation began to take its toll on the Company's finances, a situation made worse by the agricultural depression which reduced rental values after 1815, and by the loss of income from freedom fines following the Kauter case, vacancies for pensions and places in the almshouses had to be frozen.[45] This remained the situation until the 1830s when the leases on the garden outside Micklegate Bar were sold off to yield an annual income nearly three times the £30 that the land had commanded before building development.[46] New names could now be added to the pensioner list and by 1844 there were five men and one woman, each in receipt of £2 a quarter.[47] A sign of easier times was the decision in 1842 of the junior members of the Quarterly Court to vote the senior members (some of whom were their fathers) £20 each in compensation for expenses not refunded them while they were in office "at periods when the Finances of the Company were inadequate (in consequence of considerable Debt)".[48]

A review of income and expenditure in 1849 showed that the annual income from rents and investments now totalled £171 1s. 0d., over half of which came from ground rents on the Park Street properties: the average annual expenditure over the past four years had been £171 3s. 6¼ d., of which half had gone on repairs and just over a quarter on the poor.[49] It was agreed therefore to curtail other expenditure in order to increase charitable giving, raising from £8 to £10 a year the payments to each person on the poor list.[50] Yet even when it could not afford it, the Company was never backward to recognise and relieve immediate distress among its members. The case of James Masser noted above was extreme but not unique. In 1849 £5 was given to two of the oldest members, Thomas Atkinson (admitted 1799 and Master in 1802) and Joseph Walker (admitted in 1807 and Master in 1817, 1831 and 1839).[51] In 1850 Walker, who had already been allowed a loan of £100, half of it interest free, was put on the poor list to receive £10 a year, and after his death of heart disease six weeks later, his widow continued to receive his pension for a further thirty years.[52] Payments were already being made to his son, William Slade Walker, who had been put on the pension list in 1844 and, after his premature death in York Asylum in 1865, his widow continued to receive support.[53] Occasional payments were also made to Joseph Walker's three daughters, the last of whom received her final payment in 1894, 87 years after her father had first been admitted to the Company.[54]

Freedom of the Company carried benefits rather like a friendly society, as is illustrated by the case of William Coupland, a tailor who was a Searcher in 1844. In 1853 he applied for help in his "distressed situation". The Quarterly Court asked the Master "to express to him that the Company was surprised at this application from so young a member", having been admitted to the Company only in 1841. The request was nevertheless granted. Similar requests continued to come in over the next few years, and each time they were granted until finally in 1887 Coupland, now of Gateshead, was put on the pensioners list to receive £6 a year.[55]

None of these sums was in itself enough to live off, and if the poor had no other sources of support they would either starve or be sent to the workhouse. Old age pensions, when introduced in 1908, were at a rate of up to £13 a year for a single person, and that was barely adequate. So it is likely that many of the poor helped by one charity also sought support elsewhere. Suspicion that some poor might be "milking" the system led to a more "professional" attitude towards relief in the later nineteenth century, inspired by the Charity Organisation Society, begun in 1869. In this spirit York set up a single register to enable the 24 charitable bodies and 21 parochial charities located in the city to co-ordinate their efforts.[56] The Merchant Taylors sent a representative in 1910 when threatened by the Charity Commissioners with a consolidation of all the city's charities under the city council.[57] A list supplied to the York Charities Register Committee of those in receipt of the Company's charity in 1911 illustrates the Company's work at this time. All four men and two women being supported in April 1911 were between 72 and 83 years old.[58] Four of the six were in receipt of a state old age pension. Two lived in the almshouses and the others in their own homes. The amounts given varied between £1 and £2 a quarter. Widow Hill, for example, received only £1 12s. 6d. because her granddaughter paid 7s. a week for her lodgings. Edwin Gell, who received the full £2, was also Beadle and caretaker. Robert Dent, "an old tailor close upon 80 years of age" had been given the room over the gateway from Aldwark in 1895 and an allowance of £6 a year. This was continued to his widow in 1900, and when widow Dent died in November 1911 in one of the almshouses, her two daughters were allowed to continue living there on payment of the same 1s. 0d. a year as their mother and they also received her allowance of £1 10s. 0d. a quarter.[59] When another of the Company's pensioners, John Bean, died in December 1911, his £2 a quarter went to Charles Corp, aged 73, a widower living in the Shambles. In May 1911, £1 10s. 0d. a quarter was allowed to Caroline Nicholson, a widow who rented one of the cottages in the yard for 1s. 6d. a week. Although she had a job as an office cleaner at the North Eastern Railway, clearly this did not pay well and in 1912 she applied to have her rent reduced to 1s a week. Instead the Company increased her pension by 10s a quarter, which was more generous.[60]

This charitable activity at the beginning of the twentieth century is also typical of the record throughout the nineteenth. Numbers relieved at any one time were never high but, although some pensioners survived for years, many were near their ends when taken on to the list and there was consequently a high turn-over. The lowest point was reached in 1880, for when widow Walker died on 10 May there was no one left and a search had to be made for worthy recipients to enable the Company to meet its charitable obligations. Numbers were then built up again, though between 1899–1900 and 1901–2 there were only four pensioners, receiving £24 a year in total. By 1903–4 to 1907–8 numbers had doubled and the annual amount given to the poor then averaged £44 15s. 6d.[61]

Some assistance was also given to good causes in the city, though here the Company was discriminating. The most spectacular donation was the response in 1803 to the threatened French invasion when £100 was promised to City of York Volunteer Corps. On the other hand in 1871 £10 was subscribed to "the fund in aid of the suffering Peasantry in France, and for the supply of Seed Corn" at the time of the French Civil War; and in 1899 two guineas were sent to the Lord Mayor's appeal "for relieving the distress caused by the war in the Transvaal".[62] Most donations were local and small. Apart from regular subscriptions of one or sometimes two guineas to the County Hospital and the Dispensary, occasional gifts were made to Dr Tempest Anderson's Eye Institution which rented a cottage in the Aldwark yard.[63] In memory of John Wade junior in 1888, £2 was paid to each of the York Blind School, the Blue Coat School, the Dispensary, the County Hospital and the Industrial School.[64] The Company also recognised its obligations as a landlord in Murton, and in 1875 voted £10 for the new parish school in neighbouring Osbaldwick and a further guinea in 1905 for the school enlargement fund.[65]

Occasionally there were refusals. The Company did not subscribe towards the local expenses of the British Association visit to York in 1881 but it did give ten guineas towards the new building for the Yorkshire Institute of Popular Science and Literature in 1883.[66] In 1898 condolences on the death of Sir Joseph Terry were not followed by a donation to his memorial fund but there had been less hesitation two years earlier about subscribing £5 to the Mansion House Fund for a memorial to Canon James Raine, who had long been the Company's annual preacher.[67] In 1912 it declined to contribute to the fund to extinguish the debt on the Salvation Army's building but in August 1914 £5 was donated to the Local War Relief Fund.[68]

The high point of the year was St John the Baptist's Day, 24 June, Midsummer's Day, when the Company processed from their Hall to St. Crux church in accordance with the will of John Straker, to hear a sermon from the minister. Apart from 10s. a year for distribution to the Company's poor, Straker's will left an annual income of £1 to pay for the sermon and 10s. for wine at the Midsummer Feast.[69] This was indicative of the Company's priorities.

The annual cycle of events began with Nomination Day on 20 June, followed by the election of Master, Wardens and Searchers, usually on the morning of 24 June before the service. By the 1870s as numbers dwindled attendance at such meetings was low: in 1880 there were only ten present, including five of the six new members elected the previous year.[70] Even at the swearing-in on 24 June, only the officers and one other were present. With the list of poor pensioners being reduced to nothing a few weeks later, this was the lowest point in the Company's recent history, but even in better times numbers were never very large and attendance at Company feasts was augmented by invited guests.

The main feast was the Midsummer Feast but each occasion in the year — the Quarter Days, Nomination Day and Election Day — all merited a meal, either a dinner or a supper. Added to this was the dinner to follow the viewing of the Company's property every three years. Expenditure could seem excessive, even to the members themselves, and several efforts were made to trim the social calendar. In 1860, the accounts show that out of an income of £189 18s. 8d., £86 8s. 4d. was spent on dinners and suppers. The Midsummer Dinner alone cost £24 0s. 6d.[71] What went into such a dinner can be judged from the menus surviving from the end of the period under review. At a banquet held at the Royal Station Hotel on 23 February 1892, there were fourteen toasts and a six course meal. A special drinking custom on these occasions was the Cool Tankard filled with three pints of ale sweetened with nutmeg, sugar and orange slices and set on the table at the start of the meal; and the Loving Cup, filled with a quart of champagne, two bottles of soda water, a liqueur glass of brandy, two tablespoons of sugar, a pound of powdered ice and a sprig of green borage. This was to be brought to the Master immediately before the Game course.[72] The Company possessed two silver tankards, dating from 1681 and 1683, and a silver cup from 1639. They also possessed a silver salver "to contain the Cup for Drinking the King's Health out of", purchased in 1814 with the proceeds from selling the rest of the company's silver — two bowls, two mugs and a tumbler, dated between 1608 and 1689.[73]

The attempts of the Company to restrain itself from some of these delights were as numerous as they were unsuccessful. Dinners were a way of rewarding men for the time they gave to organising the trade and charitable aspects of the Company's work; and they were a way of demonstrating to their fellow citizens their importance and dignity as an ancient Corporation and integral part of the city's history. In that sense ritual and display were not to be taken lightly. Nevertheless, the Masters were mostly good business men. They were given an allowance for their year of office, which usually ranged between £70 and £100 depending on the Company's financial position, and they were expected to work within it. If they could not, or if the allowance could not be afforded, then dinners had to be trimmed to suppers or, later in the century as eating times and customs changed and ladies were more evident among the guests, even to luncheons and the occasional tea. In 1869, when £180 had been saved "by care and economy" this sum was distributed among the members who had served as officers and paid fines to the Company.[74] In other years, they were concerned to save money in order to augment their charitable giving.[75] After June 1880 as the new members began to play their part, the Company took a more active view of its charitable obligations and resolved in 1890 to cut back the number of annual dinners to five and to restrict the number of guests "in consequence of the increasing demand on our Pension Fund".[76] In 1892 the Master's allowance was cut back to £90 following an overspend of £28 the previous year and in 1895 it was cut again, from £90 to £75, so that the £15 saved could accumulate as a reserve.[77]

At the same time the Company was becoming more self-consciously aware of its history. Ceremonial robes had always played a part in the rituals of the Company but there are few mentions of them in the Court minutes before the 1870s.[78] Later in the century, concern about ceremonial dress increased with rising expectations of how the Company's officers should look when participating in civic ritual. A sub-committee was set up in 1873 "to consider the question of a suitable Robe to be worn by the Master" on the occasion of a Guildhall Banquet in honour of the Lord Mayor of London.[79] In 1877 the Court resolved that the Master should wear his gown at the annual sermon and at Company banquets. The next step came in 1886 when, following a proposal that gowns should be provided for some of the officials, advice was taken from the Merchant Taylors of London and the Wardens were dressed in purple.[80] The incentive might have been to put on a good show in the Jubilee celebrations of 1887, which involved a Thanksgiving Service in the Minster and a civic procession.[81] In 1897, but a little late for the Diamond Jubilee service, the balance left from the Master's allowance was spent on cocked hats for the Company's officers, and John W. Hardcastle (Master in 1891 and 1902) presented a scarlet gown with fur trimmings to be worn by the Master.[82]

Along with the Company's growing pride in personal ceremonial came an increasing awareness of the historic value of the Company's Halls. For much of the nineteenth century the Large Hall was let out to provide a useful income of between £15 and £25 a year, though the burden of repairs made it more of a liability than an asset and the fabric was much neglected with increasingly serious consequences.[83] Despite a resolution of 1804 "that the Hall shall not in future be let to any Person on any Occasion whatever, or used for any Purposes but those of the Company",[84] financial need and charitable disposition coincided when the York Central Diocesan Society applied in 1812 to use the Hall for a National School.[85] At first the school was for boys only, but when they moved to the King's Manor in 1813, a girls' National School was begun and this arrangement lasted for the next sixty years.[86] When the girls were moved to a new mixed school in the Bedern in 1873, the Hall was let for various purposes, including a dancing school,[87] but there was no long-term tenant and the deteriorating fabric made the Hall a liability. In 1894 the Company's neighbour, the brewer J. J. Hunt, even offered to buy the premises, doubtless to convert them to commercial use or even to demolish them, but the Court decided this was "not expedient".[88] Salvation came in the form of the Catholic Apostolic Church, which took the Hall from the end of 1894 and remained there for nearly fifty years.[89] A church notice board appeared on the wall of the Little Hall on the approach from Aldwark and the Court minutes even refer to the Large Hall as "the Chapel".[90]

The Merchant Taylors were now thinking only of the Little Hall as the Company's Hall. In 1901 when they approached the architect Walter Brierley for advice on the restoration of their Hall, they were rather taken aback when he recommended restoring the Large Hall instead. His estimate of £500–£600 to restore the roof and almost as much again for the walls, floor, panelling and fittings settled the matter. This sort of expenditure was well beyond the Company's means and so they continued to patch and mend as best they could.[91] The interior of the Little Hall, though, received increasing attention as a expression of the Company's identity and growing antiquarian interest, and in 1883 the stained glass was restored.[92]

The practice now developed of giving portraits, historical pictures and other artefacts to the Company, the first being a picture of the "New Walk below Ouse Bridge", presented by Thomas Walker "for the adornment of their Hall" in 1884.[93] This idealised eighteenth-century view had recently been transformed with the opening of Skeldergate Bridge in 1881. J. G. Turner followed this in 1885 with ten "Engravings of sundry ancient views of York".[94] Shortly after the death of their father in 1889 the Master (Edward Whitehead) and his sister gave two oil paintings by Henry Cave of Castlegate Postern and Fishergate Postern.[95] More was to follow, not all of it directly relevant to York: in 1886, the Master (Robert Anderson) gave a copy on vellum of the death warrant of Charles I.[96] It was now decided to commission a framed list of all Masters since 1707 and to encourage past masters to donate portraits or photographs of themselves for the collection.[97]

The secretary or clerk to the Company from 1864 to 1900, Joseph Wilkinson, was particularly active in promoting the antiquarian side of this growing collection. His obituary described his "love for the old city and such a pride in her historic monuments and institutions".[98] In 1890 he presented "an Antique Engraving" of the course of the river Ouse from Ouseburn to the confluence with the Trent and the Humber, dated 1725, and later that same year two framed items: an invoice of goods supplied by Frederick Atkinson, who had been Master in 1788, and a Calendar of Malefactors for trial before Lord Kenyon at the March assizes which dated from around the same time.[99] A few months later Wilkinson followed this up with twelve framed engravings of the months of the year taken from the original blocks of the Nuremberg Calendar of 1596.[100] In 1909 his widow gave a collection of framed invitation cards to Corporation banquets.[101] Her husband, who had been Town Clerk, apparently collected everything! Other gifts relevant to York included a lithographic bird's eye view of York presented by George Kirby in 1892 and a series of engravings of the ruined abbeys of Yorkshire, presented by William Houlden at the end of his Mastership in June 1902.[102]

The Company was increasingly aware of its own historic past. The members took the opportunity of a new gate entrance to the premises from Aldwark to commission a stone carving of the Company's coat of arms, and they were delighted to discover in 1893 the lost plate of Henry Cave's engraving of the arms in a shop in Stonegate.[103] The greatest pleasure, though, was when the lost minute books for 1641–80 and 1680–1706 were found in the Guildhall.[104] It was now possible to commission a further list of past Masters for the years 1641-1706 and extracts from the missing books were printed for sale.[105] The Charter granted by Charles II was revered as a historic object as well as a legal document. In 1891 William Houlden presented a framed engraving of the Seal attached to the Charter, and in 1905 George Potter-Kirby presented a framed copy of the Charter itself.[106]

The revival of the Company from the 1880s was also accompanied also by a growing domestication of its rituals for, while the social activities in many respects remained an expression of male sociability, the minutes indicate an awareness of the fact that members had families. Though doubtless many a Master's lady had supported him behind the scenes, in 1891 the vote of thanks to the outgoing master, Thomas Rodwell, was extended "also to Mrs Rodwell who had so gracefully assisted him in the duties of that office" and when George Arthur Potter-Kirby became Master in 1911 at the age of 32, he felt able to say that although he had no wife he had a mother — who had, of course, been

Master's wife on three occasions already.[107] As the younger generation took over, attitudes were changing. In 1895 the Master, R. W. Anderson junior, married during his year of office and in 1904 a silver bowl, spoon, fork and serviette ring were presented to Mabel Gertrude Beckwith in recognition that this was the first recorded time that a child had been born to a Master in office.[108] The presentation took place during an outing to Scarborough. These social outings were but one of the ways in which families were brought together in an extended circle of sociability. The first summer outing recorded in the minutes was to Bolton Woods in May 1893 and in subsequent years such outings became a regular summer occurrence.[109]

In addition to their own ceremonials and rituals, the Merchant Taylors were also important in civic life. As one of the two surviving ancient guilds of York, they expected to play their part alongside the Merchant Adventurers and the City Corporation in marking civic and national occasions. Such events became more frequent and more elaborate as the nineteenth century progressed. The Court minutes give little indication of the Company's role within the city until 1881, when an invitation was received to take part in the civic procession at the opening of Skeldergate Bridge.[110] The next major occasion was the Thanksgiving Service in the Minster and Civic Procession on the occasion of the Queen's Jubilee in June 1887.[111] Royal occasions now became the fashion. Whereas the coronation of Queen Victoria had been marked by gifts to the poor and there had been no loyal address to the Queen on the death of Prince Albert, letters of condolence to the Queen and Prince and Princess of Wales in 1892 on the death of the Duke of Clarence were duly sent and elicited formal replies which were loyally framed and hung on the Hall walls.[112] The Jubilee of 1897 was another occasion for a major civic display, with a service at the Minster, Lord Mayor's procession and of course a Loyal Address.[113] A member of the Company, Christopher Annakin Milward, was Lord Mayor in that year and so was awarded a knighthood. On the death of Queen Victoria the Company was represented at the Guildhall for the proclamation of Edward VII, followed a few days later by attendance at a civic memorial service in the Minster and then an Address of sympathy from the Company to Edward VII. The acknowledgment was duly framed and hung in the Hall.[114] The coronation of Edward VII was significant because George Potter-Kirby was Sheriff in that year and responsible for the civic celebrations.[115] On the death of Edward VII there were similar rituals – the proclamation of George V, the memorial service in the Minster and the Address to the new king.[116] On a lighter note, the Master agreed to appear as himself in the York Pageant of 1909.[117] The Merchant Taylors were indeed part of the pageantry of York.

This was, however, only half the story, for the real interweaving of Company and City is to be seen in the roles paid by the members themselves in civic life. Sir Christopher Milward's service as twice Lord Mayor was but the climax of a long relationship between members of the Company and the city. Between 1780 and 1914 the Company produced four Lord Mayors of whom three had also been Sheriffs; five other Sheriffs, and six Aldermen, all of whom had also been Sheriffs. In addition there was a sprinkling of councillors, both before and after 1835. However, it may be significant that no Master of the Company who first became Master after 1835 went on to become Lord Mayor. The last was Richard Evers, Master in 1835 and 1850, who was also Sheriff in 1849, an Alderman from 1851 and Lord Mayor in 1853 and 1860. On his death in May 1871, the cathedral bell of Great Peter tolled in mourning.[118] The only comparable figure for the latter half of the century, Sir Christopher Annakin Milward, was never Master. He was elected a councillor for Bootham ward in 1885–92 and then became an alderman. He was Sheriff in 1890 and Lord Mayor in 1896 and 1897.[119]

Beyond formal politics there were other networks of service and sociability which brought together the men who were Merchant Taylors in the nineteenth century, though they came from diverse political and religious backgrounds. Richard Evers was a Liberal; George Potter-Kirby (Master in 1888, 1899 and 1907) was a Conservative and Milward was described as "a staunch Churchman and an energetic member of the Conservative party".[120] Thomas Rodwell (Master in 1884, 1890 and 1900) was for 35 years deacon of Salem Congregational Chapel. The Whiteheads were prominent Wesleyans, W. J. Whitehead having been the first treasurer of the Centenary Chapel trust in 1840. Robert Buckle (Master in 1893) was a Wesleyan Sunday school teacher and class leader, and a member at Centenary Chapel since 1859. "That chapel knew him for over sixty years and was the centre of his life. All his life was wrapped up in Methodism", recalled his obituarist.[121] Robert Anderson was churchwarden at St. Martin-le-Grand, as well as a feoffee of the church, as were his son, R. W. Anderson, George Arthur Potter-Kirby and Christopher Annakin Milward. William Catton (Master 1846 and 1854) was a senior feoffee of St. Crux. Thomas Rodwell and George Potter-Kirby were both members of the Ancient Society of York Florists. The Potter-Kirbys and Milward were freemasons. William Catton, George Potter-Kirby, and Christopher Annakin Milward were all directors of the York Gas Company. R. W. Anderson senior, Robert Anderson, George Potter-Kirby and Christopher Annakin Milward were all involved with the Grand Yorkshire Gala. Robert Anderson was a governor of Bootham Park Asylum and the York County Hospital, as were George Potter-Kirby, his son George Arthur, and Christopher Annakin Milward. The same names recur. By the later nineteenth century those family firms which provided leadership to the Merchant Taylors were also central to the social and philanthropic networks of the city. They were never a closed group, and the Company may not have been their principal interest –

clearly for Milward it was not – but they were a defining group.[122]

Others operated in different circles, sometimes partly overlapping. Robert Bousfield, admitted in 1888, had begun in York as a journeyman tailor before starting out on his own in lowly Margaret Street and working his way up to "a high class trade" in Castlegate. He had been both Searcher and Warden, but never Master. His obituary noted how he "was prominently identified with the Brethren" of the Company, yet in character "He was a quiet, unassuming gentleman, and took no part in Municipal or Imperial politics, though he always evinced a keen interest in whatever was for the advancement of morality and the public weal".[123] W. T. Beckwith ran the family firm begun by his father in 1852. "He was never identified with public affairs, but was among the best known citizens and freemen of York".[124] W. J. Whitehead declined to be appointed an alderman and like his father devoted his spare time to Wesleyanism. He was a trustee of the York Charities and "a liberal supporter of numerous religious, philanthropic and educational agencies, and in every respect his career was a most worthy and useful one".[125] Of William Catton, woollen draper of Pavement and trustee of Haughton's school, William Camidge wrote: "He was a man of active habits and genial disposition, being greatly respected as a tradesman, and by an extensive circle of friends".[126] Richard Evers was "a gentleman of benevolent disposition and supported our local charities in a ready and liberal manner".[127] Obituaries of an earlier age used a different style of language to convey the same sentiments. John Walker, Master in 1792, was "highly esteemed for his integrity and exemplary piety".[128] Of Robert Rhodes, Master in 1797 and Lord Mayor in 1808, it was recalled that "the urbanity of his manners was commensurate with the integrity of his conduct".[129] Though there were some poor businessmen like Stephen Priestman (Master 1798) and even dishonest ones like John Lee (Master 1803),[130] most would probably have deserved the words bestowed on Frederick Atkinson, Master in 1788, whose invoice was to be displayed on the Company's Hall wall a century later: "He was ingenious, sensible, modest and humane; a dutiful Son; an affectionate Husband; an indulgent Parent; and an honest Man".[131]

NOTES

1. *Report of the Inquiry by the Government Commissioners into the existing state of the Corporation of York ... Extracted from the York Herald. With an Index. Also an Appendix, containing a brief notice of the Merchants' Company and the Merchant Tailors' Company ...* (York [1833]), pp.79, 80.

2. BI, MTA 2/4, Court Minute Book, f.176r, 15 December 1780 (added at the end of the Minute Book).

3. BI, MTA 2/5, Court Minute Book, f.54r, 25 March 1789.

4. See for example BI, MTA 2/5, f.72v, 29 August 1793.

5. BI, MTA 2/5, f.98v, 28 November 1799. This was more easily said than done, for in 1806 there was another resolution to seek counsel's opinion on "whether the Men who come to York for the Purpose of vending Cloth, can be prevented" – BI, MTA 2/5, f.122v, 16 January 1806.

6. In 1806 they called a joint meeting with the Linen Drapers, Hosiers and Cutters to consider what to do about hawkers and pedlars – "they being considered a great Injury to the fair Trader" (BI, MTA 2/5, f.124v, 6 May 1806). In fact they were unable to collect sufficient evidence to secure a conviction and the matter seems to have lapsed. For the Thursday Market, see W. Camidge, *York Guilds* (York, 1905), p.31.

7. BI, MTA 2/5, f.123v, 6 February 1806.

8. BI, MTA 6/3, Admissions of abled masters, 1751–1862, f.1r.

9. BI, MTA 2/5, f.110v, 18 November 1802; MTA 6/3, 24 February 1803.

10. BI, MTA 2/5, ff. 119v and 120v, 28 February and 24 June 1805; MTA 3/7, Minute book 1847–1855, ff.42r–43v, list of members of the Merchant Taylors' Company 1790–1844; MTA 6/3, 24 June 1805.

11. BI, MTA 2/5, f.156v, 23 May 1814. Whiteley, who had served his apprenticeship and therefore had to pay the lowest entry fee, took his freedom on 22 February 1821 – see MTA 3/7, f.43v.

12. BI, MTA 2/5, f.158v, 17 November 1814. The policy of exerting the Company's control continued. In February 1815 John Poole agreed not to expose any more woollen goods, or he would take his Freedom – MTA 2/5, f.158v, 23 February 1815. He did this on 15 February 1816 – MTA 3/7, f.43v.

13. BI, MTA 2/5, f.166v, 7 October 1816.

14. *York Courant*, 28 February 1814.

15. BI, MTA 2/5, f.171v, 9 April 1818.

16. BI, MTA 3/7, f.43v, 16 March 1840.

17. PP 1835 (116), *Municipal Corporations in England and Wales, Report on the Corporation of the Company of the Merchant Tailors of the City of York*, p.1765; BI, MTA 2/6, Court Minute Book, ff.70v–72r, 23 May 1844, Report of the committee appointed to enquire into "the circumstances of the needy and poor members of the Company". The latter names 27 members, but the Minutes suggest a further two (John Dodgson and Benjamin Settle) who had been omitted from this list – MTA 2/6, ff.71v –72r, 23 May 1844.

18. The last female master to be mentioned in the register of apprentices was Mary Kilner who took Jane Binns, daughter of John Binns of Heaton, Bradford, as an apprentice mantua maker on 23 March 1797 (BI, MTA 9/2, f.61r). Ann Boddy, the last woman to become a master, is recorded in the MTA 3/7 list as dead.

19. William Slade Walker, son of Joseph Walker (Master in 1817, 1831 and 1839), apprenticed to his father in 1820, admitted to the Company in 1831; John Hollins jnr, son of John Hollins (Master 1823, 1834, 1841), admitted to the Company in 1831; and William Coupland, son of James Coupland (Master in 1844), admitted to the Company in 1841 - BI, MTA 9/2, Register of Apprentices 1751-1862, f.76r, 5 September 1820; MTA 6/3, 20 and 24 June 1831, 24 June 1841. All three had financial problems: Hollins, snr, had to mortgage his house to the Company for £220 in 1840 and in 1853 the loan was called in shortly before his death - BI, MTA 2/6 ff.49v and 50r, 27 August and 23 September 1840; MTA 3/7 f.29r, 7 May 1853. For Coupland and Walker, see below.

20. BI, MTA 9/2, ff.76r-79r.

21. BI, MTA 2/6, ff.10v and 11v, 17 February and 20 June 1831.

22. BI, MTA 6/3, *passim*.

23. BI, MTA 2/6, f.138r, 27 May 1870.

24. BI, MTA 2/6, f.170v, 23 May 1878. He had already tried earlier, in 1866, so the young man could claim his freedom, but Court had postponed the decision and it had not been returned to — MTA 2/6, f.120r, 22 February 1866.

25. BI, MTA 3/11, Draft Minute Book, f.1r, notes.

26. BI, MTA 3/7, Draft Minute Book, ff.26v-27r, 5 April 1852 [sic, actually 1853]: Anderson was Master in 1860, 1868, 1876 and 1882; Annakin in 1861 and 1869; and Atkinson in 1862, 1870 and 1877.

27. BI, MTA 2/6, f.155r, 24 June 1874. Nicholson was the son of George Nicholson (Master in 1859, 1867 and 1875); Anderson was the eldest son of R. W. Anderson (Master in 1860, 1868 and 1876).

28. BI, MTA 2/6, ff.174v-175r, 20 February 1879.

29. BI, MTA 6/3, *passim*.

30. BI, MTA 2/7, Court Minute Book, f.55v, 23 February 1888.

31. BI, MTA 3/7, Draft Minute Book, ff.33v and 39r, 23 February 1854 and 1 March 1855; MTA 3/8, Draft Minute Book, ff.10r and 18v, 13 May 1857 and 20 June 1859; MTA 2/6, Court Minute Book, ff.110r and 128v, 18 May 1864 and 14 May 1868; MTA 8/3, Letter from member requesting help 1854, James Masser to The Master, Wardens, & Searchers & Members of the Merchant Tailors Company, 29 November 1854. For his bankruptcy, see *Yorkshire Gazette*, 16 December 1848. His father, John Masser, had been admitted to the Company in 1805 and his brother, Thomas, in 1860 — BI, MTA 6/3, 28 February 1805 and 28 February 1860.

32. Details taken from Court Minute Books, BI, MTA 2/4-2/7 and Draft Minute Books, MTA 3/7-3/8, *passim*. See also *Yorkshire Gazette*, 13 October 1860 and York Reference Library, York Scrapbook 1852-1891, p.203.

33. York Reference Library, Card Index to newspapers, inserted notes under R. W.

Anderson. See also *Yorkshire Gazette*, 24 October 1846 (W. Evers), 20 May 1871 (R. Evers), 25 August 1888 (J. H. Anderson), 2 July 1887 (R. W. Anderson), 10 February 1906 (Milward), 18 June 1906 (R. Anderson), 12 January 1918 (Hayler), 2 January 1953 (R. W. Anderson, jnr); *Yorkshire Herald*, 5 February 1906 (Milward), 23 June 1906 (R. Anderson); York Scrapbook 1914–1923, p.181 (Hardcastle); *Yorkshire Evening Press*, 2 January 1953, 1 June 1965, 2 October 1968 (the business).

34. *Yorkshire Gazette*, 14 May 1825, 11 April 1840, 28 July 1849, 3 January 1880 (G. Nicholson), 25 June 1887 (G. Nicholson, jnr), 11 October 1924 (G. Potter-Kirby); *Yorkshire Evening Press*, 25 March 1967 (G. A. Potter-Kirby); *Yorkshire Who's Who* (London 1912), entry for George Potter-Kirby. There was a different George Nicholson, who moved to premises in Coney Street in 1823 and died in 1850 (*Yorkshire Gazette*, 7 April 1821, 10 May 1834, 1 May 1850).

35. *Yorkshire Gazette*, 18 November 1882 (Todd), 19 January 1884 (W. Whitehead), 10 December 1892 (W. J. Whitehead), 13 May 1905 (J. Whitehead), *York Herald*, 24 August 1889 (W. J. Whitehead), 3 February 1928 (E. Whitehead). For William Whitehead, snr, see passing references in J. Lyth, *Glimpses of Early Methodism in York* (York and London, 1885), pp.193, 259, 264, 272. See also *York and District Directory* (York, 1900), p.190.

36. Leak was elected sheriff in 1884 and was a leading Wesleyan in York for 57 years – see *York Herald*, 26 March 1887. Leak and Thorp became a major department store in York during the twentieth century, along with W. P. Brown, founded by Henry Rhodes Brown in 1891. Brown, like Leak, was a leading citizen of York, Lord Mayor in 1914, but not a Merchant Taylor – see York Reference Library, MS. Y352, T. P. Cooper, Lord Mayors and Sheriffs of the City of York.

37. BI, MTA 3/12, Minute Book, ff.5r and 40r, 18 February 1909 and 22 July 1912; *Yorkshire Gazette*, 20 July 1912, 27 June 1914.

38. BI, MTA 3/11, Draft Minute Book, notes inside front cover.

39. BI, MTA Add 3/7, Digest of charities chargeable on the Havergarths.

40. BI, MTA 2/5, Court Minute Book, f.221v, 6 April 1829; MTA 11/2, Schedule of Deeds, 19 October 1831, 9 April 1832, 14 May 1832 and 9 November 1835.

41. BI, MTA 2/5, f.126v, 20 November 1806; MTA Add 17/3/2, 'An Account of Benefactions to Poor Members of the Merchant Taylors' Company and Other Persons who, although not Members of the Company, were in some measure, connected with the Trade'.

42. BI, MTA 3/11, Draft Minute Book, ff.95v–96r, 23 August 1900.

43. BI, MTA 2/5, ff.65r, 66r and 130v, 17 November 1791, 16 February 1792 and 19 November 1807.

44. BI, MTA 2/5, ff.79r, 87r, 87v, 88v and 151v, 19 February 1795, 24 November 1796, 23 February 1797, 20 June 1797 and 18 February 1813.

45. BI, MTA 2/5, ff.138r and 147v, 17 August 1809 and 20 February 1812.

46. BI, MTA 2/5, f.220v, 22 December 1828.

47. BI, MTA 2/6, ff.71v, 72r and 75r, 23 May and 5 September 1844.

48. BI, MTA 2/6, ff.55v–56r, 11 January 1842.

49. BI, MTA 3/7, Draft Minute Book, note of income inside back cover.

50. BI, MTA 2/6, ff.97r–98r, 16 November 1849.

51. BI, MTA 2/6, f.98r, 16 November 1849.

52. BI, MTA 2/6, ff.43v, 52v and 101v, 23 May 1839, 27 May 1841 and 29 August 1850; MTA 2/7, f. 2r, 23 August 1880; *York Herald*, 12 October 1850.

53. Walker may have been suffering from mental illness for, if he were 14 when apprenticed to his father in 1820, he would have been about 36 when he first received aid in 1842 and only 59 when he died in the Asylum – BI, MTA 9/2, Register of Apprentices, f.76r, 5 September 1820; MTA 6/3, Admissions of abled masters, 1831; MTA 2/6, ff. 61v, 71v, and 117v, 25 August 1842, 23 May 1844 and 20 June 1865.

54. BI, MTA 3/7, f.25v, 24 February 1853; MTA 3/8, f. 19v, 24 June 1859; MTA 2/6, f.169r, 22 November 1877; MTA 2/7, ff.119r–119v and 123v, 20 June 1893 and 24 August 1893.

55. Coupland's apprenticeship is not recorded in BI, MTA 9/2, but he was admitted to the Company by servitude – MTA 6/3, 24 June 1841; MTA 3/7, f.32v, 1 December 1853; MTA 3/8, ff.3v, 13r, 18v and 25v, 21 February 1856, 11 May 1858, 20 June 1859 and 20 June 1860; MTA 2/6, f.144r, 27 November 1871; MTA 2/7, ff.44v–45r and 52r, 24 March and 29 August 1887.

56. See the list in BI, MTA Add 17/2/3, York Charities Register Committee, 1911.

57. BI, MTA 3/12, Minute Book, ff.19v–20r, 20v–21r, 21v–22r, and 22v with insert, 14 October, 21 November, and 5 and 15 December 1910.

58. BI, MTA Add 17/2/2, Correspondence re York Charities Register, William Houlden to H. W. Badger, 17 January 1911. John Waind, tailor of High Ousegate, was admitted 1879 and died 1884 (MTA 2/6, f.175r, 20 February 1879 and MTA 2/7, f.25r, 21 February 1884); his son, Frederick Waind, was admitted 20 November 1884, Master 1895, and died in 1910 (MTA 2/7, f.29v, 20 November 1884 and MTA 3/12, f.13r, 27 April 1910).

59. BI, MTA 3/11, ff.16r, 19r and 95r–95v, 20 June, 22 August 1895 and 23 August 1900; MTA 3/12. f.33r, 15 December 1911.

60. BI, MTA Add 17/2/1, York Charities Register Committee; MTA 3/12, ff.26r, 34r and 37r, 18 May 1911, 22 February and 30 May 1912.

61. BI, MTA Add. 17/1/1, Charity Commission Returns to the Charity Commissioners.

62. BI, MTA 2/5, f.114v, 15 August 1803; MTA 2/6, f.141r, 23 February 1871; MTA 3/11, f. 87v, 22 September 1899.

63. BI, MTA 2/6, ff. 157v and 169v, 18 February 1875 and 22 November 1877.

64. BI, MTA 2/7, f. 56r, 23 February 1888.

65. BI, MTA 2/6, f.160r, 19 August 1875; MTA 3/11, f.156r, 23 November 1905.

66. BI, MTA 2/7, ff.4v, 6r and 20v–21r, 24 February and 19 May 1881, and 24 May 1883.

67. BI, MTA 3/11, ff.58v–59r, 65v and 41v, 18 January and 20 June 1898, and 13

August 1896.

68. BI, MTA 3/12, ff.43r-3v and 58v, 5 September 1912 and 20 August 1914.

69. BI, MTA 2/5, ff.227v-228v, Copy of John Straker's will, died October 1669. This land, amounting to a cottage and about twelve acres in four closes, lay in Holtby parish, just beyond Murton – MTA Add 17/3/3, Appointment of new feoffees under the will of John Straker, 5 February 1897, and G. Lawton, *Collections relative to Churches and Chapels in the Diocese of York* (new edition, York, 1842), pp.444-45.

70. BI, MTA 2/7, f.1r, 21 June 1880.

71. BI, MTA 12/3, Annual Accounts, 1827-1869.

72. BI, MTA Add 19/1/5, Menu for Banquet at Royal Station Hotel, Tuesday 13 Feb. 1892; MTA Add 19/1/6, Memorandums.

73. BI, MTA 2/5, f.158v, 17 November 1814; MTA Add 13/7, List of Plate, 1868. The only other silver possessed by the Company in the nineteenth century was a snuff box purchased in 1839.

74. BI, MTA 2/6, f.134r, 28 May 1869.

75. BI, MTA 2/6, ff.97v-98r, 16 November 1849.

76. BI, MTA 2/7, f.84r, 22 May 1890.

77. BI, MTA 2/7, ff.111v-112r, 17 November 1892; MTA 3/11, f.12r-v, 19 February 1895. In 1914 it was cut again to a mere £50, but this time because the accounts were in deficit – MTA 3/12, ff.56r and 58v, 20 February and 20 August 1914.

78. In 1794, John Haxby, who was to be Master in 1796, was fined 2s. 6d. for not wearing his robe when sworn in as a Searcher and another 10s. the following year for appearing four days in the Hall without his gown - BI, MTA 2/5, ff.76r and 83r, 24 June 1794 and 12 November 1795. New hats with silver lace were provided for the beadle and porter in 1819 – MTA 2/5, f.178v, 18 November 1819.

79. BI, MTA 2/6, f.152v, 11 September 1873.

80. BI, MTA 2/7, ff.42r and 43r-v, 25 November 1886 and 24 February 1887.

81. BI, MTA 2/7, ff.48v-49r, 26 May 1887.

82. BI, MTA 3/11, f.52v-53r, 5 July 1897. However, the members left "in abeyance" the suggestion of George Potter-Kirby that they should subscribe towards a badge of precious metal embodying the Company's arms, to be worn by the Master with his gown – MTA 3/11, ff.56r-v and 57r-v, 26 August and 18 November 1897.

83. See M. Mennim, *The Merchant Taylors' Hall* (York 2000), chapter 8.

84. BI, MTA 2/5, f.116v, 20 June 1804.

85. BI, MTA 2/5, f.147v, 23 March 1812.

86. *VCH York*, pp.441, 449.

87. BI, MTA 2/7, f.38v, 20 May 1886.

88. BI, MTA 2/7, f.127r-v, 22 February 1894.

89. BI, MTA 2/7, ff.131r-v and 132r-v, 14 September and 22 November 1894.

90. BI, MTA 3/12, ff.42r-43r, and 31r, 5 September 1912 and 16 November 1911. There is a photograph of the notice-board in Mennim, p.172.

91. BI, MTA Add 14/2, Walter H. Brierley to The Master, Wardens and Fellowship of the Society of Merchant Taylors of the City of York, 19 September 1901; MTA 3/11, ff.102v–103v and 112r–114r, 16 May and 20 September 1901.

92. BI, MTA 2/7, f.19r, 22 February 1883.

93. BI, MTA 2/7, f.25r, 21 February 1884.

94. BI, MTA 2/7, f.34v, 20 August 1885.

95. BI, MTA 2/7, f.78r–v, 21 November 1889.

96. BI, MTA 2/7, f.41v, 25 November 1886.

97. BI, MTA 2/7, ff.83v–84r, 85v, 89r and 95r, 22 May, 20 June and 29 September 1890, and 21 May 1891.

98. *Yorkshire Gazette*, 31 March 1900.

99. BI, MTA 2/7, ff.84r–v and 91r, 22 May and 20 November 1890. Kenyon received his peerage in 1788.

100. BI, MTA 2/7, f.98r, 20 June 1891.

101. BI, MTA 3/12, f.6r, 20 May 1909.

102. BI, MTA 2/7, f.107v, 19 May 1892; MTA 3/11, f.121r, 20 June 1902.

103. BI, MTA 2/7, ff.47r–v, 53v and 125v, 28 April and 14 November 1887, and 16 November 1893.

104. BI, MTA 3/11, f.104r, 16 May 1901.

105. BI, MTA 3/11, ff.133v, 143r and 149v, 19 November 1903, 18 August 1904 and 19 May 1905.

106. BI, MTA 2/7, f.92v, 19 February 1891; MTA 3/11, f.150r, 19 May 1905. The growing antiquarian outlook of the period, reflected in the interests of the members and of the age, also found expression in the social activities of the Company, especially at the November Dinner in 1893. This was held "Atte ye house of Halliwell y'clept ye North Eastern" and the menu was similarly cast in pseudo-Old English, with toasts to "Ye Queene" and "Ye Good Wishes to ye Antient Companye of ye Merchante Taylors". The eight course meal included oysters, and the cheese was "from ye Yorkshire Dales". Drink, as was customary, was from "Ye Antient Tankarde" containing "ye Spicey Beer" and of course there was "Ye Lovinge Cup" – MTA Add 19/1/5, Menu for Dinner, 3 November 1893.

107. BI, MTA 2/7, f.98v, 24 June 1891; MTA 3/12, f.29r, press cutting inserted in minutes, 21 June 1911.

108. BI, MTA 3/11, ff.12v and 138v–139v, 19 February 1895 and 20 June 1904.

109. BI, MTA 2/7, ff.117v–118r, 20 June 1893, and printed leaflets in MTA 3/11 *passim*.

110. BI, MTA 2/7, f.5r–v, 4 March 1881.

111. BI, MTA 2/7, ff.48v–49r, 26 May 1887.

112. BI, MTA 2/6, f.40v, 20 June 1838; MTA 2/7, ff.104r–106r, 20 January and 18 February 1892.

113. BI, MTA 3/11, ff.45v and 47v–49r, 19 May and 21 June 1897, and insert at f.50r, 22 June 1897.

114. BI, MTA 3/11, ff.97v–98r, 98v–100v and 102r, 25 January, 2 and 21 February, and 16 May 1901.

115. BI, MTA 3/11, ff.122v–123r, 26 June 1902.

116. BI, MTA 3/12, ff.13v and 15r–16r, 10 and 26 May 1910.

117. BI, MTA 3/12, f.5v, 20 May 1909.

118. *Yorkshire Gazette*, 20 May 1871.

119. York City Library, MS Y352, T. P. Cooper, "Lord Mayors and Sheriffs of the City of York".

120. *Yorkshire Herald*, 5 February 1906.

121. *Yorkshire Gazette*, 22 June 1918.

122. *Yorkshire Gazette*, 20 May 1871 (Evers), 16 March 1912 (Rodwell), 11 October 1924 (G. Potter-Kirby); *Yorkshire Herald*, 5 February 1906 (Milward), 18 June 1906 (R. Anderson), *York Herald*, 24 August 1889 (Whitehead); *Yorkshire Evening Press*, 2 January 1953 (R. W. Anderson), 25 March 1967 (G. A. Potter-Kirby); William Camidge, *Ye Old Streete of Pavemente* (York, n.d.), p. 215 (Catton).

123. *Yorkshire Gazette*, 6 August 1904; BI, MTA 3/11, f.141r, 2 August 1904.

124. *Yorkshire Gazette*, 27 June 1914.

125. *York Herald*, 24 August 1889.

126. Camidge, *Ye Old Streete of Pavemente*, p.215.

127. *Yorkshire Gazette*, 20 May 1871.

128. *York Courant*, 31 May 1813.

129. *York Courant*, 16 August 1813.

130. For Priestman, see Brotherton Library, University of Leeds, Yorkshire Society of Friends Archives, K. 2.2, York Monthly Meeting, Disownments, Stephen Priestman to the Friends of York Monthly Meeting, 6 March 1805 and *York Courant*, 9 December 1805. For Lee, see Yorkshire Society of Friends Archives, D.7, York Monthly Meeting Minute Book, 1793–1815, 1 May 1805 and BI, MTA 2/5, ff.132v and 134v, 12 May and 25 November 1808 and MTA Add 23/15, Case for the Opinion of Mr Raine.

131. *York Courant*, 22 August 1803.

THE MERCHANT TAYLORS IN THE TWENTIETH CENTURY[1]

E Royle

Between the Great War of 1914-1918 and the end of the twentieth century the structure, purpose and finances of the Merchant Taylors' Company were transformed. At the beginning of the period, the members were, with one exception, still all tailors, though recruitment since 1879 had been mainly by invitation and Order of the Court. By the end of the period the requirement was only that a reasonable proportion of the membership should be connected with the trade. At the start of the twentieth century, the Company Hall was the Little Hall and the problems of conservation and its associated costs had only half-heartedly been faced. At the end of the century the Large Hall had been fully restored and the premises had become a major source of income.

Pressures working this transformation in the Company's history were partly external. Inflation during the First World War and, especially, after the Second World War, undermined the value of traditional investments as well as of the benefits paid out to the Company's pensioners, and the development of state welfare in any case made the traditional charitable activities of the Company less relevant. The rise in historical consciousness in the city and Company alike in the late nineteenth century was matched in the twentieth century by the growth of conservation movements which both offered new opportunities to and imposed additional responsibilities on the Company as curator of a major historical building. Internal changes within the tailoring trades were also making their impact. The Company had been able to survive as a guild of master tailors thanks to the continued existence of a number of family tailoring and drapery firms within the city. Gradually during the course of the twentieth century the majority of these closed, either completely, or as part of mergers with national companies often based in Leeds.

MEMBERS AND THEIR ACTIVITIES

At first recruitment to the Company continued as it had since 1879. Six new members — three prominent local tailors, two woollen drapers and a linen draper — received their freedoms by Order of the Court in 1916 and subsequently furnished the Company with its Masters between 1920 and 1925.[2] Exceptionally, following the precedent set only for the former secretary, Joseph

Wilkinson, in 1888, the chaplain (Canon John Watson) and secretary (Henry Walter Badger) were elected as non-trade members in 1917.[3] The ceremonial and social life of members also continued in the pattern set in the late Victorian period. In June 1921 at the triennial View Day, fifty were entertained by the Master to a "sumptuous feast" which was followed by a ladies versus gentlemen cricket match. It is not reported who won.[4] The Master continued to receive an annual allowance of £50, supplemented in View Day years, to cover such expenditure.[5]

If the 1920s represented, as in so many other aspects of life, an attempt to get back to the normality of the pre-war years, by 1930 there was a growing awareness that this was no longer possible. In that year a Minute to the effect that to elect anyone a member who was outside the trade of draper or tailor was against the Charter, suggests that the issue of a wider membership had been raised, though it was not until 1936 that the decision was finally taken to admit non-trade members as a matter of course.[6] Before this, in 1926 and 1931, further batches of four new members, all of them tailors or drapers, had been elected to introduce new blood to replenish the ranks depleted by the deaths of such stalwarts of the Company as George Potter-Kirby, admitted in 1885 and Master for his fourth term in 1917; James Cattle, admitted in 1893 and Master for the second time in 1904; Edward Whitehead, admitted 1885 and Master for the fourth time in 1912; and William Houlden, admitted 1885 and Master for the second time in 1901.[7]

The change in policy was precipitated by the death of the secretary, H. W. Badger, in 1934. Badger, who had held the office since 1900, was a respected city solicitor and partner in a local firm. On his death at the age of 84 he was succeeded as secretary by another solicitor, Herbert Edward Harrowell, son of a Wesleyan minister and, at the time of his appointment, Lord Mayor of York. Harrowell might have been expected in any case to have brought new ideas to the Company, but what was desirable became a necessity when the financial consequences of Badger's death were realised.[8]

In 1900, shortly after Badger became secretary, £1000 was invested by the Company with Edwin Gray on the security of Yorkshire Insurance Company shares. The terms were varied over the years, and by 1929 when Gray died the sum stood at £750. The interest of about £35 a year continued to be paid into the Company's accounts, in Gray's name, until 1932, then by Gray's representatives and finally in 1934 in the name of "late Gray". However, it appears that on Gray's death Badger, who was in personal and business difficulties, had retained the loan, unsecured. On his own death in 1934, his liabilities were greatly in excess of his assets and the estate was declare bankrupt. After adjustments for interest, all the Company received was £118 0s. 2d.[9]

This loss of a major investment coincided with the increasingly urgent need to raise funds for the restoration of the Company's Hall. This had been talked about since the late 1920s and plans had been commissioned, but each new initiative had failed over the question of funding. The matter was now addressed with greater urgency. The Master's annual allowance was cut from £50 to £35 and all members agreed to pay an annual subscription to the Company of one guinea: 29 payments were received in the financial year ending 24 June 1936, which just about made up for the loss of interest on the former Gray loan.[10] In October 1935, proposals were put forward that in future nominations for membership could include up to twelve "men who are not in the occupation of Taylors" in addition to "suitable members of the trade". Harrowell brought forward a list of names. Twelve new members were duly sworn in. Apart from Harrowell himself and Canon Gill, the new chaplain, the names included F. T. Penty, the architect, W. H. Birch, the builder, G. S. Bellerby, the decorator and A. Harrower, shortly to become General Manager of the Yorkshire Insurance Company. These were men with business expertise likely to be able to serve the Company in a wider capacity than had hitherto been the case. At the same meeting of the Annual Court in 1936, a sub-committee of six, including three of the new members, was set up "to go thoroughly into the question of the renovation of the Hall".[11] The following year, Harrowell was elected Master, the first non-trade member to hold this office; his immediate successor, Harrower, was another non-trade member. There was no further major election of members until the Second World War was drawing to a close in 1944. On this occasion six tailors and five non-tailors were elected, bringing total membership up to nineteen tailors and fourteen non-tailors.[12]

The next major change in membership policy came in 1962 when it was decided to extend membership to "outsiders". There had always been some members who did not live in York but with a few exceptions these were members of York families such as the Whiteheads who had retired to Scarborough. The target now was Leeds and some of the leading figures in the national tailoring trade. Such "outsiders" were not to exceed half the total membership and, as the rule requiring half the membership to have trade connections remained in place and neither category of outside membership was to outnumber the equivalent of inside members, that strictly limited the number of non-York people from outside the trade. The intention was that in extending the membership, the Company would continue to recruit active members, whether from the trade or not.[13]

Some York trade members may have retained doubts about the new policy.

One asked "whether the Company had ever actively searched for practising tailors now working in the City who may feel able to accept membership?" The answer suggests the distance the Company had travelled since the days when it had compelled local tailors to take their freedoms: "there had never been any necessity to search for members in this way" — which was true only because of the decision in 1935 to recruit from outside the trade. There was also concern about expense: the sort of people who had replaced the employees and members of the old family firms, the shop managers for the new multiple firms, tended to be moved frequently and they might not "feel able to accept Mastership when their turn arose". In other words, they would have neither the time nor money. The implication was that it was better to go for the owners of the multiples if they had an interest in the traditions and history of the Company. The five members elected in March 1963 included Arnold Burton (of Montague Burton) and Gordon May (of Maenson). Bernard Lyons (of John Collier) became a member shortly afterwards.[14]

This broadening of the potential membership was inevitable if the Company were to survive. As Harrowell explained when soliciting donations in 1937, the decision had been "brought about by the gradually lessening number of tailors in the City eligible by virtue of their occupation for membership" as a result of increasing competition from multiple shops.[15] Family firms which had been the bedrock of Company membership were gradually disappearing or being merged with the multiples. Whiteheads on Foss Bridge had been taken over by the Bradford Manufacturing Company as early as 1900. G. A. Potter-Kirby sold Kirby and Nicholson to Rowntrees of Scarborough during the Second World War — Ralph Rowntree was admitted a member in 1949 — but the shop in Coney Street then passed to Debenhams in the 1970s. R. W. Anderson & Sons sold their Coney Street premises to meet death duties in 1969.[16]

The changing economy of York was reflected in the membership of the Company. When the new University of York was established in 1963, several of the leading citizens who had worked to that end were also connected with the Company and so it was perhaps natural that the first Vice-Chancellor, Lord James of Rusholme, should be admitted in 1964. These ties were subsequently strengthened both through members of staff, with Mathematics lecturer, Victor Hale, becoming Master in 1979, and through lay members of the University Council or Court, such as Arthur Gladwin, Master in 1954 and 1964, and Richard Wheway, Master in 1978.[17]

The move towards non-trade members to some extent began to blur the distinction between the Merchant Taylors, a trade guild in origin, and the Merchant Adventurers, which appealed to a wider membership among the business

166

men of York. Of the new members admitted in 1936, Cuthbert Morrell (Master in 1944) had been a Merchant Adventurer since 1930. Bernard Johnson, whose family firm were printers, became a Merchant Adventurer by patrimony in 1930 and was their Governor in 1956, as well as being admitted a Merchant Taylor in 1938 on account of his transcription of the records of the Company (of which he subsequently wrote a history). He was Master in 1946, 1947 and 1963. Arthur Gladwin became a Merchant Adventurer in 1943 and a Merchant Taylor in 1947. This relationship between the two Companies was reciprocal. Robert Tusworth Collinson (Master in 1948) was admitted in 1944, two years before joining the Merchant Adventurers; and in 1945 two of the leading Merchant Taylors, Herbert Harrowell and G. A. Potter-Kirby, became Merchant Adventurers.[18]

One consequence of this wider occupational and geographical recruitment was a steady increase in the number of members. In 1951 it was resolved to restrict the membership to fifty "in order better to preserve the selectivity of the Company" and also to keep down the costs of entertainments. In 1963 the total membership was forty-eight of whom forty lived in York, and in 1977 it was fifty-two, of whom eight were rarely seen. By 1993 the maximum had been increased to seventy-five though it was agreed not to increase further to 125.[19] By the end of the century the membership was ninety. A preference for selectivity and comfort on the one hand could be countered by the facts that new members paid an entry fee, ten guineas in 1935 but £50 by 1982 and £150 from 1990; and the entire membership paid an annual subscription, one guinea when introduced on a regular basis in 1935 but £50 in 1987 and £100 in 1990.[20]

This policy of requiring members in effect to pay for themselves both underlined the financial cost of being a member and marked an important switch in policy as well as attitude. One qualification for membership was now the ability to sustain the financial burden it imposed: there was no longer room in the Company for poor tailors. John Lofthouse, admitted in 1916, was the last Master to return to the Company as a supplicant: he was granted five guineas in 1932 and the following year was given an annual pension of £10 – on condition he resigned his membership.[21]

In the 1920s, the social and ceremonial rounds of the Company's activities were paid for out of the Master's annual allowance of £50, reduced to £35 in 1935. This sum was far less in real terms than the £100 available through much of the previous century and social events were duly curtailed, often to little more than the Charter Day tea and an Annual Dinner. The latter was always held off the premises as the Large Hall was throughout the period until 1939 leased to the Catholic Apostolic Church as well as being in poor repair. In 1928 the Master, G. W. Harding, suggested instead of a Dinner giving his £50 allowance and a further £50 to the Fabric Fund: the members resolved to give him "a free hand to expend the money as he thinks fit during his year of office". George A. Potter-Kirby did the same the following year. In 1940 R. W. Willsdon likewise returned his £35 allowance and added a further £15 to it.[22] This became the usual pattern. If the burden were not to fall wholly on the Master other means of financing social events would have to be devised – which meant members paying for themselves. Thus when the Master suggested a Livery Dinner be added to the calendar of events in the Spring of 1956, those attending were asked to contribute £2 10s. 0d. each and thereafter the price was raised until a small profit was shown on the dinner.[23]

The question of the place of ladies in the Company was not an easy one. Although until the early nineteenth century female mantua makers had been encouraged to purchase their freedoms of the Company, no new female masters were admitted after 1806. A similar pattern is found in the records of the Merchant Adventurers, with the exception of two honorary members.[24] When the question of female membership was raised in 1991, "It was stated that if women members were to be admitted, different membership rules could not be applied to them from those applicable to male members."[25] Despite the increasing numbers of women in business and public life thus qualified, by the end of the century no further action had been taken.

There was some room for women at social events, though in December 1963 the Master, Bernard Johnson, thought "it was unfortunate that it was the Members' Ladies who, in fact, made least use of all of the Company's Hall". After some discussion over whether to hold a dance or a dinner, a Ladies Dinner was held the following November. It was judged a great success and became an annual event in the form of a revived Martinmas dinner. Members' – and especially Masters' – wives did a great deal of work behind the scenes, in recognition of which the latter were awarded their own Master's Lady's badge of office in 1989.[26]

The range of activities performed by the Master, often accompanied by his lady, is illustrated by the notes left by Michael Dryland following his year in office in 1984–1985. His year began with a speech at the Reception following Charter Day – held on 20 June because there was a York Festival service followed by tea at the Mansion House on 24 June – and ended with the Court of Assistants meeting the following 29 May. Between these dates he attended the Company's four dinners, seven other guild dinners in York, eight guild dinners elsewhere in the country, mainly in London, eight religious services (not including the installation of a new Dean in York Minster) as well as the regular meetings of the Company's Court, Court of Assistants, and Fabric and Finance Committees. Together with the odd funeral and social and civic events, the tally amounted to a total of forty-two engagements during his year of office.[27]

FROM CHARITY TO CONSERVATION

Speaking at the Livery Dinner in April 1964, Sir James Ritchie, Master of the Merchant Taylors of London, admitted that "We are too often thought to be nothing more than a wining and dining club, there being no regard to our contributions to charity, education, commercial life and many other things."[28] That this was an impression easily formed of the York Company is not surprising.

The Company was obliged by the terms of several bequests to dispense charitable income to the poor. In 1935, Harrowell ascertained these sums to be £2 a year from John Straker's charity of 1669, £1 a year "for the benefit of the hospitallers" under John Napier's will of 1732, £2 a year for the poor from the Charity of Thomas Neville and £10 a year "for the use of the poor brethren and sisters"of the Company.[29] In practice the Company supported a small number of regular pensioners, some living in and some outside the almshouses, made regular payments to local "good causes" and gave occasional sums to cases needing temporary relief. The sums involved were very small and became increasingly irrelevant as the century progressed. In 1915 and 1916, six pensioners were maintained at a cost of £35 but thereafter the number never rose above four and in some years, between 1926 and 1932, and again between 1948 and 1954, fell as low as one. Average annual expenditure on pensions between the wars was £22. The same pattern continued after the Second World War until 1966, after which no further payments were recorded under the heading "Pensions under Foundation Charter".[30]

The sort of people who merited a Company pension were, as in earlier years, old tailors and their widows. A number of those nominated were workmen or former workmen for family firms whose heads were leading members of the Company. Andersons, for example, in 1917 put forward James Taylor, aged 71, who had been in their employ for forty years; in 1930 they had another nomination at a time when there was a danger of there being no pensioners on the list at all; and in 1937 they proposed a former employee who now lived in Hereford. Frederick Stanley Fletcher Frost proposed a £10 pension for a 77-year-old journeyman tailor in his firm as late as 1963.[31]

However, as alternative state provision for welfare developed so the need for the Company's traditional pensions and donations declined. In 1942, for example, it was decided not to award a pension to William Lord as the extra income he gained from the Company would have caused him to lose his shilling a week payment from the Public Assistance Board. When further vacancies occurred in 1946, two nominees both declined "as they were in work and feared a loss of pension from state sources". There was also less need for the usual annual guinea subscriptions to the County Hospital and the York Dispensary. These were maintained only until the establishment of the National Health Service, final payments being made in 1947 and 1948 respectively.[32]

The generosity of the Company could vary with circumstances. In 1954 the brothers William and Harry Hardy were both given pensions. On the death of Harry Hardy less than three years later, his widow was allowed to continue his pension, "she being in the tailoring trade in her lifetime" and the same was done for William's widow a few months later. Here was some recognition of the claim that female tailors (admittedly pensioners' widows) might have on the Company's charitable funds.[33] Charity however, ran out in the treatment of Harold Bell, the caretaker. When his wife died in 1965 it was proposed to dismiss him from his job and evict him from his accommodation on the grounds that he had needed her help with such tasks as cleaning the toilets; he was finally allowed to stay on promising that he would find additional help himself if necessary. He left shortly afterwards and was replaced by a married couple.[34]

While the Company remained conscious of its legal obligation to make certain charitable payments it also sought alternative and more relevant ways of fulfilling the spirit of what was required. At the same time the members were becoming aware of the tax advantages of establishing the Company's own charitable status, as by 1944 half its income was being paid out again as tax. A new Trust Deed was therefore executed in 1945 and members were asked in future to covenant their annual subscriptions. Being a charity, however, was not without its complications, for members of a charity may not gain a material benefit from it.[35] The Objects of the Company under its Ancient Charter and the Trust Deed of 1945 were:

> the maintenance upkeep and repair of the said Hall premises Almshouse and documents and the payment of pensions to decayed Taylors of the City of York or the suburbs thereof or in or towards such other purposes for the benefit of poor and deserving persons of the said City and suburbs as are charitable.[36]

The first of these objects took priority and the Charity Commissioners were informed of this in 1948.[37] In parallel with this change in emphasis, the income of the Company also shifted from what could be realised from its earlier charitable investments in real estate, stocks and bank deposits, to the Hall itself.

170

During the course of the century the Company's real estate was gradually sold off until only the Murton land and a few head leases on the Mount remained in addition to the Aldwark site.[38] There was also a policy of acquiring land in Aldwark, which was helped by the clearance of many old industrial and slum properties from the vicinity of the Hall and then the redevelopment of the area following the Esher Report of 1967.[39] In 1920, the income for the year amounted to £167 10s. 0d. of which nearly half came from investments. For the rest, £56 came from leases on The Mount; £21 1s. 0d. was rental income on the Aldwark premises, chiefly the Hall which was let to the Catholic Apostolic Church; and £14 15s. 0d. came from the Murton land. By 1950, apart from the special Fabric Fund, income amounted to £486 16s. 2d., of which the major components were Investment Income (£87 1s. 10d.), members' subscriptions (£59 17s. 0d.) and Admission Fees (£43 7s. 0d.). Rental from the Mount leases had fallen to only £42 0s. 0d. following the sale of some ground rents in Park Street in 1937. Thirty years later still, income was now £1,788 of which the major components were £798 from subscriptions and £336 from reclaimed tax. Of the original real estate only the Murton land was yielding a significant income. Whereas The Mount land had been sold off on long leases for housing in the early 1830s and the freehold of the Havergarths land off the Hull Road had been sold for building in 1917, the low-value agricultural land between Osbaldwick and Murton had been retained. This meant that the rent could be raised at least to keep pace with inflation. Though there was little movement in the rent between the £30 of 1940 and the £39 of 1970, by 1980 the net yield was £330 and this had risen to £820 by 1999.[40]

Despite some essential repairs in the mid-1920s, by 1930 the Company's halls were in poor condition. The general level of income was scarcely adequate for the Company's routine needs and left little to spare for property conservation on a large scale. An estimate in 1936 was that £2,000 would be needed to put the Large Hall in order with a further £450–£500 for the Little Hall. Serious fund-raising now became a priority. By 1938 £700 was in the Fabric Fund, including a gift of £250 from the Pilgrim Trust and the promise of a similar amount from the Merchant Taylors of London. In February 1939 restoration work started on the Large Hall, with Company members Penty as architect and Birch as builder. The Catholic Apostolic Church was served with notice to quit. The roof was repaired before the war brought a halt to further works. After the war, a new appeal was launched to complete the restoration work with the aim later set of having it completed in time for the York Festival of Art in 1951. With the help of a further £1000 from the Pilgrim Trust and £525 from the Wolstenholme Trust (of which G. A. Potter-Kirby was a trustee) this was achieved and the incoming Master, Herbert Harrowell, was able to hold the Charter Day ceremonies in the newly-restored Large Hall. The premises were now scheduled under the Ancient Monuments Acts of 1913 and 1931. Three years later, in 1954, they were listed as of Special Architectural or Historic Interest under the Town and Country Planning Act of 1947.[41]

Meanwhile the Company was expanding its Aldwark site. In the late 1930s the Company's neighbour to the south-east, the brewer J. J. Hunt, was interested in disposing of the now-redundant Rose and Crown inn, which stood to the left of the archway entrance to the courtyard in front of the Hall. When there was no money for this, Harrowell bought it personally on behalf of the Company, transferring ownership to the Merchant Taylors in 1946. By this date, the Bow-man property between the Hall and the street was also largely derelict and the Company purchased it in 1948. The open courtyard in front of the Hall was then laid out in 1950–1952. The final major extension to the site came in 1968 when Camerons Brewery, now owners of J. J. Hunt, offered the site of the Ebor Vaults on the south-eastern boundary of the property jointly to the York Civic Trust and the Merchant Taylors. Despite a resolution a few months earlier to incur no further capital expenditure for three years, this offer was too good to miss and so a special appeal was launched to cover the cost of clearing and landscaping the site: the Merchant Taylors of London sent 200 guineas. When the overdraft at the bank was finally cleared in 1970 the Master, Geoffrey Lavers, hoped that the Company would now be able to resume its charitable work.[42]

Old properties never stay in a good state of repair for long. Apart from routine maintenance, painting and decorating, there was always something need-ing attention or some desirable embellishment requiring new expenditure, not least because standards and expectations were continually rising, both among members and with the local authority and chief fire officer. By 1956 the almshouses were in thorough need of renovation, but yet more work was needed in 1973 when the premises were declared by the Public Health Officer to be unfit for habitation.[43] New kitchens were built at the east end of the hall in 1961, helped by £1,250 from the Pilgrim Trust, but the lack of adequate kitchen facilities was back on the agenda in 1972 and in 1981 further improvements were needed to satisfy the Environmental Health Officer.[44] In 1954 dry rot was found in the floor of the Little Hall and in 1963 further repairs included re-newal of the Large Hall floor.[45] Though toilets were built, after much discussion and delay, to the west of the entrance passage in 1954, comment on the inad-equacy of these continued to recur in the Minutes until 1994 when a new recep-tion wing was completed – though two members were not being entirely fair when they dismissed this new wing as "essentially a toilet block": it did provide rather more, with the small upper room above the screens passage being con-verted from the ladies' toilet into a meeting room.[46]

Having instituted a quinquennial review of the condition of the property in 1982 to ensure a rolling programme of maintenance and the avoidance of sudden crises, the cost of such a programme was estimated at £22,000 over five years. To help fund this one suggestion was to redevelop the Aldwark frontage, as envisaged in the Esher report, to give the hall more privacy and to create a "Cambridge College" effect. This, however, "did not find favour". Nevertheless it was decided to go ahead with an even more ambitious programme of further restoration at a total cost of about £60,000. An appeal was launched in the summer of 1984 which had soon attracted £10,500 from English Heritage, £9,000 from various Trusts, £6,500 from other guilds, £5,300 from commerce and industry, £3,500 from individuals and £11,000 from the estate of a recently deceased member, William H. Vine (Master in 1966). The balance was borrowed from the bank and stage one of the work was completed by the beginning of 1986.[47]

The purpose of all these improvements to the hall was partly conservation and partly to provide the Company with worthy premises to enhance its image and reputation as one of the ancient guilds of York — two not incompatible aims. This emphasis on the historic nature of the premises is to be understood against the background of the wider conservation movement in England and York at this time, epitomised in the formation of the York Civic Trust in 1946, to which the Company affiliated. Ownership of a grade 1 listed building had its advantages and disadvantages. The latter included the bureaucracy involved in getting permission to make any structural changes to the building — the new reception block required thirteen different permissions. The advantages included the ability of the Company to attract grants, such as those from the Pilgrim Trust and, above all, English Heritage.[48]

The English Heritage grant, however, was conditional on the Hall being open to the public on at least 30 days each year and this raised an important issue related to the charitable status of the Company. How far was the Hall now the Company's to do with it what it chose, and how far had the Company accepted public responsibilities more akin to exercising trusteeship of an important historic part of the public heritage?

The members' idea was that the Hall should be made to pay for its own upkeep and maintenance, and that it should therefore be let out for functions to create the necessary income stream. However, the Company could not charge a commercial rent as this might bring its charitable status into question, even though all income was being ploughed back into what on one occasion was actually called the "Charity Hall".[49] The device was therefore adopted of setting a donation rate for lets. Initially catering was contracted out, with the York

Coffee House Company covenanting fifteen guineas a year for seven years as a free gift in gratitude for the franchise, but much of the work administering the lets fell on the clerk who, following Harrowell's retirement in 1961, was Richard M. Stanley, a young partner in Harrowell's firm. After a decade of development with an increasing volume of work, Stanley offered his resignation. This prompted the decision to split the clerk's job, and a separate Hall Manager was appointed on a salary of £250 a year who took on the catering in-house.[50] The effect of the new arrangements can be seen in the level of "donations" fixed for various events. A wedding reception, for example, in 1974 cost £17.50. (£20 on a Saturday), and an evening function £25. Gradually fees were raised. Even so, in 1979 the income from the hall was judged not to be matching the running costs of the Hall and so donations were raised "substantially".[51]

This more commercial attitude towards the Company's finances coincided with the appointment 1979 of Peter Smith, an accountant, as Chancellor. This office, originally called Chamberlain or Treasurer, had been created in 1960 and the first holder, Jack Darley, had done a great deal to bring order to the Company's accounts.[52] After 1979 there was a notable surge in turnover. Hall receipts, which went up in 1980 by over 27 per cent, increased in 1981 by a further 52 per cent, from £7,642 to £11,628. The historic value of the Hall was evident. The rise in the level of donations at first did little to cut demand, but in 1986 the Hall Manager thought there was a danger that further substantial increases might prove counterproductive.[53] This intensive use of the Hall meant extra work for the caretaker and, in what was becoming a residential area, was not necessarily well regarded by the Company's neighbours. The dilemma was that a high level of letting was needed to raise income sufficiently to cover costs, however inconvenient this might prove. During the renovations of the mid-1980s the annual number of lets fell as low as forty-six but then began to recover again and offered the prospect of putting the Company on a sound financial basis.[54]

The Merchant Taylors had in effect become a company in the modern commercial sense as well as the historical sense of the Charter. Its operations and activities were substantial. This demanded new structures at every level. Richard Stanley, the new clerk, recognised that the Company could not continue to be run, in effect, by the Master for the time being and the clerk. It was necessary to have a committee structure in place with a smaller executive group meeting regularly and taking responsibility for running the Company's business and social affairs. The Court of Assistants was accordingly set up in 1963. This Court comprised ten members: the Master, Senior and Junior Wardens (who were the next two members in line for becoming Master), the immediate past Master, two other past masters, and four other members who had not previously held office. The clerk, chancellor and architect could be "in attendance". In 1993 the Finance and Fabric Committees were reminded to report to the Court of Assistants and not the full Court which now met only in January and September. The new Court in effect became a Board of Directors, with the Master as Chairman of the Board and the clerk as Managing Director.[55]

The new structure was soon reflected in the social calendar of the Company. Having held a successful tercentenary dinner in September 1963, the Master that year, Bernard Johnson, proposed that a September dinner be held annually for the members of the Court of Assistants. He also promoted the revival of the ancient Martinmas feast as an occasion at which ladies could be entertained in the Hall. Together with the Livery Dinner in April and the Charter Day tea in June, this created a regular programme of activities to which in 1973 was added a Members' Dinner early in the New Year.[56]

The second major change in 1993 was the creation of a separate trading arm to handle commercial operations. This was made necessary by new legislation affecting charities but for some time the Company had been aware that certain of its activities might be interpreted as incompatible with its role as a charity. For example, members were allowed to park in the courtyard to the hall. This was clearly a benefit of some tangible value so the simplest and most profitable thing to do was to charge for it: a donation was mooted in 1983 when sixteen members donated £382; by 1994 the yield was £4,560. The trading company was set up in 1993 with Richard Stanley, Peter Smith (Chancellor) and Ray Bradley (Accountant) as directors and the clerk (Ronald Pontefract) as secretary. The Merchant Taylors' Company held a £1 share in the trading company, all profits of which were to be covenanted to the Merchant Taylors with the charitable object of maintaining their Hall. This was neat and tax efficient. Around £30,000 annually was and continues to be transferred to the Company's accounts in this way.[57]

The minutes of the Company suggest from time to time that members were aware that the conservation and decoration of their Hall might not be all they should be doing to fulfil their historic role within the city and community of York. Concerning the Hall, had it been preserved only for themselves or did they have a responsibility towards the general public, beyond the thirty days' opening a year required by English Heritage? Most members valued their privacy. When the Ebor Vaults site was divided between the Merchant Taylors and the Civic Trust in 1969, the former wanted a high boundary wall and the latter a low one; when there seemed a distant prospect of a compulsory purchase order establishing a right of way across the Company's land in 1972, there was distinct unease alleviated only by the expectation that it would never happen. In

1975 it was decided that the Hall should be kept locked except for four hours a day during the summer when tourists would be charged to cover the cost of the attendant. In 1984 two members suggested that the fact that the hall was open to the public might be made more widely known. They were asked to prepare a paper, and that was an end to it. Though in 1986 the Court decided to continue to open the hall to the public, in fact there was no choice, having accepted an English Heritage grant the previous year. Members discussed in 1993 whether the Hall could be closed to all outside functions, but in the absence of such a decision, there was a clear conflict of interest between the commercial lets necessary to support the Hall and public opening throughout the week. In 1996 the Hall was completely closed to visitors after a theft was reported, but the English Heritage conditions obliged the Company to re-open it again at least for the minimum period of thirty days a year, which in practice meant Tuesdays throughout the summer months.[58]

If the tension between custodianship of a part of the public heritage and the privacy of a private Company was unresolved as the twentieth century drew to a close, there was less hesitancy about the wider charitable obligations which might fall on the Company once the major problems of the Hall had been settled. In 1970 the Master proposed a fund to build new almshouses in the form of an old people's home, preferably as part of the redevelopment of Aldwark. An appeal was launched but a site could not be found and the idea was dropped. It had been too ambitious. Money was also needed to make the existing almshouses habitable for the caretaker.[59] Small donations were made, however, to various worthy causes with which the Company was associated. For example, in 1979 £100 was given to the Civic Trust towards the £575 needed to renovate the pulpit in All Saints church where the annual Charter Day sermon was preached. The following year £60 went to the "Lords of Misrule", a student troupe of amateur actors who were performing the Hosiers' Play on their waggon. Finally, in 1982 a working party was set up to answer the major question: "whether the Company should participate in charitable works beyond the maintenance, repair and improvement of our Hall". Coming just before a decade of major expenditure on the Hall, this was perhaps inopportune, but in 1988 it was agreed to award an annual prize to the best student in the Textiles department at York College of Arts and Technology; and, as a concession to the needs of local charities, the Master was allowed to nominate one charity each year to be granted a reduced booking rate for the Hall.[60]

The matter of charitable giving was returned to again in 1991 when a Charity Committee was set up "to see what the Company might be able to achieve in the furtherance of our general charitable aims" and two years later consideration was given to a "more active charitable function". Members meanwhile went ahead with their new toilet block and economised by paying for their own Charter Day tea. After so many false dawns, in September 1995 the Court of Assistants finally decided to set aside £2,000 a year for charitable work. Though at first spending this money "was proving difficult", a start was made when a wheelchair was bought for a disabled person at a cost of £500. With healthy reserves at last, it was felt "that charitable donations should be increased" and "awards and donations" became a regular heading in the annual accounts.[61] This object was greatly strengthened in 2001 when a member generously gave £100,000 to "pump prime" the charitable funds of the Company. After taking advice from the City Council, an area of need was identified and a "restricted fund" set up

> to provide financial support to deserving and needy young people, principally within York and the surrounding area, pursuant to their advancement, encouragement and skill development in the fields of Art, Craftsmanship and Music.

By 2003 further donations and interest had augmented the fund to £125,000.[62]

The company had come a long way during the twentieth century. Until the 1930s it was surviving rather than thriving, still with remnants of its original charitable activities and its direct links with the trade. Thereafter there were many changes, necessary to the survival of both the Company and its Hall. After years of being a liability and a drain on funds, during the second half of the twentieth century the Merchant Taylors' medieval hall in Aldwark was converted into an asset, not only for the Company but the city. This achievement was in no small measure due to the energetic efforts of a sequence of clerks from Herbert Edward Harrowell onwards and to the commitment of a series of Masters, for whom the burdens of office meant rather more than eating a few, well-appointed dinners.

Notes

1. I am grateful to Richard Stanley (clerk 1961–86 and Master 1986–87) for sharing his recollections with me and commenting on a draft of this chapter.

2. BI, MTA 3/12, Minute Book 24 June 1908–20 November 1930, f.74v, 13 October 1916; MTA Add 22/3, Court Roll, 1916. Occupations are given in MTA 6/3, Admission of abled masters, 6 November 1751–19 November 1931.

3. BI, MTA 3/12, ff.85v–86v, 21 June 1917.

4. BI, MTA 3/12, f.118v, 8 June 1921.

5. BI, MTA 3/12, f.124r, 22 November 1921.

6. BI, MTA 3/12, f.196r, 20 November 1930; MTA Add, 6/1/2, Minute Book 19 February 1931–12 February 1953, 21 May, 3 October 1935, 15, 30 January, 26 May and 19 June 1936. The folios in this volume are not numbered.

7. BI, MTA 3/12 f.161v, 21 May 1926; MTA Add 6/1/2, 21 May 1931. George Potter-Kirby, d. 1924; James Cattle, d. 1925; Edward Whitehead, d. 1928; William Houlden, d. 1930.

8. BI, MTA Add 6/1/2, 19 June and 25 September 1934. Harrowell resumed the practice of calling the secretary the "clerk" in accordance with the Trust Deed – 6 December 1934.

9. BI, MTA Add 6/1/2, 29 March 1935; MTA Add 20/10, Correspondence. For the loan to Gray, see MTA 3/11, Draft Minute Book, 23 May 1894–20 June 1908, ff. 96v–97r, 22 November 1900; MTA 3/12, ff.66v and 122v, 18 November 1915 and 14 December 1921; MTA 12/4, Cash Book, 1869–1962, accounts for financial years ending 24 June 1932, 1933 and 1934.

10. BI, MTA Add 6/1/2, 21 May 1935; MTA 12/4, accounts for financial year ending 24 June 1936.

11. BI, MTA 6/1/2, 3 October 1935 and 19 June 1936.

12. BI, MTA 6/1/2, 13 April 1944.

13. BI, MTA Add 6/1/4, Minute Book, 1 July 1953–2 April 1997, p.86, 27 June 1962.

14. BI, MTA Add 6/1/4, pp.91, 93-4, 4 March and 30 May 1963, and information from R. M. Stanley. In 1963 the Master wrote to Sir Henry Price, founder of Price's (Tailors) Ltd and The Fifty Shilling Tailors, inviting him to become a member but Price died before he was able to reply - MTA 8/5, Folder for September–December 1963, B. P. Johnson to Sir Henry Price, 28 October 1963, and MTA 6/1/4, p.103, 17 December 1963.

15. BI, MTA Add 20/1, Correspondence, H. E. Harrowell to Merchant Taylors of London, May 1937 (draft letter).

16. For Whiteheads, see *York and District Directory* (1900), p.190; for Kirby and Nicholson, see *Yorkshire Evening Press*, 25 March 1967; for Andersons, see *Yorkshire Evening Press*, 2 October 1968. The business was then continued under the old name in new premises at 13 Blake Street.

17. BI, MTA Add 6/1/4, pp.108-109, 24 June 1964 (James); p.135, 22 June 1966 (Hale); p.144, 21 June 1967 (Wheway). Gladwin had been admitted in 1947 – MTA

Add 6/1/2, 6 March 1947. Other university connections included R. B. Dobson, the Company archivist, MTA Add 6/1/4, p. 307, 18 June 1980; S. B. Saul, the third Vice-Chancellor, *ibid.*, p.318, 17 June 1981; and T. R. Bradley, *ibid.*, p.384, 19 June 1985.

18. Merchant Adventurers Archives, Merchant Adventurers Hall, York, Members Lists.

19. BI, MTA Add 6/1/2, 15 March 1951; MTA 8/5, Correspondence of B. P. Johnson, 1963-1974, Folder for 1963, list of members; MTA Add 6/1/4, pp.270 and 466, 26 September 1977 and 9 December 1993.

20. For figures, see BI, MTA Add 6/1/2, 21 May 1935, and MTA 12/4, accounts for year ending 24 June 1936; MTA Add 6/1/4, pp.340, 416 and 450, 13 December 1982, 23 April 1987 and 24 September 1990; and MTA 12/5, Cash Book, 1963-1999, accounts for year ending 24 June 1990.

21. BI, MTA Add 6/1/2, 25 August 1932, and 23 February and 25 May 1933. Lofthouse remained a pensioner until his death in 1938.

22. BI, MTA 3/12, ff.181r and 183r, 22 November 1928 and 23 May 1929; MTA Add 6/1/2, 12 April 1940.

23. BI, MTA Add 6/1/4, pp.12, 16 and 22, 28 February and 6 October 1955, and 14 May 1956. In that year a loss of £34 was incurred. Although in 1957 this increased to £43 1s. 4d., in 1959 there was a profit of £5 18s. 0d. – see *ibid.*, pp.37 and 55, 15 October 1957 and 9 October 1959.

24. These were Dr Maud Sellers (1911) and the Princess Royal (1949) – see Merchant Adventurers' Archives, Members' Lists and Members' Register, vol. 3. For the last female Merchant Taylor, see above p.140.

25. BI, MTA Add 6/1/4, p.451, 28 January 1991. The matter was raised again on 30 September 1991 and then apparently allowed to drop – *ibid.*, p.452, 30 September 1991.

26. BI, MTA Add 6/1/4, pp.103, 113, 116, 408, 443 and 454, 17 December 1963, 28 September and 14 December 1964, 12 December 1986, 29 January 1990 and 27 January 1992; also pp. 229, 433 438 and 440, 1 October 1973, 26 September 1988, and 31 May and 8 August 1989. The badge, costing £1,500, was paid for out of a bequest from Carl Rosen (Master in 1971).

27. BI, MTA Add 23/14, Useful Notes, Master's Diary, 1984-1985.

28. *Yorkshire Evening Press*, 11 April 1964.

29. BI, MTA Add 17/3/4, Correspondence with the Charity Commissioners, 1917-1948, Letters to and from H. E. Harrowell, 12 November 1936 – 7 December 1948, especially 25 November 1938. Straker's Charity paid the Company £2 a year from the rental income of a cottage and land at Holtby; the Napier £1 and the £10 originally derived from the Company's land on The Mount and were secured on the Havergarths land until 1917 when the capital was invested in 2½ % consolidated stock. I have found no other references to the Neville Charity and it does not feature in the Cash Books.

30. The details of pensions are pieced together from BI, MTA 12/4, Cash Book, 1869-1962, and MTA 12/5, Cash Book, 1963-1999, supplemented by MTA

Add 7/1-18, Accounts and Balance Sheets, and MTA Add 20/9, Correspondence.

31. BI, MTA 3/12, ff.89r–90v and 196r, 23 August 1917 and 20 November 1930; MTA Add 20/9, Clerk to William Prest of Hereford, 7 December 1937 and MTA Add 20/7, Correspondence, letter from William Prest, 16 December 1937; MTA Add 6/1/4 p.92, 4 March 1963.

32. BI, MTA Add 6/1/2, 1 January 1942 and MTA Add 20/9, note by E. Poole (assistant to the clerk) on William White Lord, dated 5 March 1947, at which time Lord was given a pension of £10 a year on reaching his 75th birthday; MTA Add 6/1/2, 26 September 1946; MTA 12/4, accounts for years ending 24 June 1947 and 1948.

33. BI, MTA 6/1/4, pp.12, 41 and 46, 28 February 1955, 15 October 1957, and 18 March 1858. However in 1961, Annie Hardy of Driffield gave up her pension – *ibid.*, p.64, 21 February 1961.

34. BI, MTA Add 6/1/4 pp.129–130 and 134, 27 September 1965 and 7 March 1966. Bell had been appointed in 1958 at £3 a week – *ibid.*, p. 49, 27 November 1958.

35. BI, MTA 6/1/2, 26 October 1944, 1 March 1945; MTA 6/1/4, p.99, 23 September 1963.

36. BI, MTA Add 5/3(1), Trust Deed dated 1 March 1945; see also MTA Add 23/14, Notes relating to registration as a charity, no. 229067, 15 December 1963 and amended 6 July 1983; and MTA Add 9/1/13, Income Tax and Land Tax, 5 February 1945.

37. BI, MTA 17/3/4, H. E. Harrowell to Secretary of Charity Commissioners, 28 September 1948.

38. The Havergarths land was sold in 1917, BI, MTA 14/2/4/6, Draft Conveyance to Leonard Birch, 9 May 1917. The freehold reversion of the Abbey Park Hotel on The Mount was sold for £450 in 1962, which was invested in 5½ % Treasury Stock, leaving only the ground rents on nos. 69, 71, 73 and 75 in Company hands – MTA 12/5, List of Assets, 1963.

39. For details of the physical development of the Aldwark site, see A. M. Mennim, *The Merchant Taylors Hall, York* (York, 2000), pp.184, 200 and the plans on pp. 153 and 194, showing the layout of the site in 1891 and 1970. Also BI, MTA Add 6/1/2, 4 February 1948.

40. BI, MTA 12/4, Cash Book, 1869–1962, and MTA 12/5, Cash Book, 1963–1999.

41. BI, MTA 3/12 ff. 141v–144v and 159r, 1 April, 27 May and 20 June 1924, and 19 February 1926; MTA Add 6/1/2, 19 July 1936, 5 May 1938, 24 February 1939, 24 May 1945, 26 September 1946, 22 May, 24 June and 30 September 1947, 5 February and 7 October 1948, 29 September 1949, 11 January, 30 March, 27 June and 20 September 1951, and 14 February 1952; MTA Add 12/10–11, Rating and Planning, 24 May 1951 and 14 June 1954. For further details, see Mennim, pp.171–93.

42. BI, MTA Add 6/1/2, 15 September 1938, 26 September and 28 November 1946, 5 February 1948, 30 March and 15 November 1951, and 14 February 1952; MTA Add 6/1/4, pp.145, 149–50, 155, 167, 168, 171 and 178–79, 25 September 1967, 18 March and 4 November 1968, 22 September and 12 November 1969, and 21 September 1970.

43. BI, MTA Add 6/1/4, pp.29, 228-9, 256 and 261, 16 October 1956, 1 October 1973, and 24 May and 27 September 1976. For further details of the contents of this paragraph, see Mennim, pp.196-206 and Plan of Hall in 1981 on p.202.

44. BI, MTA Add 6/1/4, pp.61-2, 66, 210 and 321-2, 14 February and 21 June 1961, 25 September 1972, and 21 September 1981.

45. BI, MTA Add 6/1/4, pp.7 and 98, 30 September 1954 and 23 September 1963.

46. BI, MTA Add 6/1/4, pp.6, 30-1, 141, 227, 241 and 467, 30 September 1954, 16 October 1956, 27 February 1967, 1 October 1973, 27 January 1975, and 31 January 1994.

47. BI, MTA Add 6/1/4, pp.338, 344, 352-53, 357, 360, 372, 375-77 and 388-89, 13 December 1982, 26 April, 17 August and 19 September 1983, 17 September 1984, 21 January and 2 October 1985. Also, Mennim, pp.201-03.

48. BI, MTA Add 6/1/2, 16 May 1946 and 7 October 1948; MTA Add 6/1/4 ff. 453, 20 January 1992.

49. BI, MTA 12/5, List of Assets, 1963.

50. BI, MTA Add 6/1/4, pp.30, 190, 196-97, 200 and 208, 16 October 1956, 17 January, and 17 April, 22 May and 25 September 1972. The Hall Manager between 1972 and 1987 was Philip Booth (Master in 1980). Catering was then once more contracted out, to Anthony Wright who held the franchise until 1994 – ibid., pp.409-11 and 471, 12 March 1987 and 6 June 1994.

51. BI, MTA Add 6/1/4, pp.239-40 and 288-89, 19 September 1974 and 17 May 1979.

52. BI, MTA Add 6/1/4, p.58, 29 February 1960. The title Chamberlain had been dropped in favour of Chancellor within two years – see ibid., p.79, 22 February 1962. For Smith's appointment, see ibid., p.294, 20 June 1979.

53. BI, MTA Add 6/1/4, pp.309, 320-21, 335, 360 and 397, 22 September 1980, 21 September 1981, 20 September 1982, 19 September 1983 and 3 April 1986.

54. BI, MTA Add 6/1/4, pp.397, 408, 423, 434 and 437, 3 April and 1 December 1986, 28 September 1987, and 23 January and 31 May 1989.

55. BI, MTA Add 23/14, Notes, Report of Membership Committee, n.d. This report would appear to have been accepted at the Court on 27 June 1962 – MTA Add 6/1/4, p.86, 27 June 1962. At first the Court of Assistants met earlier on the same day as the Quarterly Court but it was soon meeting on different days with separate entries in the Minute Book. See also ibid., pp.462 and 479, 27 October 1993 and 8 February 1995; also Mennim, p.195.

56. BI, MTA Add/6/1/4, pp.103, 124 and 222-3, 17 December 1963, 23 June 1965 and 20 June 1973.

57. BI, MTA Add 6/1/4, pp.343, 360, 415, 455, 458-59 and 461, 26 April and 19 September 1983, 23 April 1987, 28 September and 23 November 1992, and 1 February and 4 October 1993. MTA 12/5, annual accounts.

58. BI, MTA Add 6/1/4, pp.171, 189, 249, 373, 397, 463 and 495, 12 November 1969, 17 January 1972, 29 July 1975, 17 September 1984, 3 April 1986, 27 October 1993 and 4 July 1996.

59. BI, MTA Add 6/1/4, pp.178-9, 181, 192, 220 and 233, 21 September 1970, 14 June 1971, 27 March 1972, 7 May 1973 and 21 January 1974.

60. BI, MTA Add 6/1/4, pp.288, 305, 333, 425 and 432-3, 16 January 1979, 20 May 1980, 27 July 1982, 2 January and 26 September 1988. The accounts show that £140 was spent on awards to students in 1989–1990, and in 1995 £120 was given to sponsor a model for the College annual fashion show – MTA 12/5, annual accounts, and MTA Add 6/1/4, p. 482, 3 May 1995.

61. BI, MTA Add 6/1/4, pp.452, 463, 484, 489, 501, 30 September 1991, 27 October 1993, 11 September 1995, 29 January 1996, and 27 January 1997; MTA 12/5, accounts for year ending 24 June 1999. At the same time, these accounts show £486 spent on the Martinmas Feast and £1,678 on the Livery Feast, presumably on hospitality for the Company's guests.

62. Letter circulated to Members of the Company, February 2003.

THE CONSTRUCTION OF THE TAYLORS' HALL:
A CURIOUS HISTORY

John Baily

*Taylor-hall-lane....carries you to Merchant-taylor's hall, a large and hand-
some structure; which serves, both for the meeting of that company, and
lately for the acting of stage plays in. The company have lately erected a
small hospital near this hall for four poor brothers or sisters.*

Francis Drake, 1736[1]

The prosperity of medieval York can still be seen in the city's considerable
stock of buildings of the period. A major influence in the city's growth as a
trading centre was, as with London, the rise of the guilds and fraternities. Through
the thirteenth and fourteenth centuries they established the framework that
gained control of the commercial and civic life of the City.

The wealth and power of the mature Companies can be gauged by the
description of the Corpus Christi Mystery Plays, compiled by the Town Clerk in
1415, the year the Taylors acquired the site for their new Hall. In that year 53
plays were sumptuously mounted by 96 Guilds and Fraternities.[2] This in a city
with a total population of some 15,000.[3] The smaller companies banded together to mount a play, whilst the larger companies had one to themselves. The
Taylors' play being of *'Mary, John the Evangelist, two Angels and eleven Apostles;
Jesus ascending before them, and four Angels bearing a Cloud.'* It is of note that the
major concluding plays, covering the ascension of Jesus and Mary into Heaven,
were given individually by the Tailors, Potters, Drapers, Linenweavers, Weavers
of Woollen, Hostlers and Mercers. Five of the seven worked in the clothing
trades.

It is likely that the larger Companies had their own Hall by this time or
were, like the Taylors, acquiring one. The small companies joined forces in a
common hall, or held their meetings in the hall of another guild or in the home
of a member. The Guildhall, where all guilds met together, formed the beginning of the city's local government through those elected as freemen of the
City.[4] York is fortunate to have five medieval halls still in use, all oak framed
and each an example of a different form of hall construction. The Merchant
Adventurers Hall (1357-61), originally the Guild of Mercers and Merchants,

has a double-banked Hall on the first floor. Also with an undercroft is the aisled St. Anthony's Hall (c.1446–75), a religious and social Guild, and the hall in St. William's College (c.1465), built to house chantry priests at the Minster, both being part of larger and much altered buildings. The Merchant Taylors Hall, the only surviving craft guildhall (1415), is built on the ground floor, as is Bedern Hall (1370), originally the refectory of the Vicars Choral. Bedern Hall was restored in 1980 as a common hall for the Guild of Freemen, the Guild of Building and the Company of Cordwainers. Lastly, the City Guildhall, originally of 1449–59, was to a quite different flat roofed aisled-hall design, and was rebuilt in 1960 following war damage. The development of structural systems to cope with ever increasing spans is the principal interest in tracing the history of large halls such as these. Apart from the Guildhall, these York roofs show variations of the two main truss designs, the tie and crown post truss and the arch-braced truss, of which that used in the Taylors' hall is the most curious. But more of that later.

The Hall itself had several functions; as a general gathering place for members, as a court where the Master and Wardens would manage the business of the Company and adjudicate on disputes, and for feasts on saints' days and festivals. These functions closely mirrored those found in many domestic variants generally termed 'hall houses', from large merchant's houses in York, such as 51 Goodramgate and the re-created Coffee Yard, to many a manor house across the country and to great houses such as Haddon Hall and Eltham Palace.[5]

The architectural form common to all these examples is an off-centre entrance (usually from a courtyard) into a screens passage, with to one side the great hall, with a dais at the far end, and to the other side kitchens and stores. In a great house there would be private family quarters behind the dais end of the hall, possibly double storey with a solar above for the ladies of the household. In a guildhall, such as the Taylors, the domestic quarters were replaced by rooms for the master and wardens to retire to and in which to undertake private business. The greater guildhalls, as in the greater manorial houses, would have a chapel, as that in the Merchant Adventurers' Hall. The care of the sick and elderly was (and is) a common feature of guild life throughout the country, accommodation being provided either within the building, as at the Merchant Adventurers, or in an adjacent almshouse or hospital as at the Taylors, or further afield.

The first written indication of the Taylors forming a guild was in 1387 when '128 taylors and cissors' issued their 'Ordinances'.[6] Somewhat earlier they also formed or were associated with a Confraternity of St. John the Baptist,[7] the same patron saint as the London Company of Merchant Taylors. It is possible that as Taylors built up their resources to build their own hall they were already meeting in Petre Hall, of which little is known, sited between the City Walls and Aldwark.[8] Then in 1415 the Taylors took a 100-year lease from the City for land adjacent to Petre Hall and it is likely that they built straight away, incorporating Petre Hall as the left hand or western wing. The only physical evidence for this assumption is the curious angled end to the Taylors' Hall, for there seems little reason to mess up the design of ones' new hall in this way unless it was to butt up to an existing building.

It is surprising that the Taylors, a large and influential Guild, took on a site that was an awkward shape in an awkward location, ominously described in the lease as 'a piece of ground in our ditch commonly called the Mote'.[9] As Plate 5 shows, the site was roughly triangular in shape, jammed up against the embankment of the city walls to the north, with St. Helen's church to the east and separated from the street frontage on Aldwark by a run of buildings and back yards.[10] The only access to Aldwark was by a narrow lane variously called Taylor Hall Lane, Kirk Lane or Love Lane. Hardly a prestigious site; the only points in its favour would seem to be its modest cost and its link to Petre Hall.[11] The Hall suffered this cramped and hidden site right through to 1949 when the Taylors began the acquisition of the Aldwark properties and eventually demolished them.

The size of the Hall is quite ambitious. Five bays give an internal length of 17.83m (58½ft) and a width of 8.68m (28½ft).[12] A sixth bay on the western end accommodates the entrance, screens passage and staircase to an upper room. This bay has the curious, angled end, presumably caused by a determination to build the west and north walls parallel to Petre Hall and the city walls respectively. They meet at an angle of 100°, with the result that the first bay is 5.0m (16½ft) at the front and 3.3m (10¾ft) at the back, excluding the brick casing to the ground floor. The two cross frames of this bay (A and B on the plan, Plate 1 & 11) have a principal tie at eaves level, an upper collar and a crown post in-between. A pair of curved braces between the tie and crown post infill the gable and below is a second cross tie at about 2.3m with vertical studs and corner braces. These two frames are however different in detail, a variation possibly due to the western elevation being rebuilt when the west wing was rebuilt in the sixteenth century. It is probable that the west wing was demolished in the latter half of the eighteenth century.[13]

The critical decision in the structural design of the Hall was its width, and whether the roof was to span this in one leap, or in two as at the Merchant Adventurers Hall, or in three, with aisles, as at St. Anthony's Hall. The built form of a building is determined, apart from site and functional considerations, by the availability and structural character of the materials used in its construction. The Vale of York was rich in oak and clay so medieval York was a town of oak framed buildings, clay roof tiles and brick chimney stacks. Even so, long oak timbers were scarce and therefore expensive (this was well before the importation of Baltic pine), so flat roofs spanning more than some 4.0m (13ft) were costly. Pitched roofs could achieve wider spans more economically and could be covered by thatch or tiles instead of heavy and expensive lead. This also had the advantage of a lofty height commensurate with a large hall, but the disadvantage that it produced a powerful lateral thrust, pushing the walls outwards and threatening collapse. If massive stone walls and buttresses could be afforded these would provide the resistance needed, but with timber-framed walls both the timbers and the joints flex. The solution was to hold the thrust internally by fixing a bottom tie across the span, forming a triangular truss. The truss was supported on posts in the walls and placed at about 4.0m (13ft) intervals along the length of the building, using wall plates and purlins in-between to support the rafters and roof covering.

However, there is a visual drawback to tie beams, as they interfere with the soaring and impressive space of an open pitched roof. To avoid the need for a tie the arch-braced roof was developed from its origins in cruck houses, where two curved timbers were leant together forming an arch. These were stiffened by being locked together with the rafters to the outer side of the arch and with a collar at the apex. This arrangement brought the thrust of the roof down the line of the arch so the walls had to cope with a (more or less) vertical load rather than a lateral thrust, thus removing the need for a tie.[14] Clearly the steeper the pitch of the roof the more vertical were the loads, but this had to be traded off against the resultant increase in height and weight.

The need for this explanation is that the roof trusses used over the Taylors Hall appear to be a curious hybrid, incorporating both the tie beam and the arch-brace design. Why both? Was it built like that, or were the ties — or the braces — added later? This ambiguity has created a good deal of debate. (Plate 13 & 14)

The generally accepted position as to the original date and design of the roof goes back to Bernard Johnson's book published in 1949. Johnson cites several authorities who date the roof between 1360 and 1420 and describes it as a transitional design between that of the Merchant Adventurer's Hall (1357) of tie, collar and crown post, and that of St. Anthony's Hall (1453) of arch-brace and collar.[15] The Royal Commission on Historical Monuments took Johnson's description for their volume on the Central Area of York, and added a key statement that the original arch-brace trusses 'have inserted tie-beams of rougher quality than other members' and that the roof may have been rebuilt to incorporate the ties in 1567.[16] Michael Mennim in his history of the Hall inclines to the view that the trusses were an 'intermediate' form of an arch-braced design, the ties being added about 1450, that is some 35 years after the roof was built.[17] The conflicting view comes from Katherine Giles who, in her doctoral thesis, argues that the ties form part of an original crown post and collar truss and that the arch-braces were added later.[18]

Much of this speculation can be clarified by obtaining the age of the various timbers. The felling date of oak can be determined by dendrochronology, the study of differentials in the annual growth rings. When the timbers in the hall roof were dated in 1991 the arch-braces were inexplicably omitted.[19] Had the braces been included and found to be of a similar date to the other timbers, there is evidence of a single construction period. Had the date been later there is evidence that the braces were an afterthought. All the timbers tested had felling dates between 1393 and 1413, which supports the suggested construction date of 1415, and as the ties were included in the dating we have evidence to support the suggestion that they were part of the original truss construction and not added later. These dates also show that it is unlikely that the roof timbers were re-used from an older building.[20]

The problem with stylistic dating, as used by Johnson's experts, is that change is not linear and constant. There is an infinite and haphazard variation in timber truss designs and the quality of workmanship; individual carpenters and different locations had their own styles, some were conservative, some innovative.[21] This leads to a blurred division between a curved brace used as part of a tied truss and a curved brace used as the principal structure in an arch-braced truss. The end frames A and B and the open truss C illustrate this (Plate 11). There is however a fundamental difference between the two types of truss which is defined by structural continuity; that is with a tied truss the tie is continuous and with an arch-braced truss the brace is continuous. The key factor in considering the truss used in the Taylors Hall is that the tie runs *through* the brace and not *past* it. The tie is continuous and the brace is cut.

Bearing in mind this definition together with the felling dates of the timbers, what conclusions can be reached on how the trusses were built, as illustrated in Plate 13 & 14?

Hypothesis 1. That the roof truss was built as an arch-braced design to which ties were later added as a safety measure because the roof was spreading.

Firstly there is the problem of the felling dates, which indicate that the timbers were contemporary with other roof timbers. Whilst it is possible the

Taylors purchased the ties at a later date, it was common, because of their high value, to use oak 'green', that is soon after they were cut. Hence the query as to whether the ties were second-hand, as this would explain the pre-1415 felling date; but this does not appear to be the case.

Secondly, irrespective of the date, surely the ties would have been fixed against the side of the unstable arch-braces to form the necessary restraint, as has occurred in the Small Hall roof? It would need a brave and very foolish carpenter to cut through the structural arch-braces on both sides, thus inviting a catastrophic collapse before the tie could be put in place. It would also be impossible to cut and fit tenons and mortises with the braces in-situ, so the logic is that the whole roof must have been dismantled and rebuilt if this hypothesis is correct. To undertake such a huge enterprise simply to have the ties run *through* the braces rather than *past* them is most unlikely.

Hypothesis 2. That the roof truss was built as a tie, crown post and collar design which was adapted later by removing the crown post and adding the arch braces.

As far as the author is aware, the only person to have inspected the trusses close up was F. V. Rhodes who was responsible for the re-roofing repair work in 1947. He wrote to Bernard Johnson that he was convinced from his observations that the truss was never fitted with a crown post.[22]

The other odd thing is the substantial size of the arch braces, as their introduction must have been primarily for decorative effect. They are much closer akin to the massive braces used in earlier crown post roofs such as that in the Bowes Morrell house at 111 Walmgate, so the date of their insertion becomes critical. If they are early, say 1425, experimentation with a new idea could be the cause of their heavy appearance. But if they are later in the century, say 1470, surely the refined elegance and economy of the arch-braced roof in St. Anthony's Hall, just built and a near neighbour would have been used as a model – even in the negative sense of realising it was not possible to compete? (Plate 3) If the Taylors' fitted the arch braces soon after the roof was completed their attempt to enhance the roof appears clumsy, whilst if the work was much later (and even 1567 has been suggested) it appears old fashioned too. In both cases it seems a poor return on the cost and effort expended.

Hypothesis 3. That the roof truss was built as we see it today, with tie and arch-brace together, making this a unique hybrid design.

This is clearly possible as a sort of 'belt and braces' approach (pun not intended!), but the arch-braces despite their size are structurally weak because they are cut either side of the tie. If the tie and brace were built together a halved joint with *both* being continuous would be the logical procedure, so both were structurally effective.

The hypothesis must also be questioned because the decorative moulding running along the bottom edge of the braces does not occur on any of the other timbers; for example on the ties, purlins and wall plates as seen at St. Anthony's Hall and to a lesser extent at Bedern Hall. Such decorative programmes were common. Also all the other timbers used in the roof, the ties in particular, are very plain, rough and rather crudely worked whereas the braces are more consistent and finer worked, giving the appearance of the work of a different carpenter.

The only way these uncertainties can be resolved is for all the braces and ties to be dated by dendochronology, and to check if mortises for crown post tenons do or do not exist in the tie beam below and collar above. If it were proved that the roof was built as we see it today, then perhaps it would be safe to describe it as a unique design. The only thing that is certain at present is that arch-braces were employed in a tied roof. Why the Taylors chose to embellish their roof in this expensive and eccentric manner remains a mystery.

The four trusses spanning the main hall were supported on oak posts, the external wall between the posts in-filled with oak braces and vertical studs with brickwork and a plaster finish in between. ([23] & Plate 11) Most of this infill, including some of the posts, was replaced with brickwork between 1715 and 1732. Originally the posts were set on a stone plinth just above the ground except for the north wall where shorter posts sat on a brick or stone retaining wall as the building was built into the earth bank of the city walls. Today the bank is at the sill level of the windows, some 2.74m (9ft) above the floor, but it is generally thought that when built this wall was only 1.52m (5ft) high.[24] No builder would dream of constructing a timber-framed wall against damp earth, but would have used a brick or stone retaining wall, so either this assumption is a mistake or the embankment has grown in height by 1.22m. There are records of the city walls being repaired and raised between 1496 and 1569[25] so prior to this work the embankment may have been lower, possibly at 1.52m. But could the embankment have risen to its present height by 1715, when the eastern flight of steps was constructed to give access to the city walls? The answer must wait for a detailed examination of the north wall construction both inside and out. Whatever the height, it is astonishing that the Taylors required the builder to cut their new building into a high earth bank — especially in a city that is virtually flat. It was expensive, and internally produced a different wall design to the north and south elevations. Could the cause have been a somewhat desperate need to get away from the backs of the buildings facing Aldwark? (Plate 5) If this was so it gives some measure of the mean and awkward nature of the site.

The reason for replacing the timbered walls with new brick walls is another puzzle. This was a major and very expensive undertaking and by the eighteenth century the Taylors were not an affluent Company, so a financial burden of this size could hardly be put down to fashion. Having said that, the Taylors would have observed the transformation at St. Anthony's Hall where in 1656-7 the half-timbered first floor was replaced with brickwork and they may well have wanted to follow suit.[26]

It is important to appreciate that the Taylors' Hall was not 'brick faced', that is a facing placed in front of the oak framed wall. The infill walls and some of the posts were *replaced* with brick up to the wall plate, which was retained. The new brickwork is remarkably true and plumb, which indicates that the timber frame had not weakened by spreading outwards, which lends weight to the hypothesis that the ties were part of the original truss. On the other hand it is possible to construct an altogether more catastrophic suggestion already touched on in *Hypothesis 1* that the walls and roof *did* spread outwards and *both* were dismantled and rebuilt, not around 1450 but between 1715-1732 when the brick walls were built. This may fit with some of the observations made on the trusses and walls, but had such a major financial crisis and rebuilding programme occurred would it not have been recorded in the Minute Books of the Company?

The more prosaic cause for replacing the walls is poor workmanship, materials and maintenance leading to rot and decay in the timbers. From 1672 onwards the Minute Books refer to frequent but fairly minor repair activity to the Great Hall, the Counting House (Small Hall) and the Maison Dieu, which was eventually pulled down in 1702. It appears that during this period up to 1715 the Taylors gradually came to the view that patch repairs were not acceptable and that the whole Hall needed a new brick exterior. It is of interest that York prohibited the use of external timber frames in 1645 as a fire prevention measure.[27] This may offer evidence for the cause of the decision to replace the timber framed walls with brick. If the Taylors had lost an argument with the City Authority as to when a 'repair' was judged to be 'new work', it could be that the Taylors were obliged on legal grounds to undertake this extensive building programme.

Whatever the reason, the 1715 programme of work saw the east end of the Great Hall completely rebuilt some 1.16m (3ft 10in) outside the line of the original frame by a brick wall with three large windows, the middle with a semicircular head (G and Ga on the plan and section, Plate 11 & 12).[28] The north

190

elevation was rebuilt, the south elevation rebuilt west of the porch and the Little Hall east elevations rebuilt and extended. The second phase was completed in 1732, covering the remaining part of the south elevation and the west and south elevations of the Little Hall. The vertical junctions between the phases of brick-work can be clearly seen to the east of the porch and at the abutment of the extension to the Little Hall. The porch was added at this time, but this encloses the original medieval door rather than a smart new eighteenth century one.

This work raises a curious dichotomy between the extent and cost of the 1715–32 renovations and the architectural style that was employed. The pro-gramme of work was very extensive, not only the brick external walls, but inter-nally the doors to the Great Hall and the Small Hall were replaced by doors of a more fashionable design, the Great Hall was panelled and the odd 'minstrel's gallery' added.[29] The Small Hall was enlarged and the windows to both Halls replaced. Yet the architectural style adopted was ambivalent and inconsistent. Certainly an architectural 'statement' was not made, which for the period is unusual, especially as a huge amount of Georgian house building was going on in York at this time. To gauge the depth of the Taylors' ambivalence and incon-sistency compare their work to the Hall with its next door neighbour in Aldwark, Oliver Sheldon House. This was building at the same time (c.1720) with hand-some double-hung sash windows, classical doors and surrounds and a rich roof cornice. Yet at the Hall small, plain and very high windows were built into the main south elevation — why not large and airy sash windows like those being inserted into the Merchant Adventurers' Hall, or indeed like the new east eleva-tion windows? And again, a smart classical flight of steps up to the city walls was built, but the main entrance to the hall — a much more important element in the building — was left is its medieval state, with everyone clambering through a little wicket door.

The east wing, originally referred to as the Council or Counting House and now known as the Little Hall, has an uncertain history. The thickness of the wall between it and the Great Hall indicates that it was a later addition butted up to the Great Hall. It is also thought that the roof has been raised.[30] This view is reinforced by the lack of any relationship between the timbers of the two roofs, with the eaves line of the Small Hall 0.6m(2ft) higher than that to the Great Hall. The first roof truss (H, see Plate 12) has a bottom tie and collar, with intermediate braces and studs rather like an external wall frame, and the exten-sion of the roof timbers to meet the Great Hall roof is rough and *ad hoc*. It is therefore possible that originally this was an external gable wall later adapted to link up the two roofs.

But why was the roof raised? Giles and Mennim are of the view that the building had two floors, so the roof could have been raised to insert the extra floor.[31] The problem is that the present ceiling is, according to the Royal Commission, an integral part of the roof alteration[32] so raising the roof only achieved an increase in the ceiling height to the ground floor room. There is insufficient height in the attic to form a usable room, with only 1.20m (4ft) between the floor and the tie beams. Without the ties the floor is usable but utilitarian, with trusses that don't match and there is no indication of a ceiling. There is also the problem of the location of a staircase, rising 4.2m (13¾ft) somewhere through the hall below. On the other hand, could an inserted floor at a lower position have been installed when the roof was raised, to give a lower room height of say 2.4m (8ft) and the upper room the same – or more if the ties were not yet fitted? There seems to be no evidence of such a floor. Neither case seems very likely, although the inner face of the attic east wall is plastered and the attic floor is loadbearing, which indicates it was a habitable room.(Plate 10) This original east wall shows no signs of alterations to the wall timbers or the roof trusses, which indicates that the roof was never raised; if it was, all it achieved was an improvement to the proportions of the Small Hall with the original utilitarian room above.

The original wall construction differs from the Great Hall, with the timber framing sitting on a brick wall about 1.67m (5½ft) high.[33] As with the Great Hall the external framed walls were replaced by brickwork in the eighteenth century, and this included the original brick wall. The eastern extension was originally built in 1576 and rebuilt as it is today during the 1715 programme of work. The south and west walls were completed by 1732 and the junction between the two phases can be clearly seen on the south elevation. This links in neatly with the record of tiles being bought to re-roof the Small Hall in 1732-3.[34] As there is no indication on the south wall extension of the brickwork being raised to a new roof line, the logic is that the Small Hall roof was lifted at or earlier than the 1715 rebuilding of the extension. The west wall was therefore built in one lift, as can be seen, to the raised roof position and the job finished with the re-tiling. Only the top section of the posts supporting the centre trusses (Plate 12, I&J) was retained on the west elevation and these can be seen externally either side of the window. It is likely that the ties were fitted to the trusses sometime later to resist the thrust against the thin brick walls, thus nullifying the use of the attic space.

The original east wall is important as this still shows the original timbered construction from within the extension, and even better from within the attic (Plate 10). The brick lower section is largely removed for access between the hall and the extension, the low height of the wall plate giving cause for many cracked heads. But for the lack of headroom, the wall plate would have been the obvious location for the lower first floor, forming an undercroft within the brick walls.

As with the Great Hall, the problematic history of the Small Hall can only be resolved by dendrochronology. Comparative dates for the original eastern framed wall, the transverse beams in the Hall ceiling and the roof trusses would resolve the building history of the Small Hall. The problematic history extends also to the use of the Small Hall, the early descriptions as Council House or Counting House seem most likely, but there have been suggestions that it may have held the Chapel.[35] There is documentary evidence in the fifteenth century that the Taylors supported a chapel and chaplain, and as there is no evidence that this was within one of the local parish churches it may be assumed that it was at the Hall. However, its location – or indeed that of the Maison Dieu – is simply not known, and both may have been in the now demolished west wing.

The two stained glass windows in the Little Hall are rare and interesting, but they do not help with the search for the Chapel's location, as they are secular. They are by the York glazier Henry Gyles who was commissioned by the Company in 1702. The south window has a small panel surrounded by clear glass. It shows the Coat of Arms of the London Taylors (the York Company were not awarded their own until 1963) with a dedication below that it was the gift of Simon Buckton in 1662. The west window is the larger, with a fine portrait of Queen Anne with the London Company's arms below. It also has an extraordinary descriptive panel claiming that *This Company had beene dignified in the yeare 1679 by having in their Fraternity, eight Kings, eleven Dukes, thirty Earles and fourtyfour Lords.* This refers to the London Company, who actually did have such a membership (but presumably the inscription should read '..by having <u>had</u> in their Fraternity...'). The date of 1679 refers to the completion of the restoration of their Hall following the Great Fire of 1666; the mystery is why the glass is in York rather than London.[36]

The west wing of the Hall was not demolished until after the 1715–32 programme of work, possibly about 1750.[37] It is curious that the Taylors lost the use of the site, retaining only that part adjacent to the west elevation of the Hall. This may indicate that the site (and west wing?) was leased from the City. The west elevation of the Hall has remained timber framed to this day, so the desire to reface in brick was quickly lost. Perhaps the wall was in good condition, having been rebuilt in the sixteenth century. Perhaps it was because the elevation could not be seen from the entrance front, perhaps there were unrealised plans for a new wing. Whilst small extensions were built against the wall, including new toilets in the 1946 programme of work, it was not until 1994 that the site was fully exploited when a new cloakroom and toilet block was built.

The fact that there was a lane forming a public access from Aldwark to the city walls makes it very unlikely that there were ever any extensions to the east end of the Great Hall. It is also unlikely that the Taylors had any land to the east of the lane, as in 1730 they paid for a conveyance of the land needed to build their new Hospital.[38] This is a simple building, built to house four old men or women, and has a handsome dedication plaque on the main elevation. The Hospital was converted to its present use as the Caretaker's cottage in 1948, but the original layout with massive back-to-back fireplaces can still be identified on the plan. The adjoining run of buildings opposite the end of the Great Hall do not appear on Bernard Johnson's sketch plan of c.1940, so they must have formed part of the post-war restoration programme.[39] They were renovated in 1961 with a link across to the Little Hall so that they could be used as kitchens for functions in the Hall. The kitchens were enlarged and substantially improved in 2000, reflecting the growing use of the Hall as a popular venue for dinners, functions and weddings.

The Hall today is probably looking better than it ever has; certainly its setting within the Forecourt has made a fundamental improvement. It has managed to survive despite the collapse of the guild structure and of the tailoring trades within the city, but not without some difficult periods through the eighteenth and nineteenth centuries — indeed the sale of the Hall was considered in 1870 and 1893. The dilapidated state of the Hall is graphically shown in the drawing by Edwin Ridsdale Tate of 1905 (Plate 2) and by 1922 the Company had ceased to use the Great Hall.[40] In 1934 the new Clerk, H. E. Harrowell, set about revitalising the Company and establishing a programme of essential repairs. Work on the dilapidated roof started in June 1939 but was delayed by the Second World War. The programme of work restarted in 1947 and included extensive repairs to the roof timbers, new panelling and flooring to the Great Hall, general replastering, new toilets (the gents upstairs in the meeting room) and a new heating system. This work and that to the new Forecourt was complete by 1951, but having got into the way of tackling problems the Company has not really stopped since. During 1961-2 the Little Hall had a new floor and panelling and the Kitchens were improved. The Great Hall interior renovation was completed in 1978-9 with a set of new chandeliers and the erection of the handsome coat of arms on the east wall, to complement the Drapers arms over the fireplace.[41] In 1994 the new cloakroom block was completed to the west of the entrance hall, allowing the upstairs committee room to be returned to its former use. In 1998 the Forecourt was refurbished, and in 2000 the Caretaker's Cottage improved. In between these dates was a continuous programme of maintenance — redecoration, new furnishings, electrical re-wiring and so forth.

The motivation for much of this work derives from the Company's tradition of offering their Hall for use by others. Through the eighteenth century theatrical events were held, and in 1714 a 'House of Conveniency' was built for the comfort of theatre-goers and other visitors.[42] Between 1813–73 the National School for Girls used the Hall as did the Catholic Apostolic Church in the period 1894–1940. Today, as in the past, the Company's own use of the Hall is but a small fraction of its use by the people of York. They provide the income to cover the maintenance of the Hall, as the Company has little by way of endowments. There is also a growing awareness that the Hall is an integral part of the social life and fabric of the City. This will place future demands on the York Company of Merchant Taylors to initiate change and adaptations to their Hall, in response to the changing needs in society.

NOTES

1 F. Drake, *Eboracum: or, The History and Antiquities of the City of York*, (London, 1736), p.316.

2 Ibid. Appendix pp.xxx–xxxiv. (In 1785 edn. vol. II, pp.121–126).

3 RCHM, preface p.xxxv.

4 The admissions to the Freedom in York for 1500–1699 cite over 150 different trades and crafts of which 40 were in the textile and clothing trades. The dominant trades were the Merchants (peaking at 169 in 1625–49) and the Tailors (peaking at 220 in 1600–4). It is of note that 'Merchant Taylor' does not appear in the list until the time of the Royal Charter of 1662 and that by 1675 outnumbers 'Taylor'. See C. Galley, *The Demography of Early Modern Towns: York in the Sixteenth and Seventeenth Centuries* (Liverpool, 1998).

5 RCHM, preface p.lx, p.138 & fig. 84 for 51 Goodramgate, York. For house plans and general description of hall houses *see*: N. Lloyd, *A History of the English House* (London, 1931), pp.183–7; Margaret Wood, *The English Mediaeval House* (London, 1965), pp.49–67.

6 Johnson, p. 20; YMB, I, pp.94–101.

7 Giles, p.37.

8 Also referred to as Pear Tree Hall and Peter Hall. Date of construction not known. The name may relate to ownership by the Minster and location in the Liberty of St Peter. Mennim suggests (pp.17, 35) it was about 40ft by 16ft of 2 storey construction. Assuming it was incorporated into the Taylors Hall it is shown on several maps (Coffin 1775, Drake 1736, Cossin 1722, Horsley 1694, all illustrated in Mennim). It could of course also have been newly built with the Hall, but there is no documentary evidence.

9 Mennim, p.50.

10 For ease of description the true orientation has been adjusted, so that north describes true north east, south describes true south east and so forth. See Plate 12.

11 Mennim, pp.50, 88. The initial rent was 40 pence per annum. It is of note that the lease was to four tailors and the Master, brethren and sisters of the Guild or fraternity of St John the Baptist. The rent was raised to 6s. 8d. per annum in 1652 under a new lease from the City. It is not know when the Company acquired the freehold.

12 It is tempting to view the design as based on a double cube, in round terms 60 ×30 × 30ft, the height to the roof ridge being 32ft. A width of some 30ft was ambitious; the Merchant Adventurers' Hall spans about 20ft and St Anthony's Hall about 28ft. Halls of the period typically span 20–24ft, exceptional spans of 37ft can be found at Dartington Hall, Devon, South Wingfield Manor, Derbys and Eltham Palace. These spans highlight the tour-de-force of Westminster Hall at 67ft. For details see Wood, *English Mediaeval House*, p.64.

13 Assuming Petre Hall and the west wing of the hall are one and the same, it is shown on the plans of York including Coffin's plan of 1775. If this plan is accurate demolition did not occur until after that date. Mennim, p.125 however suggests Coffin's map is inaccurate preferring that of Chassereau in 1750. This shows the

Hall without a west wing. Giles, p.40, suggests that a new wing replaced Petre Hall in the sixteenth century to link with her date for rebuilding the west wall of the Hall, still visible today. It would also tie in with the gift of timber from Thomas Hughes in 1567.

14 For good general descriptions of the development of timber roof frame systems see: a) N Lloyd, Ibid. pp.33–8; b) David Yeomans ed.. *The Development of Timber as a Structural Material* (Studies in the History of Civil Engineering, vol. 8), pp.113–41.

15 Johnson, p.19 describes the roof as 'an arched truss...strengthened by tie beams' and refers to it as 'transitional'. He is silent on the question of when the tie beams were introduced.

16 RCHM, preface p.lxix & pp.89–90. The Commission is unequivocal in its view that the roof 'evidently had to be rebuilt to incorporate tie beams'. 1567 relates to the gift of timber from Alderman Thomas Hughes referred to in the Company's Minute Books. The idea was seductive because he gave four trees and there are four tie beams. However they did not have the correct dendochronological dating, and the use of the timber to rebuild the west elevation of the Hall is a more likely suggestion.

17 Mennim, pp.54, 62 & 213 suggests that the tie beams were not originally used in the construction of the trusses but were bought and held in case of need at a later date. This accommodates the dendrochronological dating.

18 Giles, p.41 'It is the arch braces rather than the tie beams which were added … at a later date.'

19 Giles, pp.39–40 and Table 4.2.

20 Johnson, pp.19–20 cites F.V. Rhodes, who was responsible for the 1939–40 renovation works to the roof, who thought that the roof could have been second-hand or heavily altered because of a regular pattern of unused dowel holes in the ties and braces. These could also have been from the crown posts and struts removed when the arch-braces were added, as Giles suggests.

21 The tie beam frame and the crook/arch-brace frame are thought to be two separate geographical families. See J.T. Smith, *Archeaological Journal*, CXIII, pp.211–14; also Yeoman and Wood. However there is clearly a great deal of cross-pollination between the two.

22 Johnson, p.20. He comments that the work to the roof entailed 'the taking down and re-erecting of the main timbers'. This means that Rhodes saw the tie beams *before* the strengthening works had been carried out to the top of the ties, which would mask the crown post mortise holes – if indeed they are there at all. He makes a catagoric statement that the truss never had a crown post in it which flatly contradicts Giles' proposal. It is also worth noting that the tie to truss G has notches in it, as if for joists. These could be attributed to the ceiling that was put in before 1688 and removed *c*.1940. (Mennim, p.100).

23 RCHM, p.88; Giles, Fig. 64. See Plate 11.

24 RCHM, p.89.

25 Mennim, pp.22, 24; RCHM, *The City of York, Vol.2. The Defences* (1972), pp.19–21.

26 Giles, pp.47–55 & Figs. 88 & 89 for timber framed upper floor.

27 Mennim, p.3.

28 Why was the wall built only 1.16m outside the original wall line? Hardly a significant increase in floor space. Possibly the old wall was used as the scaffolding support to provide working space for the bricklayers working on the new wall. It would also ease the problem of replacing or extending the roof timbers. Once the new structure was in place the old wall could be dismantled.

29 The 'Waits' Gallery' is one of the real curiosities of the Hall. There are references to its erection in 1649, but RCHM (p.90) believes on stylistic evidence that this was replaced with the present gallery c.1725, that is when the hall was panelled. However, it is far too small and frail to have ever been used, it has no means of access (other than a brought-in ladder) and has no proper support. It does not fit with the present 1945 panelling either.

30 RCHM, p.90.

31 Giles, p.43; Mennim, p.60. RCHM and Johnson do not mention a second storey.

32 RCHM, p.91.

33 RCHM, p.88; Mennim, p.60.

34 Johnson, p.108; RCHM, p.89.

35 Johnson, p.19; Giles, pp.42-3.

36 1702 was the date of Anne's accession to the throne so the Company would not have acquired Anne's portrait from Gyles before this date (they paid 10s. for it). However the Minutes refer to the purchase of the Arms from Gyles in 1700 for £4. There is no date for the acquisition of the other Arms or the 'Kings and Dukes' panel. The two dates – 1662 and 1679 – indicate that the Company had collected various panels over a period of some years (they bought a box for the Arms in 1700 for 2s. 6d.), but did not commission Gyles to assemble and install them until after March 1702. The main west window reads as a piece, and is only signed once, on the bottom panel. How the York Company acquired the 'Kings and Dukes' panel and why they used it is not known. Perhaps it was an aborted commission for the London Company that Gyles off-loaded to his acquaintances in the York Company. There is not a similar panel in the present Hall of the London Company and no record of one being in the previous Hall, bombed in the Second World War. Information on the London Company and Hall kindly given by Dr Ann Saunders.

37 Mennim, p.38.

38 Mennim, p.121. Mr Tompkinson was paid £1 5s. 0d. for drawing up the conveyance of land for the Hospital.

39 Mennim, p.192 & Fig. 43. Johnson describes the open area to the east of the Hall as the 'Little Garth'.

40 Mennim, p.184.

41 Johnson, p.41. The Drapers Company joined forces with the Taylors in 1551 the overmantle Coat of Arms above the fireplace, is those of the London Drapers.

43 Johnson, p.107.

INDEX

Kepwyk, William 36
Kerrigan, Thomas 96, 135 n.105
kersey 43
Kidcote prison [York] 61
Kilner, Mary 156 n.18
King's duty 133 n.89
Kingston upon Hull, *see* Hull
kinship 59
Kirby family 143
Kirby, George 151
Kirby and Nicholson 166
Kirby Underdale 63
kirtles 42
kitchen 43, 172
Knaresborough 42
knighthoods 65, 152

labour shortage 20
labourers 18–19, 59–60; Statute of (1351)
    15
Lancashire 59, 63
Lane, Robert 115
Last Judgment (mystery play) 7
Lathom 59
Lavers, Geoffrey 172
law courts 73, 85, 87
lawyer 67, 100
Layland, John 95
lead 43
Leak, William 143
Leak and Thorp 143, 157 n.36
leather workers 20
Lee, John 154, 161 n.130
Leeds 59, 163, 165
lent money 94
licence, royal (1453) 41
Lichfield 36
light(s), candles, maintenance of 10, 12–
    14, 34–6, 65
Lincolnshire 57, 63
litsters 35
livery 53
Livery Dinner 168–9, 175
loans 94, 156 n.19; granting of 12
lobbying activities 95
Lofthouse, John 167
London 25, 36, 43, 49 n.57, 53, 68, 78,
    80, 85, 98, 143; companies 8,
    27, 32, 40-1, 67, 75–6, 98, 100,
    132 n.77, 168; Great Fire of 75,
    193; Lincoln's Inn 100; lord
    mayor of 149; Merchant
    Taylors of 75, 149, 169, 171,

    178 n.15, 184, 193, 198 n.36;
    Middle Temple 100
Lord, William 170
Lord's Prayer Play (mystery play) 11
Loving Cup 148
Lowther, John 130 n.40
Lunde, Robert 58
Lyons, Bernard 166
    - Henry 69

macebearer 134 n.98
Maenson 166
Maisondieu (Maison Dieu, Masendue,
    hospital, almshouses of
    Company) 44, 88-9, 94, 143,
    146, 169, 190, 193; demolition
    and reconstruction 88, 194; *and
    see* almshouses
malnutrition 53
Maltby, Christopher 58, 67, 71 n.41
Malton 56
Mann, Peter 64–5
mantua-makers 85, 140, 156 n.18, 168
Margaret (of Anjou), queen of England 40
Margaret, seamstress 42
marshalls 16
Marske in Swaledale 63
Marston Moor, battle of 66
Martinmas Dinner 168, 175
Mary I, queen 64–5
Mason, John 140
    - Richard 87
masons 18
Masser, James 142, 145, 156 n.31
    - John 156 n.31
    - Thomas 156 n.31
masses, memorial 10–11, 16, 39, 65; *see also*
    trentals
Master of the Company 54, 57–8, 63, 66,
    87, 98, 113, 148, 174, 184;
    framed list of 150; refusal to
    serve as 53; master's lady 151
master tailors, *see under* tailors
Master Tailors' Association 143
May, Gordon 166
meetings, compulsory 16
members, non-trade 163–4
membership trends 76–86, 140–2, 165–8;
    membership size 119–25; tables
    101, 103, 116
Mennim, Michael 2, 37, 187, 191
mercers 7, 13, 17–18, 21, 30, 43, 54, 64,
    78, 94, 105, 124, 183

taxation 8, 30-1, *and see also* pageant silver; subsidies
Taylor, James 169
Terry, Sir Joseph 147
textile manufacturing industry 20, 73, 88, 124
theatre companies 96; performances 39, 195
Thompson, Edward 115
- John 141
- William 133 n.88
Thoren (Thorne), Richard de 34
Thornton, William 115
Tireman, Henry 71 n.41
tolls 14, 68
torches 44
Town and Country Planning Acts 172
town clerk 142, 151, 183
traitors 39
Transvaal 147
treasurer (of Company) 174
Trent, river 151
trentals 10; *see also* masses
trestles 43
Trew, Andrew 71 n.41
Trust Deed (1945) 170
tumbler, silver 148; *see also* plate
Tunnock, Richard 15
Turner, Charles 73-4, 96, 98, 115
- J. G. 150
- Lancelot 67
turnpike, opposition to 95

upholsterers 87

Vavasour family 64
vestment makers 32-3
vestments, ecclesiastical 32
Victoria, queen 152
victualling trades 54
View Day 164
Vine, William H. 173
vintners 61

Wade, John 140, 143
- John junior 143, 147
wage, maximum (for journeymen) 84
wages 15, 139
Wagoners' Case 100
Waind, Frederick 158 n.58
- John 158 n.58
waistcosts 31
Waite, Robert 133 n.88

Wakefield 68
Wales, prince and princess of (1892) 152
Walker, John 154
- Joseph 145, 156 n.19
- Thomas 99-100, 150
- Widow 147
- William Slade 145, 156 n.19
Wallace, James 99
Walsall (Staffs.) 36
War Relief Fund 147
wardens (of Company) 87, 94, 98, 113, 136 n.121, 148-9, 154, 174, 184
washerwomen 28
Waterman, Dudley 38
Watson, George 64
- Canon John 164
wax payments 10, 14, 16
weavers 14-15, 19-20, 30-1, 43, 183
weaving (work for the poor) 67
Wensleydale 63
Wentworth, Geoffrey 115
- William Ward 141
West Riding cloth manufacture 43, 68
Westminster Hall 196 n.12
Westmorland 57, 59, 63
Wetherell, Owen 5
Wetwang 63
Wheway, Richard 166
White, Richard 43-4, 65-7, 71 n.41
Whitehead, Edward 150, 164
- W. J. 143, 153-4
- William 143
Whiteheads 165-6
Whiteley, George 140
Wilford, Graham 5
Wilkinson, Joseph 142, 151, 163-4
William I, king 28
wills 3, 9, 42-4, 66, 148
Willsdon, R. W. 168
Wilson, Thomas 133 n.88
Wiltshire 57
Winchester 19
wine 148; bottle of, as entry fee 67
Wingfield, South, Manor (Derbys.) 196 n.12
Wistow 64
Wolstenholme Trust 171
women, *see* tailors, female
Wood, James 130 n.40
wool 31, 67
workhouse 146
working day, length of 84
workshop, tailor's 43
World War I 163

208